Baile
Dubl

MAKING 1916

Making 1916

Material and Visual Culture
of the Easter Rising

Lisa Godson and Joanna Brück

LIVERPOOL UNIVERSITY PRESS

First published 2015 by
Liverpool University Press
4 Cambridge Street
Liverpool
L69 7ZU

British Library Cataloguing-in-Publication data
A British Library CIP record is available

ISBN 978-1-78138-122-9

Typeset by Carnegie Book Production, Lancaster
Printed and bound by CPI Group (UK) Ltd, Croydon CR0 4YY

Contents

Figures

Tables

Contributors

Nicholas Allen is Director of the Willson Center for Humanities and Arts and Franklin Professor of English, University of Georgia

Mary Ann Bolger is a lecturer in design history and critical theory, School of Creative Arts, Dublin Institute of Technology

Joanna Brück is Reader in Archaeology, Department of Archaeology and Anthropology, University of Bristol

Justin Carville teaches historical and theoretical studies in photography in the Department of Film and Media at the Institute of Art, Design and Technology, Dun Laoghaire

Ciara Chambers is a lecturer in film studies, School of Media, Film and Journalism, Ulster University

Pat Cooke is Director of the MA in cultural policy and arts management, University College Dublin

Elizabeth Crooke is Professor of Heritage and Museum Studies, School of Creative Arts and Technologies, Ulster University

Brian Crowley is Curator of the Pearse Museum, Dublin

Jack Elliott is an associate member, Centre for the History of Medicine, University of Warwick

Orla Fitzpatrick is a PhD researcher, Ulster University

Lisa Godson is a lecturer in history of design and material culture, National College of Art and Design, Dublin

Brian Hand is an artist and a lecturer in art and design, Wexford Campus School of Art and Design, Institute of Technology Carlow

Daniel Jewesbury is a lecturer in film, School of Media, Film and Journalism, Ulster University

Lar Joye is Curator of Military History, National Museum of Ireland

Róisín Kennedy is a lecturer in modern and contemporary Irish art, School of Art History and Cultural Policy, University College Dublin

Laura McAtackney is a historical/contemporary archaeologist based at the School of Social Justice, University College Dublin

Bill McCormack was Professor of Literary History at Goldsmiths College, University of London, until 2002 and subsequently served as Keeper of the Edward Worth Library, Dublin

Brenda Malone is a historian in the Department of Registration and Documentation, National Museum of Ireland

Catherine Marshall was Head of Collections, Irish Museum of Modern Art, 1995–2006 and is co-editor (with Peter Muray) of *Twentieth Century: Art and Architecture of Ireland* (2014)

Franc Myles is the principal of the Dublin-based consultancy *Archaeology and Built Heritage*, with a research interest in urbanism and the archaeology of the recent past

Hilary O'Kelly is a lecturer in the visual and material culture of dress at the National College of Art and Design, Dublin

Damian Shiels is a conflict archaeologist, Rubicon Heritage Services Ltd, Middleton, County Cork

Elaine Sisson is a senior lecturer in visual culture, Faculty of Film, Art and Creative Technologies, Institute of Art, Design and Technology, Dun Laoghaire

Jane Tynan is a senior lecturer in cultural studies, Central Saint Martins, University of the Arts London

Approaching the material and visual culture of the 1916 Rising: an introduction

Joanna Brück and Lisa Godson

The Easter Rising is a key element of Irish national consciousness – a foundation myth around which shared identities have been constructed, sometimes emphasising, and sometimes obscuring the bitterness of the subsequent Civil War. Yet, the Rising itself has long formed a focus of heated debate: what happened, how and why; its role and significance in the emergence of the Irish state; the wisdom – military, political and ideological – of the leaders. It is no surprise, then, that there is a wealth of detailed historical research on the 1916 Rising and its aftermath, with the release of new material (such as the launch of the online Military Service (1916–23) Pensions Collection in January 2014) treated as newsworthy by the national media. Yet, in popular imagination and experience, the period is often evoked in other terms: mementoes passed down from grandparents, images of Patrick Pearse encountered on classroom walls and coins, the bullet-scarred facade of the Royal College of Surgeons. It is this body of material and visual culture that forms the focus of this volume.

A wealth of objects and images survive from the Rising – as well as from later events that commemorated it – in museums and archives, as part of the streetscape, and in private ownership. These range from the informal to the formal, from buttons cut from the tunics of Volunteers, to photographs of the ruined General Post Office and objects looted during Easter Week, each drawn into practices that rework the meaning and significance of the Rising by and for different audiences. The objects of the Rising – from the Proclamation of the Republic to scrapbooks containing memorial cards for the leaders – are key to the construction of both personal and official histories. However, such items have yet to form a focus of sustained academic enquiry. This volume does not aim to summarise or critically evaluate the events of the Rising (for this, see the many published historical analyses of the period, e.g., Townshend 2005; McGarry 2010; Foy and Barton 2011).

Instead, it considers what the material and visual culture created around, by and in response to the Rising can tell us about the varied perceptions and experiences of this seminal event, as well as the changing ways in which it has been drawn into political debates and public spectacle over the course of the past century. We understand the material and visual culture of 1916 to include not only inert, bounded artefacts but also material practices, whether of the body or the ways places are interacted with; as such, the chapters in this volume are attentive to both a praxeological and a phenomenological approach (Naji and Douny 2009). In this 'decade of commemorations', responses to these objects, images and practices – cherished and vilified, remembered and forgotten – have much to tell us about contemporary concepts of nationhood and identity.

The focus of this volume, then, is on the role of material and visual cultures in the creation of different narratives around the Rising. It has its origins in a conference we convened in April 2013: while there has been much revisiting of the events and aftermath of the Rising, we felt it germane to bring together perspectives grounded in research that takes as its focus how objects, images and spaces operated in relation to the Rising and its by-now long aftermath. As the first book-length treatment of this topic, we seek to illustrate the range and potential of visual and material culture to illuminate the Rising; the book therefore comprises 17 short case studies discussing a variety of phenomena alongside five longer and more in-depth essays. The volume does not aim to provide a comprehensive or definitive statement but instead to act as a springboard and signpost to future research. The essays and case studies include contributions that focus on the events of 1916 themselves, alongside others that consider how these resonated across time – re-imagined and recontextualised in the materiality of political discourse and commemorative practice from the Civil War to the present day; here, then, we conceptualise the 'limits' of 1916 as both a topic and an event in relatively broad terms. The rest of this short preface will outline the different sections of the book, exploring both the specificity of the individual contributions and how together they illuminate different aspects of this most multivalent event. It will then explore recent discussions around the power of the material world and its significance in processes of identity formation and remembrance. In doing so, it will consider how the contributions to this volume link to broader scholarship on materiality and visuality.

Themes in the material and visual culture of the 1916 Rising

The book is divided into four sections that each addresses different themes. The seven chapters in 'The Fabric of the Rising' explore the relationship between materiality and discourse in relation to artefacts and spaces that were physically part and active agents of the Rising in 1916. In 'The fabric of a deathless dream', Brian Hand addresses multiple readings of one of the most iconic 'fabrics' of 1916 – the Irish tricolour, hoisted by Seán Connolly on the roof of City Hall on Easter Monday, and described by Hand as 'equally as large a field of significance where its meaning echoes the republican French and Italian flags, the socialist and emancipatory Chartist and Suffragette flags'. Jane Tynan examines in detail tensions between the 'official' and improvised uniforms of the insurgents, noting that this suggests the modernity of the Rising in terms of 'the yawning gap between the fantasy of perfectly designed uniforms and the reality of the fugitive power of clothing to wage an urban guerrilla war'. In 'Beating the retreat', archaeologist Franc Myles presents the results of his 'battlefield assessment' of the route taken by the volunteers as they left the General Post Office on the Friday evening of Easter Week until their surrender to British forces the following afternoon. He combines an account of fieldwork that uncovers new physical evidence with an assessment of recent debates about the preservation of parts of this site, in particular demonstrating how any research into the material remains of the event needs to encompass an understanding of the human experience of the conflict.

Daniel Jewesbury and Bill McCormack each assess a document, the 'Half-Proclamation' and the 'Castle Document' respectively, drawing attention to how the material form of words on paper carry import and meaning beyond what they ostensibly 'say'. Object-categories are also brought into play here, from the authenticity of forgery to the way, in different hands, surviving object-agents from the Rising could serve on the one hand as precious relic, on the other as criminal evidence. Authenticity, and the nature of mediation, are considered also with Ciara Chambers's examination of two surviving newsreels in terms of the impact of the Rising not only on the streets of Dublin but to a watching audience.

The second section, 'The Affective Bonds of the Rising', considers how objects and images worked and were worked on to sustain and transform the interpersonal relationships and social identities of those involved in the Rising. This could involve the conscious constructing of tableaux of affect. In 'Portraits and propaganda', Orla Fitzpatrick analyses the way the *Catholic Bulletin* emphasised the 'normalcy and respectability' of the 1916 leaders through its presentation of photographs of their widows and children, the 'repetition of near-identical family groupings' creating 'a photographic typology of grief'. Jack Elliott explores a less slick, but no less affecting phenomenon in terms of how individuals appropriated images from newspapers, postcards and other sources to create their own mementoes of the dead and to display their allegiance to the ideals for which the 1916 leaders had died. Both Elliott and Fitzpatrick then demonstrate the necessity of taking material and visual culture seriously in tracing the change in public opinion between 1916 and 1917, attributing an agency to the consumption and reconfiguration of the images of the dead and those they left behind.

Two chapters in this section address objects created by prisoners and demonstrate the ways private and public identities were materialised through them. Joanna Brück explores craftwork made by internees in the aftermath of the Rising, the War of Independence and the Civil War. As might be expected, these often drew on established formal tropes expressing Gaelic and religious identity. Perhaps more surprising were the domestic objects – tea cosies, training reins for children and handbags for sweethearts, much of this prison art 'evoking enduring structures of sociality that transcended the physical boundaries of confinement'. Laura McAtackney presents work on the autograph books of female prisoners during the Civil War. She shows how this 'often-forgotten source' gives significant insight into the self-perception of the women involved in the Civil War as well as providing important recordings of commemorations of 1916 held within the prison. One way the Rising was invoked by these women who laid claim to its memory was the appearance in their autograph books of the iconic photographic portrait of Patrick Pearse in side-profile, an image that is central to Brian Crowley's chapter. In this, Crowley gives an extensive analysis of Pearse's 'self-cultivated physical image'. He traces the genesis of Pearse's self-fashioning from his early 'sophisticated visual sensibility' and notes how the Pearse profile became a 'quasi-state symbol' post-independence. Crowley further argues that the side-profile as rendered in a monumental idiom transcended the flesh-and-blood Pearse, not only because of the almost hagiographic reverence with which the icon was treated, but also because of the specific nature of the depiction.

In the third section, 'Revivalism and the Rising', different contributors address the reconfiguring of artefacts and even personages associated with Easter 1916. They consider the ways material and visual practices articulated a certain position in relation to the Rising and subsequent political and cultural developments. Elaine Sisson explores theatrical representation in her 'Dublin Civic Week and the Materialisation of History'. Through her analysis of a historical re-enactment by Micheál MacLiammóir she evokes how 'performance's emphasis on the temporal, ghostly and mutable' might be set against the 'fixed and documented historical text', and suggests closer attention might be paid to the experience of pageants and performances to better understand how 1916 was refashioned in the 1920s. In Mary Ann Bolger's 'Redesigning the Rising', she takes as her central focus the typographic reinterpretation of the Proclamation of the Republic, described by Charles Townshend as 'the title deed of Irish republicanism' (Townshend

2005, 160). Bolger examines not the original artefact, printed in circumstances of 'haste, secrecy and danger' on the eve of the Rising, but Liam Miller's later productions of the text in pamphlet form in 1960 and 1972, tracing his efforts to give the text a 'typographic patrimony'.

The importance of the *Capuchin Annual* in its treatment of the revolutionary period in Ireland has been well noted. Róisín Kennedy here addresses its significance in bringing together modern art and the legacy of the Rising, and how Jack B. Yeats's work in particular was configured in the Annual to become 'part of a wider non-art agenda'. The last chapter in this section is by Hilary O'Kelly, who addresses revivalism from the perspective of dress. She traces the 'visible and significant role' Celtic Revival dress played in how Irishness was re-imagined and embodied before 1916 and its subsequent critical fortunes.

The final section of the book, 'Remembering the Rising', explores how the 'material memory' of Easter 1916 has been forged and represented – what is brought to attention, what is maintained, what is forgotten, and how the materiality of the event has been used to create different narratives. One key agent in this has been museums. In 'Displaying the nation', Lar Joye and Brenda Malone trace the origins and building of the National Museum of Ireland's 1916 collection. They explore how it brought into play differing attitudes to the role of a national museum, drawing out the tension and activation of specific curatorial approaches, and the acquisition of everyday objects that, due to their association with Easter 1916, had become relics. Elizabeth Crooke tells the very different story of the way the Rising was scarcely 'remembered' in museums in Northern Ireland until recently, and indicates how a more pluralist approach to the history of Ireland has lately been materialised through innovative curatorial and research strategies. In 'History, materiality and the myth of 1916', Pat Cooke accounts for the difficulties of creative curatorship at sites that have become sacralised, such as Kilmainham Gaol. He describes collaborations with artists on-site as one way of troubling the 'material contexts and contents of myth', enabling difficult histories to be 'opened up to interrogation and exploration'. A deep consideration of cultural understandings of place is central to Damian Shiels's chapter. He raises questions about the 'long neglect of the physical remains' of specific sites where significant events in the central revolutionary period occurred. He argues that 'the continued focus on memory at the expense of place and landscape' has stymied understanding and inhibited a crucial, material way of 'interacting with the history of this period'.

A single, and singular, work of art is the focus of Catherine Marshall's '"Of all the trials not to paint …"', about Sir John Lavery's painting of the trial of Roger Casement. The surrounding and subsequent political context marked its critical fortunes, a theme that Marshall demonstrates has more recent resonance with other such work, history painting and sculpture remaining 'vulnerable to the whims of patronage and political expediency'. If the memorialising in Lavery's painting denuded it of the power to hang in particular places, more demotic visual formats were more easily circulated, particularly photography. In '"Dusty fingers of time"', Justin Carville examines photographs in relation to 1916 'not as historical documents of a fixed and immutable past', as others have considered them, but in terms of their affective qualities in relation to commemoration and the nature of the photographic image as 'materials memory'. Lisa Godson also takes commemoration as a theme, looking at ceremonies to remember the dead of 1916 in the early years of the Free State, and explores how differences in what was considered a 'usable past' and by whom, tended to cast public ritual at that time in religious terms.

The volume's epilogue, Nicholas Allen's 'Lost city of the archipelago', locates the Rising in the broader context of imperial history and explores the totality of material connections in which those who lived through the Rising were embedded. Allen examines the interrelationships between the 1916 Rising and the circulation of exotic goods, arguing that the 'intensity of Irish separatism can be understood better in relation to … imperial counterparts of exchange and capital flows', and describing how the sensual world of Dublin in 1916 was suffused with the smell, touch, sight and sound of the material culture of Empire. Here, the Rising is contextualised as an element of the globalising and inherently material flows of imperial relations.

Materiality and the making of meaning

Objects, images and spaces lie at the heart of research in many different fields of academic enquiry, and this volume is therefore multidisciplinary, involving contributors whose perspectives and methodologies are shaped by their expertise as artists, field archaeologists and museum curators, those working in history of design, English literature, cultural history, typography, film studies and history of art. As such, the essays and case studies emerge from a variety of disciplinary contexts and embrace a diversity of approaches and theoretical frameworks. Yet, while their disciplinary perspectives and allegiances may not be formally aligned to the academic fields of material and visual culture studies, they all contribute in productive and challenging ways to our knowledge of the visual and material culture of the Rising. Here, we will consider how the chapters in this volume relate to recent scholarship on material and visual culture across the humanities and social sciences more broadly. Although not all of the contributions to this volume explicitly engage with the theoretical debates outlined below, our discussion aims to introduce some of the key themes in material culture studies and to signpost their potential for future research on the material worlds of 1916. In this section, we will explore the material and visual as closely related phenomena, requiring sensitivity to the artefactual nature of images and the ways in which these are drawn into social practice, as well as to the somatic attributes of the object-world. As such, discourses of materiality encompass visuality as a dimension of material culture – the interplay between the two fields has recently been expressed as visuality/materiality (Rose and Tolia-Kelly 2012).

Material culture has become an increasing focus of interest over the past quarter of a century across a range of disciplines, including anthropology, history, philosophy, literature studies, design history, archaeology, science and technology studies, art history and digital media. Drawing on a range of theoretical frameworks including Marxism, structuralism and phenomenology, scholars have explored diverse and often eclectic perspectives on the significance of materiality (e.g., Attfield 2000; Brown 2001; Candlin and Guins 2009; Hicks and Beaudry 2010; Miller 1998; Trentmann 2009). With a few notable exceptions (e.g., Barnard 2005; Moran and O'Brien 2014), however, there has been relatively little interest in these approaches amongst Irish scholars. Elsewhere, though, this fascination with objects derives perhaps in part from their ambivalent ontological status in contemporary society. On the one hand, the rapidity of social change and the expanding role of the virtual world have resulted in the fetishisation of the tangible – as if the apparent permanence and authenticity of the material world offer an antidote to the postmodern condition. At the same time, environmental concerns have led to appeals for a profound reorientation of the balance of power between humans and the material world, with an appreciation for the significance of its non-human components inspiring calls for a 'posthumanism' (Braidotti 2013) or an 'object-oriented democracy' (Latour 2005, 14). On the other hand, longstanding anxieties that objects might one day come to supplant people – from the fears of the Luddites of the Industrial Revolution to the cyborgs of late twentieth-century science fiction – alongside ethical objections to consumer culture locate the source of alienation and oppression in our obsession with objects. In these very different discourses, objects are at once reassuring and destabilising, real and imagined, tyrannical yet in need of protection. In this volume, McCormack (Chapter 5) and Cooke (Chapter 18) discuss how discourses of authenticity are constructed around particular objects, while Allen (Afterword) explores the disruptive character of commodities so central to the complex and often chaotic processes of early twentieth-century globalisation. Our understanding of the relationship between people and the material world is therefore crucial to how we define humanity and our place within it (Miller 2005, 2).

But this concern with things is not solely a feature of the last quarter-century of academic scholarship. From the displays in Victorian museums that sought to order and aestheticise objects into schemes that legitimated colonialism, to seminal works such as Mauss's *The gift* (1990 [1924]) or Heidegger's *Being and time* (1962 [1927]), objects have long been a focus of interest in the humanities and social sciences. Nor, indeed, is the centrality of objects to contemporary conceptions of personhood and identity a product of Capitalism: studies by archaeologists and anthropologists illuminate the ways in which objects mediate social relations in very different cultural contexts (e.g., Tilley 1999; Battaglia 1990). Although common-sense understandings of objects in the modern western world emphasise their functionality – they allow us to cook food, mend a bike, or keep draughts out of our homes – they also play a significant social role. Objects are bound up with human biographies, forming inextricable elements of personal identity and memory: they are loved and hated, given and received, remembered and forgotten (Hoskins 1998). In this volume, the lockets and autograph albums discussed by Elliott and McAtackney (Chapters 8 and 10), for example, demonstrate the emotional impact of cherished objects and their significance in helping people negotiate the vicissitudes of history. In museums, as Cooke's chapter (Chapter 18) illustrates, it is often the everyday and the personal – objects such as Connolly's fedora hat – that make the most profound impact on those who view them.

Objects are therefore central to the construction of memory and, implicitly or overtly, reflections on the ways memory and history are materialised and visualised suffuse the chapters in this volume. Since the early 1980s, and gathering pace since the mid-1990s, there has been an avalanche of studies on memory, or even a 'memory epidemic' (Bodeman 2002, 24). This has often been framed in terms of 'collective memory' following Maurice Halbwachs (1877–1945), the French philosopher and sociologist considered the founding figure of studies that pay attention to how concepts of the past are socially mediated (Halbwachs 1992 [1951]). Halbwachs has been criticised for his overly unitary concept of collectivity and his concern for continuity at the expense of a sensitivity to historical change in memory itself. Due possibly to the naive organicism implied by the term 'collective', other historians often use the term 'social memory' as proposed in the book of that name by Chris Fentress and James Wickham (Fentress and Wickham 1992). In an Irish context, there have been a number of studies on how the Easter Rising has been remembered, and by whom, but material culture is not a central concern (Daly and O'Callaghan 2007; Graff-McRea 2010; Higgins 2012; McCarthy 2012).

In the introductory essay to the influential collection *Material memories* (Kwint et al. 1999), Marius Kwint notes how objects are central to the creation and maintenance of memory. He classifies the different ways this works. First, he suggests that 'they furnish recollection; they constitute our picture of the past' (Kwint 1999, 2) – a theme particularly apposite when we consider the ways 'memory' of 1916 has been represented and mediated through images and objects. In this volume, Crooke (Chapter 17), Godson (Chapter 22) and Shiels (Chapter 19) comment on the politics of memory: not only are particular events and people remembered while others are forgotten, but the materialities of commemorative practice inevitably construct the past in ways that are shaped by contemporary political conditions. Secondly, Kwint describes how objects stimulate remembering 'not only through the deployed mnemonics of public monuments or mantelpiece souvenirs' (Kwint 1999, 2) (see Shiels (Chapter 19) and Brück (Chapter 9)) but also through what Marcel Proust termed 'involuntary memory'; many of the personal objects, hidden in drawers and boxes until they were donated to museums, often many years later (see Joye and Malone (Chapter 16)), doubtless embody this experience. Thirdly, Kwint says, 'objects form records: analogues to living memory, storing information beyond individual experience' (Kwint 1999, 2–3). This speaks to the nature of social memory, as mediated by forms of visual culture, such as the innovative 1966 RTE series *Insurrection* that evoked an almost personal experience of the Rising for those who were too young to have personal recollection of the event (see Higgins 2012).

Material culture, then, is a profoundly social phenomenon: it is the very stuff of relationships, marking and making categories of person, and defining social boundaries through appropriate modes of consumption (Miller 1987). Our material surroundings – clothing, architecture, everyday things – give us a place in the world and tell us how to act in particular contexts (Bourdieu 1977). In this volume, Brück (Chapter 9) demonstrates how internment camp craftwork helped reinscribe dominant gender ideologies, while the ways in which national identities have been given material form are also a focus of discussion – expressed in typography (Bolger (Chapter 13)), for example, and the spectacle of the stage (Sisson (Chapter 12)). In this way, objects enshrine tradition by upholding systems of meaning, value and morality yet they also provide opportunities to subvert social norms (Miller, Rowlands and Tilley 1989). O'Kelly (Chapter 15) explores the contested meanings ascribed to 'national dress' in the first decades of the twentieth century, while Tynan (Chapter 2) argues that the informal character of the Volunteer uniform gave it a subversive character that challenged the norms of imperial militarism. As such, objects inevitably speak of wider political and cultural processes.

In this sense, it would clearly be simplistic to argue that objects have a single meaning – that a particular artefact 'stands' for a particular type of person, for example. Meaning is not an a priori given, but the product of social practice: the context in which an object is used – who uses it, how and when – gives it particular significance (Bourdieu 1977). In this volume, Hand (Chapter 1) discusses the variety of meanings that have been ascribed to the tricolour over the past century, while Crowley (Chapter 11) explores the remaking and reappropriation of the image of Patrick Pearse. The politics of representation are addressed in chapters by Chambers (Chapter 6), who examines how ideologies of imperialism were reiterated in contemporary newsreel coverage of the Rising, and Marshall and Kennedy (Chapters 20 and 14) who discuss how paintings by Lavery and Yeats were used to depict the events and legacy of the Rising in specific and often contradictory ways. In other words, images and objects do not simply mark the 'fact' of social identity; rather, they create the context in which particular identities are constructed. Similarly, Carville (Chapter 21) argues that photographs should not be seen as authentic historical evidence, but objects enmeshed in 'practices of looking' that create different mnemonic regimes. This is what gives the material world its social power: as Bourdieu (1977) demonstrates, habitual practice (the routine, non-discursive ways in which objects, buildings and other elements of the material world are encountered and employed in the course of daily life) upholds the systems of cultural value that underpin the social order. This is why material culture seems so inconsequential yet is actually so central to the reproduction and transformation of society – a point eloquently made in Cooke, Joye and Malone's discussions of the narrative power of 'ordinary' things in the National Museum of Ireland (Chapters 18 and 16).

Importantly, locating objects in particular cultural practices means that things must be seen in relational rather than categorical terms. Nor, indeed, are objects in themselves fixed and unchanging. Objects have lifecycles intertwined with those of humans (Kopytoff 1986): they are made, used and re-used; they break and are mended or recycled; they decay and are discarded. In popular culture, materiality is often used to articulate ideas of permanence, but objects are not stable: the visual and mechanical properties of wood, stone and metals change, for example, depending on whether they are wet or dry, old or new, hot or cold (Ingold 2007). This state of flux makes things hard to define and ensures that the relationship between subject and object is constantly shifting. It is hardly surprising, therefore, that the meanings of things are so frequently contested (see, for example, McCormack's discussion of the 'Castle document' (Chapter 5)) or that they should change so dramatically over time (as Hand shows for the tricolour (Chapter 1)). In this sense, then, objects are always emergent – the product of particular conjunctions of human desires and competences, material affordances and social conditions (Ingold 2000): as Jewesbury argues (Chapter 4), objects are as much about absence as presence, so that even the most salient symbols of the Rising frequently resist definition.

Importantly, these points require us to reconsider the relationship between subject and object – between the 'material' and 'culture' of material culture (Ingold 2000, 340). Historically, such Cartesian dualisms facilitated colonial modes of exploitation allowing active, knowledgeable and usually male subjects to exert power over a passive, feminised and objectified 'other' (Cosgrove 1984). This conceptual framework is clearly problematic on both ethical and theoretical grounds. Objects are so closely bound into our lives that it is evident that things make people (e.g., Weiner 1992) – it is not just people who make things, a point illustrated by the recursive relationship between the lockets and their maker explored in Elliott's chapter (Chapter 8). The boundary between subject and object is therefore often rather hazy: special objects are so much part of the self that to remove them would fundamentally alter – and perhaps even unravel – the subject; as such, personhood is always distributed (see also Strathern 1988). The idea of either subject or object as an a priori given is therefore problematic; both subjects and objects are constituted through particular social practices (Foucault 1979), whether that is the wearing of the brat and léine (O'Kelly (Chapter 15)) or the creation of autograph albums (McAtackney (Chapter 10)). This challenges the idea of objects as inert matter to which humans apply meaning as a cultural gloss (Pinney 2005). Objects are not passive markers of social identity but act back on us. They dazzle, frighten, excite and comfort (Gell 1998); at the same time, their materiality generates affordances that allow us to do certain things in particular ways, but impede other forms of action – particularly, for example, if they stop working as they should (Latour 1992). In this volume, Fitzpatrick discusses the emotive power of photographs of the 1916 widows and orphans (Chapter 7) and the significant impact these had on perceptions of the Rising. Indeed, Pearse's image can be argued to have taken on a life of its own, evading definition and control (Crowley (Chapter 11)). Those chapters thus not only illuminate the role of visual culture in forming perceptions of the Rising but exemplify Gillian Rose's advice on how to develop a critical approach to images, in particular her counsel to think 'about the social conditions and effects of visual objects' (Rose 2012, 17). A consideration of the effects of objects means that there has been increasing debate in recent years regarding the extent to which they can themselves be said to have agency – a move towards a more 'symmetrical' approach in which life unfolds in a constellation of creative engagements between the human and material world (Latour 1999; Witmore 2007). Inevitably, in such a world of flux and hybridity, objects challenge our understanding of subjectivity, agency and the social. For the 1916 Rising, this is especially so: as the contributions to this volume so clearly illustrate, the 'things' of 1916 inevitably call into question comfortable perceptions of Irish political and social identity, past, present and future.

Acknowledgements

We would like to take this opportunity to thank those who provided financial support for the production of the volume and for the conference from which it arises: the Graduate School of Creative Arts and Media (GradCAM), the Design History Society, Dublin City Council, An Post, University College Dublin, Senator Fiach Mac Conghail and the National College of Art and Design. We would like to thank all our colleagues and volunteers who helped with the organisation and smooth running of the conference, particularly Noel Fitzpatrick and Martin McCabe. We are grateful also to those who participated in the conference but for one reason or another were not in a position to contribute to the volume. They include Professor Mary E. Daly, who spoke on '1916 as the national commemoration? The paradox', Linda King on 'Collages and composites: the visual evolution of the Proclamation', Ellen Rowley on 'Conflict and concrete: the architecture of reconstruction in post-1916 Dublin', Kevin Rockett on 'Changing representations of Ireland's past in films made during the 1910s' and Éimear O'Connor on 'Men of the West and 1916: an emblem of presence and absence'. Finally, thanks to Simon O'Connor for kindly designing the cover of the book and to Brian Cregan, photographer, for the images on the cover.

I   The fabric of the Rising

Introduction

The contributions to this section share a concern with the significance of materiality and its effects. Each addresses a very different element of the material world of 1916: the physical contexts in which both rebels and non-combatants found themselves during the Rising and in its immediate aftermath were formed of buildings and landscapes, objects, images and documents, all of which had profound social, political and emotional impacts. On the one hand, as these contributions make clear, examining these as forms of material culture helps to illuminate the events of 1916 in new ways. Myles's forensic discussion of the surviving architectural fabric of the Moore Street 'battlefield zone', for example, provides insights into civilian experiences of the conflict and calls into question some of the 'myths' that have grown up around the events of the Rising: this is especially timely, as several of the buildings in question have until recently been in imminent danger of demolition.

Yet, to assume that the material evidence of the Rising is just that – 'evidence' for some kind of singular historical truth that has been lost in the mists of time – would be to miss much of the social potency of materiality. As Hand demonstrates, the assumption that objects' materiality makes their meaning somehow self-evident and incontestable is problematic: the network of symbolic and cultural references within which the Irish tricolor emerged is such that it was subject to multiple readings. Of course, some narratives around objects are suppressed, while others are made prominent: this is the politics of materiality. In the newsreels discussed by Chambers, the smoke-filled shells of half-demolished buildings in Dublin were framed so that they called to mind the ruined cities that other Irish soldiers were at that same moment encountering in France and Belgium. Here, the materiality of the Rising was employed to evoke a sense of horror and futility, while the juxtaposition of these images with pictures of Britannia helped cast those events in pro-Unionist terms.

Debates around the meanings of things also come to the fore in Jewesbury's treatment of the 'Half-Proclamation' – viewed at once both as sacred text and criminal evidence. Yet, as he shows, its 'evidential' status was considered problematic even at the time. Here, Jewesbury demonstrates that it is more fruitful to examine the 'Half-Proclamation' not as a document (for the words it contained soon slipped to the margins of consciousness) but as an object with its own distinct and powerful aura. McCormack's discussion of *Secret Orders* takes a related approach, examining both the conditions of its making and the materiality of fabrication so that the problematic boundary between 'reality' and 'falsehood' is called into question. The fluidity of objects is perhaps most powerfully addressed in Tynan's contribution, which explores the process of bricolage involved in the creation of 1916 military uniform: the transitory, improvised yet transformational qualities of rebel dress was one reason why it was so effective in challenging colonial forms of military power. Together, the contributions to this section explore the materiality of the Rising in various forms, addressing issues of authenticity, interpretation and ownership that are key to the social and political power of objects.

1

The fabric of a deathless dream: a short introduction to the origins and meanings of the 1916 tricolour flag

Brian Hand

'Right proudly high over Dublin town
they hung out the flag of war.'

'The Foggy dew',
Ballad by Canon Charles O'Neill, *c.*1919

The 1916 tricolour appears as a rather discontinuous symbol. With the events of the Rising, the flag was revealed as something that was both old and new. It appeared untethered to historical time, as if it floated free of sequential history like a dream image. The tricolour, then, has a mimetic relationship to our understanding of the oath-bound secret Irish Republican Brotherhood, a hidden symbol, camouflaged and cloaked. It is not that it was unknown as a republican separatist symbol before the Rising – it was centre-stage during the funeral of Jeremiah O'Donovan Rossa in 1915 – but it had not been officially baptised and named as the flag of the new Republic. To do so of course would have been to reveal the secret plans for the revolution. The 1916 Proclamation declares a feminine Ireland 'who having resolutely waited for the right moment to reveal herself' summons Irishmen and Irishwomen to her call, to her flag, to her strike for freedom. James Connolly's dispatch near the end of the Rising stated that 'for the first time in 700 years the flag of a free Ireland floats triumphantly in Dublin city' (Ryan 1949, 148). The flag stands for this abridged interval and at the same moment is reinstated as an original, new, imperishable, Messianic symbol. As Walter Benjamin (1968, 261) writes, 'the awareness that they are about to make the continuum of history explode is characteristic of the revolutionary classes at the moment of their action'.

The Rising is the origin of the tricolour, the place of its singular historical performance. Nearly all occupied buildings could be identified by the flying of this flag as the fighting progressed: there were two on the General Post Office according to Desmond Ryan (1924). There are many good descriptions of these tricolours in the Bureau of Military History statements but no good photographs. Incredibly, there are no authenticated surviving tricolour flags in national museums. However, if we distinguish between the artefact of the flag and the event of the Rising what is revealed is a fascinating montage of different, colourful fabric tricolours used by oppositional and revolutionary movements in these islands since the French revolution. A decade ago, I encountered a photograph of Emily Davison at Tattenham Corner during the 1913 Epsom Derby holding up a tricolour to the King's racehorse. This was not the Irish tricolour, however (black-and-white images can easily confuse the viewer in terms of the indexicality of colour as monotone), but the suffragette tricolour of purple, white and green (Figs 1.1 and 1.2). In this short case study, I want to examine the 1916 flag as a complex, material, historical artefact and explore and rediscover what has been overlooked in terms of its design, production and multiple meanings.

The newsreel films of the Derby and Davison's death are shocking indexical documents: they are among the earliest films of someone dying, the first films of a live horse race and the first film of a tricolour-associated attack on the Crown forces. Davison chose her location based on the position of the cameras on the opposite side of the bend but also, as the films show, on the proximity of an enormous Union flag that flew in the corner. In the Museum of London one of two blood-stained tricolour flags that were stitched into Davison's jacket is shown beside a sickening looped video of her death. There is no text explaining republican feminism in the display. The newsreels of Davison's death and mass public funeral were a lesson in publicity that was not lost on Irish, Indian or South African republican separatists. The effects can be seen in the publicity campaign and spectacle surrounding O'Donovan Rossa's funeral, jointly organised by the Irish Republican Brotherhood (IRB) and the Irish Citizen Army, which featured a tricolour for the first time on a Fenian coffin.

Given the patriarchal and conservative culture of post-independence Ireland, it is no surprise that the official account of the origin of the national flag, produced as a small bilingual booklet (*An Bhratach Náisiúnta*/The National Flag) by the Stationery Office, contains no mention of mass usage of suffragette tricolours throughout Ireland and Britain in the twentieth century, or the historic use of tricolours by Chartists and socialists. As Margot Gayle Backus has argued, the new Free State would 'push to the margins every trace of the socialist, feminist, queer, liberational impulses that infused its birth' (Gayle Backus 2008, 76). Both old and new versions

1.1   The important tradition of tricolours in Britain. Sylvia Pankhurst addressing a crowd from a scaffold-like platform outside the headquarters of the East London Federation of Suffragettes, Old Ford Road, Bow, 1912.
Courtesy of the Museum of London; NN22843

1.2   Christabel Pankhurst holding a Women's Social & Political Union (WSPU) tricolour flag and waving from the window of a house that overlooks Holloway Road Prison, 1909.
Courtesy of the London School of Economics and Political Science, Library Collections; 7JCC/O/02/108b

of the booklet betray the same agenda. There is, however, an interesting contrast between the two in their opening paragraphs. The older edition (undated, but illustrated with pen-and-ink and priced at three pence) describes the tricolour as:

> essentially a flag of union. Its origin is to be sought in the history of the early nineteenth century and it is emblematic of the fusion of the older elements represented by the green, with the newer elements, represented by the orange. The combination of both colours in the tricolour, with the white between in token of brotherhood, symbolises the union of different stocks in a common nationality. (*An Bhratach Náisiúnta*, 5)

The newer booklet (also undated, but with photographs, and priced at £2.36 or €3.00; this is the edition still available on the internet at the time of writing), in the pluralist spirit of the Good Friday Agreement (but not the citizenship referendum of 2004), tones down much of the above racialised male-centred discourse and describes the flag as 'intended to symbolise the inclusion and hoped-for-union of the people of different traditions on this island, which is now expressed in the Constitution as the entitlement of every person born in Ireland to be part of the Irish nation' (*An Bhratach Náisiúnta*, 4). This statement is more realistic in expressing a 'hoped-for-union' than the Proclamation, the idealistic mission statement of the Irish Volunteers, or the 1937 Constitution.

What does a flag of union or brotherhood mean in the context of an armed rebellion? What is obvious is that, from the rebel perspective, 1916 reconciles divergent strands in the rainbow composition of the insurrection itself – for example, the language movement of the Gaelic League, the feminist militant suffrage movement, the Larkinite activists, anti-conscription campaigners, the bourgeois nationalists, the IRB in Dublin and Clann na Gael in New York. Reconciliation here means that the fields of struggle converged into the rebellion: James Connolly reconciled himself with Tom Clarke; Constance Markievicz with Patrick Pearse. Therefore a flag for such an event would have to have a sense of the principal movements that joined forces in common cause. The nationalist Volunteer flag of the gold harp on green, the plough and the stars of the Citizen Army, the GWV (Give Women Votes) green, white and violet of feminism, and finally the internationalist red flag of socialism all needed to be superseded in this strategic yet fragile union. Robert Mitchel Henry, in *The Evolution of Sinn Féin*, writes that:

> on Palm Sunday 1916, the union of Irish Labour and Irish Nationalism was proclaimed in striking fashion. In the evening that day, Connolly (dressed in military uniform for the first time) hoisted over Liberty Hall,

the headquaters of the Citizen Army, the Irish tricolour of orange, white and green, the flag designed by the Young Irelanders of 1848. (Mitchel Henry 1920, 212)

Note the incorrect order of the flag's colours. There are conflicting accounts of this event as to whether a new tricolour or an old green flag with gold harp was flown.

Connolly had learned from his time in the British Army during the Land War, from Davison's funeral in London, and from fellow activists like Maud Gonne and Hannah Sheehy-Skeffington, the value of pageantry, flags, songs and magic lantern projections, or what could broadly be described as the theatricality of resistance (Levenson 1973, 290; Ó Broin 1976, 85). He published his speech in advance of the flag-raising event in the *Workers' Republic* newspaper (8 April 1916) as 'The Irish Flag', writing how this flag (again, Connolly avoids calling it a tricolour) meant

> that in the midst of and despite the treasons and backslidings of leaders and guides, in the midst of and despite all the weaknesses, corruption and moral cowardice of a section of the people, in the midst of and despite all this, there still remains in Ireland a spot where a body of true men and women are ready to hoist, gather round, and to defend the flag made sacred by all the sufferings of all the martyrs of the past. (Connolly 1949b, 173)

Connolly, just a month before this event, wrote and produced at Liberty Hall a one-act play set in the Fenian rebellion of 1867 called *Under Which Flag*. This revival-style drama by the Irish Workers Dramatic Company finished with a tableau where Seán Connolly (no relation to James), Abbey actor and Citizen Army commander, held up a large tricolour to the audience. Seán Connolly carried this same flag to the roof of City Hall on Easter Monday of the Rising and was shot dead trying to hoist it above the building (Connolly O'Brien 1980, 202; Ó Ceallaigh Ritschel 1998, 67).

Both versions of the official narrative agree that substituting yellow for orange destroys the original symbolism of reconciliation. The 1916 tricolour was a new dawn, a new hope, a utopian future and here is perhaps the symbolic justification in which sunburst gold (from the Fenian flag) or yellow (from the Papal colours) often substitute what is perceived by some as an ill-fitting loyalist orange. A difficulty remains, though, because a suffragette tricolour of green, white and gold was in widespread existence in the years before 1916 and was known to the leadership of the Rising, particularly Connolly. The flag belonged to the Women's Freedom League who broke from the Women's Social & Political Union (WSPU) over a number of issues in 1908; their

1.3   Republican, socialist, feminist and ribbonman, Francis Sheehy-Skeffington; portrait, oil on canvas, 78 cm × 68 cm, by Sarah Cecilia Harrison, 1916.
Courtesy of the Hugh Lane Gallery, Dublin

tricolour of green, white and gold was chosen by a large majority of members through a referendum of its branches (Tickner 1988, 265). The WFL was led by its president, Charlotte Despard, sister of Lord French and joint leader with Hannah Sheehy-Skeffington of the Irish Women's Franchise League. The WFL was generally (though not exclusively) opposed to acts of violence and was much more socialist and anti-colonialist in direction. Unlike the WSPU it did not cease its activism with the outbreak of the First World War. Despard had an incredibly long and active career in Irish and British radical politics and is buried in the republican plot in Glasnevin. After the murder of Francis Sheehy-Skeffington in the Rising, the artist (and politician) Cecilia Harrison was commissioned to paint his portrait. In the painting, which is now in the Hugh Lane Gallery, Sheehy-Skeffington is sporting a green, white and gold ribbon and badge (Fig. 1.3). Fox (1935, 149) writes of seeing this portrait of Sheehy-Skeffington and comments that 'he was wearing his votes for women badge and a ribbon in the suffrage – which were also the National – colours'.

The Sheehy-Skeffington portrait shows how confusing the emblems and symbols of resistance can be and how historians need to look very closely at the symbolism and contingent differences between specific symbolic objects used by participants in the Rising. Townshend (2005, 159; 2013, 31–2) associates the tricolour with popular images of Robert Emmet dressed in a green, white and gold uniform and notes how a Trinity College student from Belfast on seeing the tricolour fly over the College of Surgeons could not understand why one part of this was orange. The martyrdom of Emmet is recognised as an influence on the Rising, as too is his Proclamation announcing the formation of a provisional government. Connolly eulogised and constructed an image of Emmet in *Labour in Ireland* as a Dublin leader of 'working class proletarians' (from the Liberties) with an internationalist and democratic outlook. Interestingly, Connolly laments how every recurring anniversary of his ill-fated rebellion continues to bring forth 'its crop of orators who know all about Emmet's martyrdom, and nothing about his principles' (Connolly 1949a, 86). Connolly elsewhere (1991) [1900] disparages such shallow imitators of Tone and Emmet, stalwarts of bourgeois nationalism, and echoes Marx's insights (1852) into the anachronistic borrowing and hollowing-out of slogans, uniforms and symbols from the revolutionary past by those seeking to maintain the status quo through the rapid expansion of capitalist oppression and exploitation.

Although tricolours appeared in 1798 and intermittently thereafter, 1848, a year of appalling famine, is recognised as the date when the tricolour was first proposed as a possible national emblem of independence. Thomas Francis Meagher, William Smith O'Brien and Edward Hollywood, who together formed a deputation sent from the Irish Confederacy to the new republican government in Paris, returned to Dublin with a gift of an embroidered republican flag made of French silk. Hollywood is the least-known of the three: he was a third-generation silk-weaver from the Liberties whose father fought with Emmet and he was a recognised leader in the nascent trade union movement in Dublin. In recent years, his contribution to the story of the flag has been commemorated at Glasnevin Cemetery (it would be good to see the commemoration extend to the contribution of Charlotte Despard). This Young Ireland tricolour is recorded in the *Freeman's Journal* as orange, white and green. Tricolours were prominent in demonstrations throughout the southeast of Ireland during that year. In the town of Enniscorthy, County Wexford, one large flag charged with the slogan 'unity is strength' is recorded (Tobin 1964).

Tricolours are also associated with the emergent trade union movement in the chaotic industrial cities of Liverpool, Belfast and Manchester to symbolise the common cause of the mobile armies of Catholic and Protestant workers in the larger class struggle. The Chartist movement from the 1830s had a significant Irish dimension to its leadership and a tricolour of red, white and green. For the bourgeoisie and later social reformers and socialists, the geometric design of the striped cloth standard was rational, modern and even; the tri-band division had no obvious hierarchy or feudal ties, and its horizontal form suggested both equality and democracy. The *Oxford English Dictionary*, however, struggles to present an objective definition of the word 'tricolour', where it defines the adjective in a bizarrely heterotopic fashion as, first, a 'black, white and tan [breed of] dog', followed by 'the national flags of France, Italy, and Mexico', with no mention of the modern states (and former colonies) of Ireland, South Africa or India, and the entry concludes with a certainly less-than-positive definition of the word as 'the green, white, and orange Irish Republican flag'. In the conventional discourse of British society, the French and Italian flags act as clear signifiers, but there is much more confusion over the referent of the Irish tricolour, variously described as 'Ireland', 'Éire', 'the Republic of Ireland' and 'Southern Ireland'; the tricolour is a metonym for both imperialism and anti-Britishness, while seeming self-evident as the flag for a paramilitary movement.

Not surprisingly, flags and emblems are not at all straightforward in the political, economic, cultural and religious conflicts in these islands. Visual evidence recording and depicting riots and conflicts at any point during the past 200 years includes colourful rosettes, banners, costumes and flags. Much of this visual culture was informed by racist eighteenth- and nineteenth-century stereotypes, where the childlike, wild, subhuman and simian caricatures of the Irish underclass (almost a third of the UK population in 1841) were seen as needing strong governance, strict control and innovative social engineering. The more irrational the Irish could be represented in the popular and elite imagination, the less legitimate their demands for justice and democracy. The proposed economic and social reforms of Irish agriculture (which was the vital breadbasket of industrial Britain) in something like the Devon Commission of the 1840s sought to bring a modern and enlightened approach to the perceived fragmented illegible patchwork of the rural communal lifeworld in Ireland (Lloyd 2007; Nally 2011). The violently imposed rationalisation of Irish geography through the orderly geometry of colonialism (combined with the repression of industry) is a fertile area for thinking about the homomorphic design of the tricolour with tripartite statistical tables and their units and measures of exchange, striped prison and workhouse clothing, and new maps with even strips of subdivision. Once tested in Ireland, larger geographies like Africa were subjected to similar rigid lines of colonial subdivision, banding and boundaries.

The semiotician C.S. Pierce identified three dimensions to all signs in relation to their referent: the indexical, where meaning is related through causation and there is a real, existential or ontological link; the iconic, meaning the similarity, analogical or mimetic resemblance between the sign and referent; and finally the symbolic. Flags are typically understood as symbolic signs (like words), their meaning understood through the shared conventional language of a group or people. Symbolic signs have a general meaning that can be learned and passed on through generations. The 1916 tricolour deserves a whole book to pull together and investigate the multiple threads of its significance, including Seán Connolly's performance mentioned above; the role of Mary Shannon, a machinist from the Liberty Hall Shirt Making Collective who made the tricolours that Connolly brought to the General Post Office (Tallion 1996, 27); or the archives of British Army regiments which may still be holding confiscated flags from the rebellion. The indexical register of the tricolour is found in the qualities of the immediate flag-as-object, for example a flapping sound, wind direction, the gesture of looking up skyward, or an awareness of death with a flag at half-mast. In terms of the Rising, some of the immediate outcomes of Dubliners' awareness of the new flag were that all the firms opposed to the 1913 Lockout now had their windows smashed and their buildings occupied, and that Sheehy-Skeffington's ribbon in the portrait mentioned above was misinterpreted. Other examples of indexicality would range from films and photographs to how to pronounce the word 'tricolour' as the slower 'try-colour' or the faster 'trick-colour'. The iconicity of the tricolour is as interesting a field of potential research, where its meaning echoes the republican French and Italian flags, the socialist and emancipatory Chartist and Suffragette flags, the rainbow collation in the insurgency, and traditions of decorating maypoles with furze and ribbon. I hope this chapter has shown how rich such a study of this flag could be.

2

The unmilitary appearance of the 1916 rebels

Jane Tynan

In Easter 1916, a group of rebels caused chaos on the streets of Dublin. It may seem trivial to ask what they wore, but clothing was significant to the conflict, so much so that the image of insurgency the rebels created later echoed across the world. Staging any military conflict involves dressing up: uniforms advertise allegiance and discipline troops. My discussion centres on the rebels' lack of uniformity and what this meant to the legacy of the Rising. First, irregularities are not so unusual in the outward appearance of soldiers: perfect uniformity is rarely achieved. Exploring the minutiae of military clothing, even its deregulation, is potentially revealing. The paradox of non-uniformity first struck me when researching the military clothing worn by British combatants during the First World War: soldiers adapted their uniforms for battle, while many new recruits who eagerly awaited regulation issue had to contend with inferior civilian uniforms. Understanding the source of resistance to uniform and the effects of improvising military clothing brought me closer to an understanding of how soldiers contested official narratives of regulation and discipline. Here, I consider how rebels embodied their military identities for what was to become a key episode in the history of modern insurgency, the 1916 Rising in Dublin.

A spirit of militarism gave rise to a range of military-style organisations in Ireland in the 1910s. According to Michael Adams (1990), this militarising of civil society was consistent with social values established in late nineteenth- and early twentieth-century British culture. In both countries, these quasi-military organisations generated a whole discourse of military participation, often expressed in the 'call to uniform'. As Keith Jeffery (2000) argues, the First World War and the Easter Rising in 1916 were intertwined events. In the years preceding 1916, volunteers could be seen drilling openly on the streets, to which Seán Ó Faoláin (1965, 130) responded with the criticism that they were 'rudely accoutered fellows, with no uniform other than a belt around their ordinary working clothes'. Volunteer units were self-financing, with weapons, equipment and uniforms paid for by each recruit or, failing that, from a central fund (Durney 2004, 8). Volunteers were typically young, urban, educated, skilled, unmarried and most had little or no previous military experience (Durney 2004, 8). However, lack of means seemingly did not deter many young people from concocting some kind of outfit to express their militancy.

What they wore

The Rising began on Easter Monday 1916 and lasted for six days. Led by Patrick Pearse and James Connolly, the plan for the rebels was to stage an armed revolt in order to gain Irish independence from the United Kingdom. An account written just after the Rising witnessed the reactions from onlookers on the tram cars, suggesting that even those enjoying the holiday were curious about the rebels: as one helpfully explained to his companions, those 'dressed in the dark-green uniforms, with the slouch hats, are the Citizen Army, and the others in green-grey are Irish Volunteers' (Ó Cathasaigh 1919, 59). They were a familiar enough sight, and people could correctly identify their allegiance through the design of their military uniforms.

However, in the ranks of the Irish Citizen Army, doubts were raised about whether uniforms were a good idea for an armed revolt. In Seán O'Casey's autobiographical *Drums under the windows*, he recalls a debate about uniforms, recounting his own contribution to a meeting in Liberty Hall:

> the question of belligerency doesn't exist for us. We will be rebels; worse – we will be traitors, even terrorists to England, and she will strike without stop or mercy … If we flaunt signs of what we are, and what we do, we'll get it on the head and round the neck. (O'Casey 1945, 267–8)

He wanted the rebels to blend with civilians as far as possible, to compensate for their lack of resources and poor military organisation. Those who desired a smart uniform vainly hoped it would lead to belligerency status. O'Casey was sceptical, and anticipated that the rebels would be forced to adopt a strategy of camouflage on the streets of Dublin, which was also, in very different ways, a key concern for the British army fighting in the trenches of the western front. Questions about how to uniform the rebels struck at the heart of what the Rising would represent for the British, and the threat urban insurgency could pose for the industrial powers.

O'Casey (1945, 268) went on to argue that everyday working clothes were the ideal ploy: 'You would slip among the throng, carelessly, with few the wiser. In uniform, the crowd would shrink aside to show you, and the enemy will pounce. In your everyday rags you could, if the worst came, hang your rifle on a lamp-post and go your way.' To create havoc with unconventional warfare and urban terrorism was, as Andrew Mack (1975, 175–200) argues, a key characteristic of insurgency, representing the refusal to confront the industrial powers on their own terms. Once insurgents recognise that they cannot defeat the enemy militarily, they avoid direct attacks, and can only resort to asymmetrical warfare. Despite O'Casey's warnings, the Irish Citizen Army leadership decided on the distinctive military uniforms: 'They were of a darker green than those worn by the Irish Volunteers, and it became the custom among the Transport Union members to fasten up one side of the big slouch hats with the red hand badge of the Union' (Fox 1943, 68). The men's uniform was a dark green serge, with a high collar, two breast pockets and a hat similar in style to those worn by the Boers.

The Volunteer uniform was also thoughtfully designed. A uniform subcommittee was appointed in early 1914 to draft its design, and a meeting of the Volunteer Central Executive in 1915 approved a new dress instruction, later published in the *Irish Volunteer* (White and O'Shea 2003, 18). It was planned that all ranks and units would wear a standard tunic with rolled collar, dark green shoulder straps and pointed cuffs, two breast and two patch pockets, a brown leather bandolier and white canvas haversack to carry ammunition and equipment (White and O'Shea 2003, 16). The chosen uniform was to consist of a grey-green tunic, trousers, puttees and a Cossack-style headdress. The *Irish Volunteer* from 1914–16 carried advertisements for officers' clothing, including bandoliers, uniform, puttees, badges, caps and even 'marching socks' (Strachan and Nally 2012). Importantly, the uniform was not compulsory for all Irish Volunteers, although it was deemed desirable for officers (White and O'Shea 2003, 18) (Fig. 2.1).

A soft hat resembling that worn by the Boers in South Africa became known as the 'Cronje hat' after the Boer general, Piet Cronje, an attempt to emulate a force that defeated the British in South Africa (Strachan and Nally 2012, 223). Clair Wills quotes Desmond Ryan recalling Pearse sitting down beside him in the General Post Office when fires blazed on the ground floor: 'He was seated on a barrel, his slightly flushed face crowned by his turned-up military hat' (Wills 2009, 54). Other accounts also suggest that Pearse wore 'exactly this type of Boer slouch hat outside the General Post Office on Sackville Street when reading the Proclamation of the Irish Republic on 24 April 1916' (Strachan and Nally 2012, 223). The rebels created a uniform using signifiers of Irishness to fashion a distinctly

2.1   Group of Irish Volunteers and one member of the Irish Citizen Army inside the General Post Office, Dublin, Easter Week, 1916.
Image reproduced by kind permission of the Military Archives, Ireland

Irish military identity. Keith Jeffery cites uniform and the appearance of military discipline as critical to the plans to use the insurrection to claim Irish independence (Jeffery 2000, 49). Uniforms are part of the logic of warfare: they promote internal discipline, convey hierarchy and status, legitimise violence and demonstrate the access the military force has to the means of production. An eyewitness account from Joe Good recalls seeing Joe Plunkett outside Liberty Hall: he was 'beautifully dressed, having high tan leather boots, spurs, pince-nez and looked like any British brass-hat staff officer' (McGarry 2011, 158). If the smart appearance of the rebel leaders constructed a distinctly Irish military masculinity, it reflected the ways in which the war created opportunities to assert national identities.

Most volunteers could not afford a uniform and wore their normal civilian clothes and a brown belt bearing an inscription 'Irish Volunteers', but many of the buckles worn were homemade, which led to much variation in their design and appearance (Joye 2013). Despite the dapper appearance of some officers of the Dublin brigade, with firms such as Thomas Fallon and Co. of Mary Street in Dublin selling badges, headdresses and uniforms to individual volunteers, the various systems of uniform provision inevitably led to a lack of uniformity (White and O'Shea 2003, 18). The same was true of the Cumann na mBan uniform, whereby women either had an outfit tailored or made it themselves, resulting in garments that were varied in style and, as one member of the organisation described, 'badly made, as if they were cut out with a knife and fork' (Matthews 2010a, 111). So a picture was emerging of the project to uniform the rebels. Legitimate regulation dress was largely the preserve of the rebel leadership, but lack of military experience and financial hardship found the vast majority of the rebel forces bearing a haphazard, homemade appearance.

Transforming bodies

Portrait photographs taken of Countess Markievicz just before the Rising reveal a woman carefully crafting a revolutionary image. In these pictures, she wears a feminine Edwardian hat with a masculine military-style uniform.[1] In a biography by Seán Ó Faoláin written in the 1930s, he describes her military appearance for the Rising: 'She made herself a uniform of dark green, high-collared to the chin, glinting with brass buttons, caught about her middle by a leather belt, and she wore a wide-awake hat whose leaf was pinned up on one side by the flaming badge of the Red Hand' (Ó Faoláin 1934, 198). Later in the 1960s, Donald Seaman of the *Daily Express* recalled her as the glamorous figure of the Rising: 'She went to war in a gorgeous, high-necked, tight-fitting, bottle green uniform made to her own design'.[2] However, as Ruth Tallion (1996, 19) observes, Constance Markievicz improvised her outfit for the Rising by combining one of Michael Mallin's old uniform jackets with riding breeches. One thing is clear: this rebel leader was not following the regulation pattern. Her training as a painter at the Slade School of Art in London might have given Markievicz an awareness of the power of images, but she was also keen to adopt a military identity normally only available to men.

Lisa Weihman (2004) argues that various women combatants deployed gender masquerade during the Rising, shifting between feminine and masculine identities. There were times when donning traditionally female clothing allowed women combatants to blend with civilians when acting as couriers; at other times they sought to blend with the mass of male rebels. She finds a photograph of Margaret Skinnider in male drag, a Fianna uniform, with a cigarette hanging from her mouth, demonstrating that rebels were subversive in more ways than one (Weihman 2004, 233). Skinnider fought

---

1   Countess Markievicz photographs, Kilmainham Gaol, Dublin.
2   Donald Seaman, *Daily Express*, 23 March 1966 (cited in Higgins 2012, 157).

alongside Markievicz in St Stephen's Green. Helena Moloney, who helped Markievicz to establish Na Fianna Éireann in 1909, described the haphazard appearance of some of her comrades in the Irish Citizen Army: 'women had no uniform, in the ordinary sense – nor the men either. Some of the men had green coats. They wore an ordinary slouch hat, like the Boer hat, and mostly a belt' (McGarry 2011, 158). So, despite plans to supply smart uniforms, many men and women of the Citizen Army were improvising. As the women's experience suggests, what the situation demanded was an equivocal attitude to uniform, not beautifully made green tunics.

Thus, if unconventional warfare involved gender mimicry, it was one of the narrow range of options open to rebel forces determined to defeat a formidable enemy. Body transformations were a critical part of the urban terrorism enacted on the streets of Dublin in 1916. Uniforming for the rebels was about camouflage, and while many commentators were later keen to emphasise Markievicz's glamorous appearance, it was not simply a reflection of her vanity. A range of quirky outfits were in evidence on the streets of Dublin, many of which were the strange solutions rebels came up with in the course of battle. As with Margaret Skinnider's drag, clothing created illusions that enabled rebels to evade the gaze of the enemy. Following the Rising, images of destruction dominated the British press, but there is a sense that the rebels' modes of self-presentation also mobilised destruction. Eyal Weizman, in his investigation of the transformation of architecture in the occupied Palestinian territories since 1967, argues that architecture is conceptual, a 'way of understanding political issues as constructed realities' (Weizman 2007, 6). For him, temporary, incomplete, constantly changing spatial organisation is a feature of modern low-level conflict. He was not interested in clothing but his notion that design can be destructive evokes the mutating bodies of the 1916 rebels as they moved through the conflict. More significant than the smart well-designed uniforms of the leaders were the transformations that rebel bodies underwent during the course of the Rising.

Civilians were being militarised in an atmosphere of chaos. Many accounts suggest that people turned up in ordinary street clothes to join the fighting, just to be given a gun and a bandolier, echoing Seán Ó Faoláin's account of men drilling on the Cork streets looking 'so shabby, so absurd, so awkward, so unheroic looking' (Ó Faoláin 1965, 100–3). Rejecting the image of gentlemanly soldiering was not their first impulse: as discussed, both the Irish Citizen Army and the Volunteers initially opted for uniform and rank insignia modelled on British army officers. However, the actual circum-stances of the fighting, the politics of the conflict, gave rise to a material reality that forced the rebels to adopt an unheroic image, in effect to become insurgents. While this unheroic image could be interpreted as anticolonial, it perhaps has more to do with the relationship between bodies, urban space and the chaotic unfolding of events. Their bodies disrupted and opposed the symbolic order, in line with Alvin Jackson's view that the 1916 rebels were 'a legion of the excluded', a ragtag army of Fenians, socialists, outspoken women and male youth who were already distanced from the establishment (cited in Ferriter 2004, 138). They spilled onto the streets wearing civilian clothes with bandoliers and haversacks. Those joining the fighting often wore outfits improvised from working clothes, following the insurgent narrative of destruction and transformation.

The insurrection had its own geography and pace, and the peculiar dynamics of the Rising demanded an equivocal attitude to uniform. For instance, according to Clair Wills, when members of the Irish Citizen Army had taken the wounded to Jervis Street Hospital through tunnellings and across the roof to the Coliseum, they returned to Arnotts department store where some changed out of their uniforms, and joined several volunteers who had been in outposts in Liffey Street, to hide from view by 'mingling with the local residents on Saturday morning' (Wills 2009, 80). Rebellious bodies mutated into soldiers, but were quick to return to civilian appearance at a moment's notice. The result was that British forces could not distinguish rebels from law-abiding civilians. These bodily transformations gave the Rising a very modern texture. The clothing worn by the rebels was not necessarily fashionable, but the way they handled their appearance was thoroughly modern, echoing Ulrich Lehmann's view of fashion as 'transitory, mobile and fragmentary' (Lehmann 2000, xii). One aspect of the modernity of the Rising was the yawning gap between the fantasy of perfectly designed uniforms and the reality of the fugitive power of clothing to wage an urban guerrilla war.

Clothing became part of a whole set of practices for rebels to engage in artifice and illusion, particularly in their efforts to disguise their bodies. If, as Priscilla Metscher (2008, 155) argues, everything had gone according to plan, the rebels would have been a formidable force, but botched schemes, inadequate resources and the reality of the fighting found them improvising; their bodies became weapons to compensate for their lack of organisation, manpower and resources. As Desai and Eckstein (1990) argue, insurgency relies more on the force of politics than the minutiae of military organisation and planning. For them, the operational doctrines of guerrilla warfare embody the energy and vision of peasant rebellion combined with the ideology of modern revolution. This requirement to shift between civilian and military identities describes how anarchic geographies and bodies shaped the material legacy of the Rising, in particular the deployment of gender masquerade, mimicry, camouflage, disguise and bodily transformation.

2.2   Easter Rising commemorative issue of *Breiz Atao* ('Brittany Forever'), May 1935. 'Easter Monday 1916! Nineteen years ago, the Irish saved their country by shedding their blood for it'. Image reproduced by kind permission of Trinity College Dublin

After the Rising

Notions of tragic heroism dominate the memory of the Rising, but a closer look at the material culture of the conflict uncovers patterns that could perhaps challenge that legacy. The violence, the chaos, the various ways in which people were enlisted to the insurrection were inscribed in bodily practices. To borrow Weizman's phrase, the mundane rituals of dress could be viewed as an instance of 'politics as matter' (Weizman 2007, 5). Combatants were constructed through the modern military practices of evasion, illusion and transformation; the rebels exploited the fugitive qualities of clothing to great effect. Consider Seán Keating's painting *Men of the West*, in which a new kind of citizen soldier emerges from the Rising, a raw figure capable of imagining and improvising military action. Abroad, militants heard of the Irish rebellion, particularly separatists, such as the Bretons and Bengalis. It has been argued that the chief inspiration for the Bengali revolutionary movement following the First World War was Irish republicanism, and the 1916 Rising in particular (Silvestri 2009, 13).

According to Daniel Leach (2008), the Rising had a profound impact upon Breton militants, who strongly identified with the republican struggle in Ireland. Indeed, for many nationalists, these Irish heroes were revered, and as a commemorative issue of *Breiz Atao* from May 1935 suggests, they were cast in novel ways (Fig. 2.2). The image chosen to represent the Rising features what appears to be a working man wearing civilian clothes and a flat cap. Grasping a gun, he combines the menace of the terrorist with the casual heroism of the citizen soldier – a figure that perhaps embodied what was by the 1930s a renewed spirit of separatist militancy. The approach to military dress in the 1916 Rising was modern, where survival depends on the very visual and material design of the body: its capacity to camouflage, to create illusions and to transform at a moment's notice. The self-presentation of the rebels offered an alternative narrative to the version of Irishness conceived by the rebel leaders and planners. Celtic and Gaelic signifiers did not succeed in de-Anglicising Irish culture, but the Rising was a pivotal event due to the velocity of subversive military identities improvised by the rebels. The material culture of the Rising was fashioned by the spatial logic of the conflict and thus the uniforms were deregulated, haphazard, quirky and often homemade. It is not clear whether or not the experience of the 1916 rebels on the streets of Dublin shaped insurgent efforts elsewhere, but by mobilising artifice and illusion they anticipated the nature of combat on the chaotic battlefields of the future.

Acknowledgements

I would like to thank Tadhg McGrath for drawing my attention to the Daniel Leach article and the image for the 1916 commemorative issue of *Breiz Atao* therein.

3

Beating the retreat:
the final hours of the Easter Rising

Franc Myles

'This was not history. It has not passed.'

M. D'Arcy and J. Arden, *The non-stop Connolly show* (1986, 448)

Setting the scene

This brief chapter is an outcome of archaeological fieldwork and documentary research, focusing on the materiality of the route taken by republican volunteers as they left the General Post Office on the Friday evening of Easter Week until their surrender to British forces the following afternoon. The study was undertaken at the request of the National Museum in the context of a large planning application covering the entire area of the battlefield, and was thereby funded by the developers. The theoretical framework within which the study was conducted was informed by work that critically assesses the 'familiar past' (see, for example, West 1999; Buchli and Lucas 2001) rather than the more traditional methodologies of battlefield archaeology. The fieldwork was grounded on the idea of making the 'familiar' unfamiliar, a central theoretical concern of any archaeological investigation of the more recent past.

An unusual aspect of this particular archaeological inquiry was the fact that it examined events which took place within a twenty-four hour period, where archaeological investigation more traditionally deals in decades at the lower end of the temporal metric. Here, known events were distorted by memory and battlefield panic; little was left of an artefactual nature apart from the historical landscape itself, and only disarticulated fragments of that have survived. By applying more investigative methods of archaeological inquiry, by interrogating written sources, historical fabric analysis, cartography, literary sources and photography, it was hoped that something of the experience of the fighting in Moore Street could be added to the grander theatre of the conflict, perhaps reassessing the focus on the General Post Office to consider a broader understanding of the homes, workplaces and lives of those Dubliners caught up in the events.

Attack or retreat? Leaving the General Post Office

The actual narrative of events is uncontested (perhaps the most useful secondary sources include Foy and Barton 2011; McGarry 2010; Matthews 2010; Wills's 2009 treatment of the events will be a classic for many years to come). As a prelude to the evacuation of the burning General Post Office, the *soi-disant* Gaelic aristocrat, The O'Rahilly, led a charge on the barricade at the northern end of Moore Street in an attempt to break out of a cordon established by the British (Fig. 3.1). The cordon comprised a series of makeshift barricades closing off streets and vistas around the General Post Office, generally located outside the direct line of fire. The troops manning the barricades would initially have been given targets and a range at which to set their sights, but amidst the smoke and confusion appear to have opened fire only as the small attacking force approached the corner of Sackville Mall. This received image of an urban battlefield is contradicted by one supplied by future Fianna Fáil politician Seán MacEntee, who reported on the initial advance down Henry Street that '[A]ll was quiet and still. It might have been a lakeshore at the fall of evening' (quoted in Foy and Barton 1999, 197).

The O'Rahilly's attack has been skilfully recreated in the literary imagination of Roddy Doyle in *A Star called Henry* (1999), where the protagonist follows The O'Rahilly before withdrawing under heavy fire into Cogan's at No. 10 Moore Street (Doyle 1999, 133–4). Oral accounts of the Rising suggest that The O'Rahilly, while still in the General Post Office, goaded members of the 'Kimmage Garrison' (Volunteers of English or Scottish domicile who had been billeted in the months preceding the Rising on Joseph Plunkett's Larkfield estate in the southern suburbs) into following him, with the words 'English speakers first, Irish to the rear' (e.g., FitzGerald 1968, 154). In any event, with the exception of Denis Daly and Charles Corrigan, his calls appear to have fallen on the deaf ears of the mostly Anglophone Larkfield Volunteers.

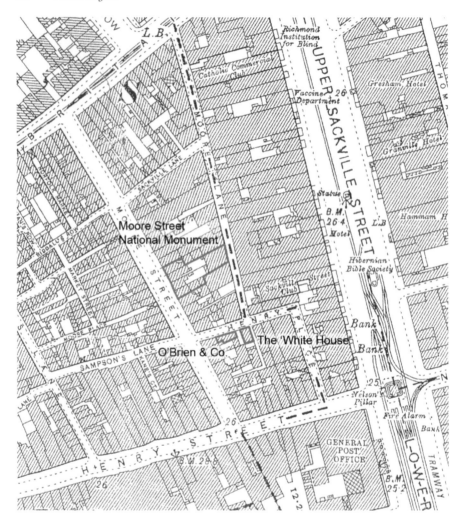

3.1   1911 Ordnance Survey 25-inch map showing the location of the Moore Street National Monument, the White House and O'Brien's.

Several republicans, including Corrigan, were killed in the assault,[1] with a few seemingly escaping into cellars to the west. The O'Rahilly himself was hit on the western side of Moore Street but managed to cross the street and crawl into cover around Sackville Mall.[2] Rumours that The O'Rahilly

1 Irish Military Archives, MA/BMH/WS/272, 1. Witness: Daniel Branniff, member Dungannon Clubs, Belfast and England, 1907; member Supreme Council Irish Republican Brotherhood, 1912–14.
2 MA/BMH/WS/428, 10. Witness: Thomas Devine, Member Irish Volunteers, 1916.

had been refused medical attention and been left to die slowly in the street resurfaced on the release of Albert Mitchell's Witness Statement in 2003.[3] Mitchell had driven a Red Cross ambulance throughout Easter Week and was prevented taking The O'Rahilly to hospital on Saturday evening:

> The sergeant drew my attention to the body of a man lying in the gutter in Moore Lane. He was dressed in a green uniform. I took the sergeant and two men with a stretcher and approached the body which appeared to be still alive. We were about to lift it up when a young English officer stepped out of a doorway and refused to allow us to touch it. I told him of my instructions from H.Q. but all to no avail. When back in the lorry I asked the sergeant what was the idea? His answer was – 'he must be someone of importance and the bastards are leaving him there to die of his wounds. It's the easiest way to get rid of him.' We came back again about 9 o'clock that night. The body was still there and an officer guarding it, but this time I fancied I knew the officer – he was not the one I met before. I asked why I was not allowed to take the body and who was it? He replied that his life and job depended on it being left there. He would not say who it was. I never saw the body again but I was told by different people that it was The O'Rahilly.

John McLoughlin and Seán MacDiarmada had, according to the former,[4] come across his body in a doorway on Sackville Lane on the Saturday morning:

> Arriving there we were still screened from the British who had no idea of our presence. I saw a number of bodies lying on the footpath and roadway – our own men. One familiar one I approached and this was O'Rahilly lying on his back, his arms outstretched, blood oozing from his body in a pool under him and flies buzzing about his head … We knelt for a few minutes and said an Act of Contrition. I then took my handkerchief out of my pocket and covered O'Rahilly's face[;] the same was done for the other three. That was all we could do.

It would appear now that The O'Rahilly was still alive at this point, which obviously questions the veracity of McLoughlin's account.

The General Post Office garrison left shortly after in three groups, crossing Henry Street and escaping out of the direct line of fire into Henry Place. Their progress was halted at the foot of Moore Lane once the British

---

3 MA/BMH/WS/196, 2–3. Witness: Albert D. Mitchell, ambulance driver, 1916.
4 MA/BMH/WS/290, 26. Witness: John McLoughlin, Officer, Irish Volunteers, Dublin, 1916.

had recognised the break-out had started. The building which became known as the 'White House' was an obvious target, closing the vista from the British barricade at the northern end of Moore Lane. At 214 yards, its limewashed facade at the end of a narrow laneway could be ranged by the Lee Enfield Mk III rifles with a reasonable degree of accuracy, given the weapon's effective range in trained hands was 550 yards. At this point, a cart was hauled across the junction to provide cover for the retreating garrison, denying the British riflemen a clear line of fire. Once the junction was safely negotiated, the republicans broke through the wall of No. 10 Moore Street and proceeded to advance north through the party walls of the buildings on the eastern side of the street, until they reached No. 25 on the corner of Sackville Lane, early the following morning.[5]

Cast and crew

Good theatre requires good actors and the *dramatis personae* of the Easter Rising in the General Post Office have become legion in Irish republican and socialist historiography. Certain more observant survivors have written their own parts in the Witness Statements. These depositions, held since the 1950s by the Bureau of Military History, and only released in 2003, became the essential primary source used in the investigation, along with the physicality of the urban theatre itself.

There are curiously few women in the cast despite the crucial role played by Nurse Elizabeth O'Farrell at the very moment of surrender (O'Farrell 1917). Hidden until recently has been the part of the Citizen Army; few of its leaders were to become prominent in the subsequent street fighting which lasted sporadically in the city until perhaps 1926 (Fox 1943). In fact, militant trades' unionism had had its day in 1913 and class struggle was never to develop to full maturity after independence. The presence of a few, previously uncredited, foreign actors has recently been written into the plot, lending perhaps something of a cosmopolitan flavour to the production, for Jewish anarchists evoke a world of docklands assignations and crepuscular conspiracies. Indeed, the presence of a handful of foreign socialists and anarchists in republican ranks has been the focus of recent research; with few participants either willing or able to receive their 1916

---

5 For example, MA/BMH/WS/242, 34–41. Witness: Liam Tannam, Captain, Irish Volunteers and Irish Republican Army, 1913–20; MA/BMH/WS/249, 53–7. Witness: Frank Henderson, Captain, Irish Volunteers, 1916, and Commandant, Irish Republican Army 1917–21; MA/BMH/WS/370, 10. Witness: Fintan Murphy, Officer, Irish Volunteers, 1914–16, and Quartermaster General, 1917–18.

pensions, their participation in the events has been expunged from the narrative (McGrath forthcoming).

This, moreover, is a theatre where the fourth wall has been removed; here, the audience partakes fully of the action with tragic consequences. The audience here represents the civilian population, many of whose stories, absent from conventional historical narratives, have been recovered by archaeological investigation.

Location and operations

The battlefield assessment undertaken here comprised three interlocking components: a survey of the surviving urban landscape (mostly carried out within what can be referred to as the public realm), a targeted physical investigation to recover evidence for the areas of fabric broken through the buildings on Moore Street, and a more general inquiry into the human experience of the conflict as it unfolded over this brief though fundamentally critical period in the mythology of the new Republic.

On one level, there is an obligation to understand what took place within the context of contemporary military praxis. As a military action, the occupation of the General Post Office sector on Easter Monday follows certain grounded theoretical practices developed and disseminated by James Connolly. Connolly published several articles (1914; 1915) on street fighting based on an analysis of the Paris Commune and indeed its theory and practice were not functionally considered by most military commands until after the Spanish Civil War, when extensive street fighting experience was gained on both sides. The General Post Office was certainly considered the centre of communications between Dublin and London and therefore a worthy target in its own right. If there is a certain truth to the idea that the General Post Office constituted an early twentieth-century manifestation of a large computer server (as is repeated in many of the walking tours available today), this very notion has since been overtaken by contemporary technology, testing the longevity of metaphor in our own phase of late modernity.

The retreat from the General Post Office is frequently read as a disorganised afterthought in the context of Pearse's concept of the blood sacrifice. Any information on an alternative plan of escape or retreat has yet to come to light. Few of the participants appear to have been fully au fait with the local geography, despite the nearby location of Tom Clarke's tobacconist shop. Clarke, a signatory of the Proclamation of the Republic, was present in the General Post Office and there are no references in the Witness Statements to his providing local information prior to the break out. Some sense can, however, be made of the retreat when the contemporary geography of the area is considered. The O'Rahilly's charge on the British barricade on the Friday evening is perhaps better understood in the light of Connolly's writings on offensive street-fighting, where traditional readings see it as his last chance to atone for his role in attempting to cancel the Rising on Easter Sunday.

From the British perspective, another more interesting truth emerges. By the Thursday evening, Crown forces had established, and were able to maintain, a cordon around the General Post Office. The unpreparedness of the state apparatus is easier to justify in the context of the received intelligence regarding the political situation at the time, where nationalist separatism was not perceived as a viable threat in the context of the thousands of Irishmen fighting on the Western Front and Gallipoli. It is apposite here, though, to remember that the type of street fighting that was developing around the republican-held strongpoints was completely beyond the ken of anything previously experienced by the British High Command. Crown forces were trained in the doctrines and procedures of more conventional, open modes of conflict and the small unit engagements associated with imperial policing. They had little experience of dealing with irregular forces in urban contexts.

Received republican accounts were also interrogated as part of this project. Reports of British snipers on the campanile of Amiens Street station and in the spire of Findlater's Church on Parnell Square[6] do not stand up to ballistic scrutiny. At a range of 570 metres it would certainly have been possible to direct fire at the General Post Office from Findlater's Church and indeed from the tower at Amiens Street some 740 metres to the east; however, given the effective range of the standard issue rifle, any such fire would perhaps have posed a greater danger to British troops along the cordon. Other accounts suggest that a machine gun position was established on the roof of Jervis Street Hospital; if this was the case, it is difficult to see how this position could have been utilised once the General Post Office had been abandoned, due to the angle of fire. Where the roof of the Rotunda Hospital would have afforded a perfect firing point directly overlooking the Moore Street area, an attacking British presence here is not supported in the documentation.

Accounts of concentrated machine gun fire down Henry Street can be compared with the German experience at the Battle of Mons in August 1914. The Lee Enfield operating system differed greatly from that of most other bolt action rifles of the period where the bolt-locking lugs were at the rear of the bolt rather than at the face, as with rifles using the Mauser system. Although this meant that the action was weaker in theory, in practice

---

6 For example, MA/BMH/WS/1686, 9. Witness: Ruaidhri Henderson, Officer, Irish Republican Army, Dublin Brigade.

it proved to be more rugged and reliable. This feature, combined with a relatively short bolt throw and a ten-round magazine created what was the fastest operating military bolt action rifle of the period. At Mons, German troops faced a small, professional British Expeditionary Force armed with this rifle (Lomas 2012): the Germans displayed an understandable reluctance to attack, believing they were facing massed machine-guns. Most accounts of the battle record the German disbelief that the heavy fire from such a small force was in fact rifle fire.

Method and materiality

The fabric investigation was led by the information collected in the Witness Statements. In the open spaces, known positions were mapped and firing arcs and killing zones worked out on the ground. Triangulated over this were the known locations of casualties, both civilian and republican.

The initial task was to establish which buildings on the route of the retreat survive today. This was undertaken using insurance mapping and a physical examination of the historic built fabric. It became evident that more fabric had survived than was previously assumed in the planning application for the site, which had focused more on the prominence of the General Post Office, located conveniently outside of the development footprint. No. 16 Moore Street (Fig. 3.2), the final HQ of the republican forces, was itself re-contested in the planning adjudication when the developers appointed Charles Townshend, a prominent historian of the Rising, to investigate the role of this building as it is enshrined in republican lore. Surprisingly, Townshend relocated the HQ several doors down the street in an insignificant premises completely rebuilt in the 1970s (Townshend 2006, 4–6). Archaeological investigation has, however, countered this reinterpretation and No. 16 has now been accepted as the building where the final conference took place prior to the surrender (Myles 2012).

Two further buildings of some significance were identified along Henry Place: the 'White House' and O'Brien's Mineral Water Stores, both of which figure prominently in the Witness Statements. The 'White House' presents intractable issues regarding its conservation as a building of significance central to the narrative, as removing the heavy cement render from the facade will undoubtedly remove the evidence of the bullet strikes in the underlying brick. O'Brien's was initially assumed to post-date the Rising, yet the brickwork and detailing are early twentieth century in date, with the painted signage under the *Goodall's* fascia still evident today (Fig. 3.3). In any case, both buildings are to be demolished.

The physicality of the fighting was investigated in terms of bullet strikes

3.2 Moore Street National Monument, nos. 17 (Studio Zee Hair salon) to 14. Photograph by Franc Myles, 2012

and physical damage to the surviving built fabric. Again, by examining British trajectories of fire, it became obvious that, at waist level, little would survive the reconstruction of the shop fronts. To the rear of Moore Street, in Moore Lane, one possible bullet strike was recorded in the reveal of a doorway. Apart from the obvious concentration of fire on the 'White House', it is likely that British rounds would have glanced off the walls along the laneway, ricocheting in all directions.

Due to their specific level of statutory protection, the formal permission of the apposite government minister, referred to as Ministerial Consent, was obtained to investigate the interiors of the four buildings comprising the National Monument. It was also considered prudent to examine those buildings outside the National Monument which appeared to retain pre-1916 fabric. No. 10, on the corner of Henry Place, was the point of entry to the buildings which extended to the north as far as what is now O'Rahilly Parade. On the side elevation of No. 10, a patch of cement mortar indicated the point at which the wall was broken through, underneath a window lighting the primary staircase. Mortar stripping on the third floor party wall revealed an area of repair where the wall had been broken through to No. 11, which was subsequently demolished.

3.3 *Goodall's of Ireland Ltd* facia, with *O'Brien's* painted signage evident underneath. Henry Place, Dublin.
Photograph by Franc Myles, 2012

As the buildings were worked through along the street, the sometimes contradictory Witness Statements guided progress and it became obvious very quickly that the repair work over the openings survived throughout the National Monument. The opportunity to associate names with archaeological traces is something that became more poignant as accounts were read of James Connolly being carried through these openings on a sheet, his stretcher being too wide.[7] The materiality of the battle from the civilian perspective was doubly evident as one looked out the front window of No. 16, where Pearse saw the former male occupants of the house lying dead on the street, their white sheet of surrender pathetically redundant in the face of British fire. The surviving kitchen range in No. 17 eloquently voiced another account of a terrified family confined to the back kitchen, unsure of what further horrors occasioned the noises emanating from behind the party wall (Fig. 3.4).[8]

7 MA/BMH/WS/284. Witness: Michael Staines, Quartermaster, Dublin Brigade, Irish Volunteers, 1913–16, Quartermaster General, Irish Volunteers, 1917–18.
8 MA/BMH/WS/889, 57–8. Witness: Seamus Ua Coamhanaigh, Dept. of Local Government, Dáil Éireann, 1921, and accountant, Sinn Féin Executive, 1918–19; MA/BMH/WS/340, 21. Witness: Oscar Traynor, Captain, Irish Volunteers, Dublin, 1913–16, and Officer Commanding, Dublin Brigade, Irish Republican Army, 1920–1.

3.4 First-floor kitchen in no. 17 Moore Street, with repair work evident in party wall to no. 16.
Photograph by Franc Myles, 2012

An examination of census returns, street directories and death certificates established the place of death of most of those civilians killed in the sector. The deaths of two children in the laneway alongside the 'White House' are especially poignant: Bridget McKane (aged 16) was killed by a Volunteer trying to gain access to her family's tenement[9] (Scully 1986), whereas William Mullen (aged 9) was shot in the thorax, possibly killed by British fire from the barricade at the northern end of Moore Lane.[10] The four bodies on Moore Street represent a grandfather, tenant and two sheltering citizens who decided to negotiate directly with the British on the unexpected arrival of republicans with picks and crowbars through their wall.[11] It was these civilian deaths that convinced Pearse to negotiate a surrender, and Nurse O'Farrell was sent out to parlay with the British just prior to the launching of another frontal attack on the British barricade.

9 MA/BMH/WS/889, 59. Witness: Seamus Ua Coamhanaigh, Dept. of Local Government, Dáil Éireann, 1921, and accountant, Sinn Féin Executive, 1918–19.
10 Death certificate for William Mullen, General Record Office, Dublin North, 1916, Vol. 2, 368.
11 MA/BMH/WS/340, 21. Witness: Oscar Traynor, Captain, Irish Voluneers, Dublin, 1913–16, and Officer Commanding, Dublin Brigade, Irish Republican Army, 1920–21.

On her way up towards the British position she passed the prone body of The O'Rahilly, who, unknown to her, was probably still alive (according to Albert Mitchell's Witness Statement).[12]

Commemoration

The Moore Street theatre has long been the site of various low-level commemorative ventures. The western side of the street was completely redeveloped in the early 1970s, removing the confusing warren of streets and laneways through which the General Post Office garrison hoped to escape. What remains today in the urban landscape is an area that was becoming increasingly derelict until the boom of the early 2000s. In more recent years, low rents have attracted a multi-ethnic clientele who operate alongside the traditional Dublin market traders. As the repair works to the houses were being recorded, the curious acoustics of the empty buildings amplified conversations in 17 different languages outside; the Irish language was not among them.

The small National Graves Association plaque to The O'Rahilly, which was placed up on the wall of a pub on the corner opposite where his body was found on Sackville Lane, has been replaced on the site's redevelopment with a more elaborate memorial by Shane Cullen, both in their own way illegible. Few, at any rate, know or care that both plaques mark the wrong spot, expressing something of the dislocation and confusion evident from the abortive mobilisation on Easter Sunday through to the government's reluctance to intervene in the development proposal. Sackville Lane has grandiosely been renamed O'Rahilly Parade and it would be challenging indeed to find a less auspicious alley anywhere in the city.

Similarly, a plaque on Conway's pub on the corner of Moore Lane purports to mark the site of the formal surrender. A re-examination of the contemporary photograph published in the *Daily Sketch* in fact demonstrates that this occurred across today's Parnell Street, with the vegetation fronting the Rotunda Hospital clearly visible in the background.[13] Another look at a later print of the exposure throws up further issues, with Nurse O'Farrell removed from the tableau of surrender. Here the photograph seems to have been doctored to depict Pearse in a more heroic light, offering the surrender on his own, by the simple device of removing O'Farrell's offending limbs.[14]

---

12 MA/BMH/WS/196, 2–3. Witness: Albert D. Mitchell, ambulance driver, 1916.
13 *Daily Sketch*, 10 May 1916.
14 See http://dublinopinion.com/2007/07/14/women-photoshop-and-the-1916-rising. Accessed 4 March 2014.

Inexplicably, this was the version of the photograph used by Tim Pat Coogan on the front cover of his *Ireland in the twentieth century* (2003).

The upper floors of the four buildings of the National Monument have been empty now for the past several years, a situation which is far from satisfactory. Where the vicarious political context of the fiftieth anniversary has been well-treated by historians recognising the official prominence of the General Post Office as the Rising's focal point, the planned demolition of the Moore Street theatre has served to encourage the development of historical walking tours and to promote an increasing focus on commemoration by the republican movement and protest fuelled by social media.[15]

Conclusion

This study was undertaken within a planning hiatus pending the preparation of final conservation proposals for the four eighteenth-century buildings making up the Moore Street National Monument. These buildings had previously been declared Protected Structures by Dublin City Council, on foot of a rather unfocused rear-guard campaign for the preservation of the entire area as a historic battlefield in the middle of the proposed shopping mall to be developed over the entire area. The original lobby group subsequently became two separate groups, each populated by several of the relatives of those involved in the Rising, one favoured by the developer and both equally vocal in their ownership of the campaign. To a greater extent, the relatives in both camps have become the self-appointed guardians of the battlefield where the state prevaricated over its preservation.

Apart from the buildings earmarked for preservation comprising the National Monument, at the time of writing the entire urban landscape faces demolition as part of the scheme which has successfully passed through the planning appeals process with some minor alterations. What remains particularly controversial is that the development is now controlled by the National Asset Management Agency (NAMA), the 'bad bank' established by the state in the wake of the economic crash of 2008. The prospect of the General Post Office sector – the site of the birth of the modern Republic – being developed into an anodyne shopping mall, facilitated by the state's jurisdiction over the notoriously secretive NAMA, is not one that has received much public support. In the context of the country's loss of economic sovereignty in a climate of fiscal austerity, opposition to the development continues to gain traction, for at play here are fundamental issues bringing to the fore concepts

---

15 See the Facebook pages *Save 16 Moore Street Dublin* and *Save Moore Street Dublin*, with 4,269 and 4,600 members and 'likes' respectively. Accessed 2 March 2013.

such as commemoration and forgetting, along with less intangible issues of urban and architectural conservation. These are all overwhelmingly contemporary concerns, which must negotiate often conflicting ideas of what is to be remembered and what is to be conserved, all set against the political background of the state-sanctioned 'decade of commemorations'. And, central to this, in the political context of a Republic without economic sovereignty, is perhaps the as-yet-unanswered question, 'what is being forgotten?' For lost in the discussion is the fundamental idea that the Easter Rising involved the furtherance of profoundly radical ideas through armed struggle.

The undeniable presence of the General Post Office as a focal point of the events was used by the developers to distract attention from the route of the retreat until they were obliged to consider the wider battlefield, well after planning permission for the scheme was obtained. If there was a failure on the part of the statutory planning authorities to recognise the significance of the battlefield, it must be said that those groups opposing the development themselves failed to exploit its materiality.

As this article was being prepared for publication, the conservation of the Moore Street National Monument had stalled as the developers negotiated with city councillors over a proposed land swap. This would have seen the National Monument, undoubtedly a future tourist attraction of some significance, handed over to the city in its entirety, its conservation and fit-out being funded by NAMA. The land swap involved a parcel of ground off O'Rahilly Parade, one crucial to the success of the development as a whole, which was in the process of being acquired from the city prior to 2008 and the renewed controversy. For its part, NAMA appeared unwilling to release the funding until the councillors supported the land swap.

In the meanwhile, the developers had further defined their vision for the National Monument as a small enclave of four buildings sequestered within the much larger shopping mall, which in the opinion of many is an architectural relic of Celtic Tiger consumerism, as inappropriate in its own way as the Ilac Centre on the opposite side of Moore Street, itself an ill-conceived exercise in faux 1970s Brutalism. Were such an accommodation made, the National Monument would house the usual museum spaces, interpretative displays, a documentation centre and bookshop, providing the opportunity to sip coffee in the courtyard to the rear. Visitors would peer through the historic holes behind perspex sheets and marvel at it all. Many, though, feared the site would simply become a heritage destination, with the politics diluted or removed altogether, where the only alternative presented was to permit the historic fabric to deteriorate further. As the councillors continued to prevaricate, knowing they had an advantage over the developers, conservation practitioners were now asking whether the preservation of this fragile row of eighteenth-century buildings was even feasible, and whether conservation would be unduly rushed to open the buildings by 2016. In any event, the councillors voted against the proposal and it appeared highly unlikely that the conservation works would proceed in time for the centenary.

Of greater interest still was the attitude of the present coalition government, whose very existence is a direct consequence of the retreat from the GPO. Where Fine Gael can boast about the participation of some of the founders of its precursor Cumann na nGaedheal, there has recently emerged a Redmondite camp within the party, one reflective of the conservative constitutional nationalism practiced by the Irish Parliamentary Party destroyed in the 1918 general election by Sinn Féin. Despite the focal point of the battlefield being a National Monument under her direct jurisdiction, the Fine Gael minister Heather Humphreys appeared reluctant in the extreme to intervene proactively in the controversy.

All this changed however when the government announced the purchase of the National Monument for €4 million on 31 March 2015, the same day it launched its revised programme of events leading up to the centenary of the Rising. While this is undoubtedly a welcome outcome, it shifts the attention back to the other buildings within the battlefield which are scheduled for demolition. In this regard, as this paper goes to press, the government has requested that the City Council place a further eleven buildings along Moore Street on the statutory Record of Protected Structures (RPS), only one of which appears to pre-date the Rising. As it stands, six of these buildings have permission for demolition, where their façades will be retained in the greater scheme. Their inclusion on the RPS will possibly save them from demolition; however, in the context of the continuing economic crisis there is little indication that the construction of the shopping mall will proceed before planning permission expires in 2017.

One can only imagine what Connolly would have thought, and it is perhaps with some justification that Margaretta D'Arcy and the late John Arden confidently placed the final words on his lips as quoted at the beginning of this chapter.

4

The constitution of a state yet to come: the unbroken promise of the 'Half-Proclamation'

Daniel Jewesbury

Introduction

The 'decade of centenaries' upon which Ireland and the United Kingdom are currently embarked brings about a renewed contest over the legitimate meaning of the events of a century ago. It is one, however, in which every protagonist has been transformed, and the contest perhaps has unexpected, albeit still very different, resonances in the different jurisdictions of Ireland, as well as in Britain, the former colonial power. The complex and ongoing negotiation of relations between the Republic and the United Kingdom has been marked by carefully stage-managed displays of post-colonial self-confidence on one side (the exhumation of statues of dead monarchs, as well as the welcoming of a living one) and equally carefully measured apologies on the other (for the Famine, for Bloody Sunday). Both contemporary states could be said to find the prospect of commemorations of the 1916 Rising somewhat awkward.

Meanwhile the pronouncements and prognoses of the founders of the state have, inevitably, declined in potency and immediacy, albeit only relatively recently. The words of Connolly and Pearse reverberated across the twentieth century and, when it suited the executive of the day (or their opponents), could be said to underwrite their actions. Today, the details of their political ideologies are seldom invoked in the political mainstream, forming a mute 'heritage' rather than an active, living current within the thinking of the state. This has not come about as the result of any single development in the recent history of the Republic as a lived entity, but arises from the general drift of its reinvention in the period since the fiftieth anniversary of the Rising in 1966. Over the course of these years, the state has finally separated itself, ambivalently at first, more definitively later on, from physical-force republicanism; it has joined the EEC, the EU and latterly the single currency; most significantly, perhaps, it has renounced its constitutional claim on the entirety of the island of Ireland, as a result of the ratification of the Nineteenth Amendment to the Constitution, in a referendum following the Good Friday Agreement in 1998.

With this last transformation, the state has become an aspiration, a willed projection into the future, rather than an assertion by right. The Irish nation is no longer held to be coterminous with the boundaries of the state, as previously (prior to the Nineteenth Amendment, Article 2 stated that 'The national territory consists of the whole island of Ireland, its islands and the territorial seas' (Bunreacht na hÉireann 1937)). The Constitution now decrees that every person born in the island of Ireland is entitled 'to be part of the island of Ireland', but it is recognised that 'a united Ireland shall be brought about only by peaceful means with the consent of a majority of the people, democratically expressed, in both jurisdictions in the island' (Bunreacht na hÉireann 2012). This decidedly post-Westphalian arrangement (see Fraser 2007) might be said to ground the state insufficiently in present fact. I hope to show, however, that it opens a door, even if inadvertently, to a radical reformulation of the basic concept of the state, through a return to its (perhaps repressed, rather than forgotten) foundational act and text.

The origins of the 'Half-Proclamation'

The circumstances surrounding the printing of the Proclamation of the Irish Republic have been well researched (see Bouch 1936; King 2001; but especially Mosley 2010a and 2010b, who offers the most definitive overview of previous literature). The peculiarities of its typographical formation have allowed originals to be reliably authenticated, and a number of confirmed copies are in archives, libraries and museums in Ireland and around the world.

In the United Kingdom's National Archives, in a dossier containing the court martial records of Seán MacDermott (who along with Thomas Clarke was one the primary instigators and organisers of the Rising), is a document that might be called the 'second impression' of the Proclamation, but that has become known as the 'Half-Proclamation' (Fig. 4.1). The Proclamation had been printed with type requisitioned from West's print shop on Capel Street, but so little of the 36-point 'Double Great Primer' required for the body of the text could be found that it had to be printed in two halves, with the forme for the top half broken up and reset for the bottom half; even then, many letters had to be improvised and scavenged from other cases. Joseph Bouch (1936, 45) explained, in a paper written for the Irish Bibliographical Society, how the 'Half-Proclamation' came into being:

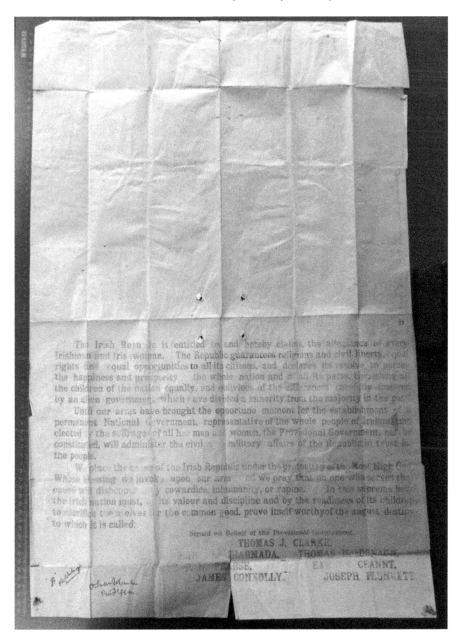

4.1   The copy of the 'Half-Proclamation' that forms part of Seán MacDermott's court martial records at the National Archives (United Kingdom); TNA/WO 71/355

although the general impression left in the mind of the machineman was … that this second forme holding the lower portion … was already effectually broken up, such was not the case … When the British soldiers entered Liberty Hall, on Thursday, 27th April, 1916, after the shelling from the *Helga*, they discovered the old Wharfdale [*sic*] machine still intact, and the lower half of the Proclamation still locked in the chase. In fact, they then proceeded to run off copies of the incomplete sheet and shortly afterwards they distributed many copies to their admirers and the sightseers.

For at least two months after the Rising, which is to say a full month and a half after the last executions on 12 May, the Dublin Metropolitan Police (DMP) and the British administration seem to have been unable to secure a full, original copy of the Proclamation, even though it had been reprinted in a national newspaper. A minute dated 11 May 1916, from Detective Superintendent Owen Brien, accompanied a 'Half-Proclamation' that the police were able to secure. It circulated between the Chief Commissioner of the DMP, Lt-Col. Walter Johnstone, and the Assistant Under-Secretary of Ireland, Edward O'Farrell, amongst other functionaries and dignitaries. Johnstone writes, on the 11th, that he has 'not been able to get a complete copy of this proclamation'. Beneath, an unidentified hand states in red ink that 'at present he [Thomas Lyster, director of the National Library, who had requested a copy] and others must be content with the reprint in the "Irish Times" Weekly issue dated 13th inst.'. A further query in this same hand, dated '20.6.16', asks 'Has a copy since come to hand?' Below, with the same date, is Col. Johnstone's terse 'no'.[1] It is important to clarify the chronology here: MacDermott was court-martialled on 9 May, and executed on the 12th. On the 11th, the Chief Commissioner had stated that he had no copy of the full Proclamation. The *Irish Times Weekly* edition dated the 13th must have been issued prior to this date, since it is referred to by 'the hand in red' on the DMP minute, on the 12th. But it is reasonable to argue that the authorities trying MacDermott had not seen a full copy of the text when MacDermott was being tried. The significance of this will, I hope, become apparent.

The copy of the 'Half-Proclamation' in MacDermott's court martial records was clearly intended to incriminate him. Barton (2002, 308) points out that the document is not mentioned in the transcript of the court martial, but in the very next line writes that MacDermott's is the only transcript which is incomplete. The 'Half-Proclamation' is marked clearly in black ink with a large upper case letter B, to which the President of MacDermott's

1 Minute from Owen Brien to Col. Johnstone, Edward O'Farrell et al., Dublin Metropolitan Police, 1916, National Archives of Ireland, CSORP/1916/8086.

court martial, Col. Douglas Sapte, has appended his signature underneath; this 'B' was the document's exhibit reference in the court. Another document, a scrap of paper bearing an order for the Volunteers to assemble at Liberty Hall on the morning of the Rising, signed in pencil by MacDermott, is similarly marked with a black letter D. This note is referred to in the court transcripts; it is reasonable to suppose that at some stage, in a part of the proceedings now lost to us, the large sheet of paper marked as exhibit B might also have been produced and discussed.

Mosley (2010a) records that in the trial of Thomas MacDonagh, the prosecutor for the court, William Wylie, argued to General Blackader, the President of this court martial (who had also not seen a full copy of the Proclamation), that a printed text could not be used to incriminate any of the signatories:

> I replied that a printed document with printed names at the end of it was not proof against any of the alleged signatories. That my name or the General's might have been put there by the printer. That unless I could get the original and prove the accused's signature to it, that it was not evidence against the accused and that I must ask the Court to obliterate all knowledge of it from their minds.

Wylie notes in this remembrance that he had, at this point, a leaflet in his pocket with the full text of the Proclamation, including all of the signatories, upon it.

Regardless of whether the 'Half-Proclamation' was examined in Seán MacDermott's court martial, his printed name at its foot was material in guaranteeing his execution. A death sentence in a court martial must be confirmed by the relevant Commander-in-Chief, in this case General Sir John Maxwell, who was present in the hearing and who was by now the supreme authority in Ireland, martial law having been declared on 26 April. Maxwell wrote to Prime Minister Herbert Asquith, explaining his confirmation of the death penalty in all 15 cases where it was upheld. The first line of his entry on MacDermott reads, 'This man signed the Declaration of Irish Independence'; many of Maxwell's confirmations were justified on the basis of intelligence not produced to the court, and thus requiring no evidential test (Barton 2002, 38).

The constitution of a deferred state

Barring a few short phrases worn shiny through use, the sentences printed on the Proclamation have long since ceased to signify in a way that registers with the actual definitions of the words used; largely disavowed by the state which is its unlikely inheritor, the document has instead become literally 'iconic'. As King (2001) notes, it is recognisable now only as an image, its words largely forgotten. Yet its authors viewed it, without question, as the sole legitimate founding text of the Irish Republic. It has no legal status in that Republic, and indeed it never has had; it is not analogous to the American Declaration of Independence (despite Maxwell's choice of words), nor to the Constitution, nor even the Bill of Rights. It is a relic, a venerated, sacred text, but one entirely lacking any subversive power, since it is now routinely taken to say precisely nothing.

The 'Half-Proclamation', meanwhile, is an especially ambivalent document, its ambivalence derived in some part from the many years in which the existence of the MacDermott copy was entirely unknown. After protracted argument, all papers relating to the courts martial (which had been heard *in camera*, contrary to the provisions of the Defence of the Realm Act) were deemed sufficiently sensitive as to be embargoed: the files are marked 'Closed Until 1992', but in fact most were not released until 1999, over 80 years after the events they concern (Barton 2002, 32). None of the individual documents in the file are catalogued separately, so MacDermott's 'Half-Proclamation' continues to exist in a measure of obscurity, the existence of other copies of the document notwithstanding[2] (and, as we have seen, it manages to be absent even from the court transcript, a cypher of rumour and indeterminacy even in this most overdetermined of spaces).

The document shares, in however diminished a form, some auratic quality of the 'original' from which it is derived; the holes punched through its centre, in order to bind it into the dossier when folded, could even be likened to mortifications, to stigmata. Not just an aura of the sacred, then, but of the martyred dead themselves clings to the document. And, unlike the Proclamation of which it is an illegitimate offspring, this sheet has some legal status: as criminal evidence. It is this doubling (through halving), this transformation from an act of *constitution* to one of *incrimination* that I argue makes the 'Half-Proclamation' so replete with potential – so *arresting* – today.

Much of this potential resides not in the poorly inked words, cast adrift from time and context, on the bottom half of the sheet, but in the huge blank space at the top, surely the most pregnant and suggestive blank space in all of Irish documentary history. Here, in place of the famously massy, close-set wooden-typed headlines of the original, is a blank into which may flow all the coloniser's fear of his untrustworthy, disloyal subjects, a space where

---

2 In 2006, an original copy of the 'Half-Proclamation' was found to have been hanging on the wall of a classroom in Wexford for several decades. Staff had apparently always presumed that it was a copy.

all the worst fantasies of violent, vengeful, bloodthirsty uprising might be projected. The absent words are nonetheless spoken by the colonial master, who can imagine only too well what they must have been.

This delay in the signification of a blank space calls to mind Homi Bhabha's reading of accounts of another colonial uprising from half a century before, the Indian rebellion of 1857, and the curious way in which rumour and panic were inscribed into its historiography from an early point: a story told in countless colonial and anticolonial histories of the rebellion is that immediately prior to the first disturbances, chapatis had begun to circulate, without explanation, from village to village, carried by messengers who urged their continued onward despatch. The British interpretation of this story at the time was that the chapati operated as some sort of secret ethnoreligious code, warning the people of trouble to come, or mysteriously mobilising them to take their part in it. Indian nationalist historians, on the other hand, have seen the chapati as symbolic of a rebel agency which cunningly and efficiently circumvented British domination. Bhabha (1994, 207; emphasis in original) asserts, however, that 'the chapati's meaning *as circulation* [of the coloniser's fear and panic] only emerges in the time-lag, or temporal break, *in-between* its social-symbolic ordering [as a sign of Indian conspiracy/Indian rebel agency] and its iterative repetition as the sign of the undecidable, the terrifying'. The meaning of the seemingly meaningless act, then, is only apparent after some delay, during which it is written about, and fantasised about, and queried, and turned into rumour, and it is its very meaninglessness which becomes so laden with terrible meaning; it is, then, not an act *done* by the Indians, but one *described* by the British, to themselves.

Following Bhabha, we can think of the 'Half-Proclamation' as a latent document somewhat in this spirit. We can think of an insubordinate agency that is not present in the text of the Proclamation as printed on Easter Sunday 1916 and read out to apathetic passers-by the next day, but which circulates instead in the indeterminacy and blankness of the 'Half-Proclamation', once the rebellion is put down and its protagonists are dead or in prison. A century later, the Irish are no longer subjects of the Crown, but once again there is a great deal of reluctance to confer legitimacy on the state and its executive. The fear of the message of 1916, the threat of popular rebellion, still circulates and resonates, anxiously, across this time-lag.

We can think of the blank space not as a mere absence, something that has been lost or erased; nor should we construe it as some mildly subversive, temporary narrative evasion in the face of the supposed certainty and might of the colonial authorities (we have already come to a point where we must question the solidity of that might, even – or especially – as it is employed in putting down the Rising). Rather, it is a space which is waiting to be inscribed, not once but repeatedly. It is the blank space in which a future state can be constituted. It now comes to signify a disowned inheritance, an unremembered commitment to republicanism as a historical and political project. Once again, as before, it exercises a dreadful power, nothing less than the capacity to delegitimise the state as currently formulated. The image of the Proclamation that will doubtless be reprinted in multiple commemorative editions, at the behest of a political class who would wish to harness its very 'meaningful meaninglessness' to their own ends, can be replaced with a genuinely empty space, *in which there is no such hiding place.*

Finally, the status of the 'Half-Proclamation' as criminal evidence is material when we come to consider a curious circular pattern that arises out of the sentencing of the leaders of the Rising. The blank space, filled up with the most masochistic colonial fantasies of revolutionary bloodlust, calls down *and justifies*, through Maxwell's briefing to Asquith, the most definite punishment available. And yet, for the British, the mysterious, irrational doctrine that all the rebels came to espouse, sanctifying the virtue and necessity of blood sacrifice, was not just deeply unsettling; it was inescapable, it pre-empted their retribution. The creation of martyrs was something that the British simply could not avoid: not just the rebels' acts, but the administration's inept handling of the events leading up to Easter Week, and their response to the Rising itself, created a situation which demanded exemplary penalties. Yet the British ended up criminalising not those they executed, but themselves. The blank, unwritten space of the 'Half-Proclamation' invites us to realise that all states must be illegitimate before they are constituted, since they can only emerge out of total rupture with the *status quo ante.* Likewise, all must become, in their turn, illegitimate, and be thrown over. This is the terrible promise of the blank space of the 'Half-Proclamation', which cannot but be fulfilled.

5

What is a forgery or a catalyst? The so-called 'Castle Document' of Holy Week, 1916

W.J. McCormack

Introducing the object

The material under consideration here, headed 'Secret Orders issued to Military Officers',[1] survives in only a small number of copies, largely because its original purpose – to sway the minds of relatively few public figures and, indirectly, to outrage its issuers' followers – did not require a large print run. Perhaps as few as 100 would have served the purpose now known to have motivated the printers, though other evidence will be considered in due course (Ó Lochlainn 1954). Additional to the question of intention and purpose, there were material factors: the paper used was fragile, not intended for mass circulation, and so likely to be casually destroyed. Even within the surviving copies it is possible to distinguish between two settings of the type and (less certainly) to propose an order in which these were run off. As no order is yet finalised, I will refer to them as the '5-dot' version and the '3-dot' version, for reasons which will become clear (Figs 5.1a and 5.1b).

The twelfth line of the purported transcript of Dublin Castle's document ends with a number of dots: an ellipsis of three dots in one version and five dots in the other. This is the most obvious difference between the two settings. A close examination of the text will reveal no verbal difference, though four variants or 'accidentals' will indicate that the settings differ in ways reaching beyond the line just specified. In order to investigate the significance of these, a fuller description of the two versions is needed (see Table 5.1).

---

1 'Secret Orders' purported to provide evidence of Dublin Castle's plans to disarm the Volunteers and arrest their leaders in the days leading up to the Rising. Printed by Joseph Plunkett, and used to persuade Eoin MacNeill of the need for immediate action, there has long been debate over whether or not it should be considered a forgery.

Secret Orders issued to Military Officers.

The cipher from which this document is copied does not indicate punctuation or capitals.

" The following precautionary measures have been sanctioned by the Irish Office on the recommendation of the General Officer Commanding the Forces in Ireland. All preparations will be made to put these measures in force immediately on receipt of an Order issued from the Chief Secretary's Office, Dublin Castle, and signed by the Under Secretary and the General Officer Commanding the Forces in Ireland. First, the following persons to be placed under arrest :— All members of the Sinn Fein National Council, the Central Executive Irish Sinn Fein Volunteers, General Council Irish Sinn Fein Volunteers, County Board Irish Sinn Fein Volunteers, Executive Committee National Volunteers, Coisde Gnota Committee Gaelic League. See list A 3 and 4 and supplementary list A 2.   .   .   .   .   . Dublin Metropolitan Police and Royal Irish Constabulary Forces in Dublin City will be confined to barracks under the direction of the Competent Military Authority. An order will be issued to inhabitants of city to remain in their houses until such time as the Competent Military Authority may otherwise direct or permit. Pickets chosen from units of Territorial Force will be placed at all points marked on Maps 3 and 4. Accompanying mounted patrols will continuously visit all points and report every hour. The following premises will be occupied by adequate forces, and all necessary measures used without need of reference to Headquarters. First, premises known as Liberty Hall, Beresford Place ; No. 6 Harcourt Street, Sinn Fein building ; No. 2 Dawson Street, Headquarters Volunteers ; No. 12 D'Olier Street, 'Nationality' Office ; No. 25 Rutland Square, Gaelic League Office ; No. 41 Rutland Square, Foresters' Hall ; Sinn Fein Volunteer premises in city ; all National Volunteer premises in city ; Trades Council premises, Capel Street ; Surrey House, Leinster Road, Rathmines. THE FOLLOWING PREMISES WILL BE ISOLATED, AND ALL COMMUNICATION TO OR FROM PREVENTED :— PREMISES KNOWN AS ARCHBISHOP'S HOUSE, DRUMCONDRA ; MANSION HOUSE, DAWSON STREET ; No. 40 Herbert Park ; Larkfield, Kimmage Road ; Woodtown Park, Ballyboden ; Saint Enda's College, Hermitage, Rathfarnham ; and in addition premises in list 5 D, see Maps 3 and 4."

5.1a   The 'Secret Orders', '5-dot' version

Table 5.1   '5-dot' and '3-dot' versions of 'Secret Orders issued to Military Officers'

'5-dot' version	'3-dot' version
Title: 're' of 'Secret' faintly printed; right serif invisible	Title: 're' of 'Secret' faintly printed; right serif invisible
't' in the word 'document' over 'u' in the word 'measures' (on the following line)	't' in the word 'document' over first 's' in the word 'measures' (on the following line)
text depth: 15 cm	text depth: 15.5 cm
37 lines of text	38 lines of text

Secret Orders issued to Military Officers.

The cipher from which this document is copied does not indicate punctuation or capitals.

"The following precautionary measures have been sanctioned by the Irish Office on the recommendation of the General Officer Commanding the Forces in Ireland. All preparations will be made to put these measures in force immediately on receipt of an Order issued from the Chief Secretary's Office, Dublin Castle, and signed by the Under Secretary and the General Officer Commanding the Forces in Ireland. First, the following persons to be placed under arrest:— All members of the Sinn Fein National Council, the Central Executive Irish Sinn Fein Volunteers, General Council Irish Sinn Fein Volunteers, County Board Irish Sinn Fein Volunteers, Executive Committee National Volunteers, Coisde Gnota Committee Gaelic League. See list A 3 and 4 and supplementary list A2. . . . Dublin Metropolitan Police and Royal Irish Constabulary Forces in Dublin City will be confined to barracks under the direction of the Competent Military Authority. An order will be issued to inhabitants of city to [remain in their houses until such time as the Competent Military Authority may otherwise direct or permit. Pickets chosen from units of Territorial Forces will be placed at all points marked on Maps 3 and 4. Accompanying mounted patrols will continuously visit all points and report every hour. The following premises will be occupied by adequate forces, and all necessary measures used without need of reference to Headquarters. First, premises known as Liberty Hall, Beresford Place; No. 6 Harcourt Street, Sinn Fein building; No 2 Dawson Street, Headquarters Volunteers; No. 12 D'Olier Street, "Nationality" office; No. 25 Rutland Square, Gaelic League Office; No. 41 Rutland Square, Foresters' Hall; Sinn Fein Volunteer premises in city; all National Volunteer premises in the city; Trades Council premises, Capel Street; Surrey House, Leinster Road, Rathmines. THE FOLLOWING PREMISES WILL BE ISOLATED, AND ALL COMMUNICATION TO OR FROM PREVENTED:— PREMISES KNOWN AS ARCHBISHOP'S HOUSE, DRUMCONDRA; MANSION HOUSE, DAWSON STREET; No. 40 Herbert Park; Larkfield, Kimmage Road; Woodtown Park, Ballyboden; Saint Endas College, Hermitage, Rathfarnham; and in addition premises in list 5 D, see Maps 3 and 4."

5.1b   The 'Secret Orders', '3-dot' version

'5-dot' version	'3-dot' version
accidentals:	*accidentals*:
line 26: 'No·'	line 14: 'A2' (no space)
line 28: '4 ǀ'	line 18: 'ǀremain'
line 33: 'PREMISES' (with first s upside down)	line 19: 'permit·'
	line 20: 'all' (with third letter raised)
	line 26: 'No' (lacks full stop)
	line 30: 'city' (first two letters off-line)
	line 37: 'Endas'

Forgery: a background

From the outset, the authenticity of 'Secret Orders' was suspect. It is unlikely that any one recipient ever held both the '3-dot' and '5-dot' versions in his or her hand at the same time; nevertheless the contents of the document raised questions in acute minds – Frank Sheehy-Skeffington's, for example. Forgery was not unheard of in the political intrigues of the late Victorian period – nor after. In Ireland, the activities of Richard Pigott came to light in 1889 as a forger of letters supposedly written by Charles Stewart Parnell and published in *The Times.* Seven years later, Captain Alfred Dreyfus was degraded from the French army, tried for treason and imprisoned on Devil's Island for years on the basis of a *bordereau* wrongly attributed to him, though further suspect documents would follow to bolster the original crime of forgery. In September 1899, the Parnellite *Weekly Independent* editorialised against Dreyfus's conviction, declaring that a nation which depended on forgery and human sacrifices for its honour was in a sorry plight (Barrett 2010, 47). More than one item was forged in the long course of the Dreyfus affair, and we may return to France in search of a terminology to describe the Dublin Castle document. In a less intensively focused instance, the virulently anti-Semitic *Protocols of the Elders of Zion* was fabricated and disseminated from 1903 onwards, its origins being Russian (Cohn 2005, 176–80; Henry Ford subsidised the printing of half a million English language copies in the 1920s). In 1924, publication in Britain of a letter urging intensive communist agitation, and supposedly issued by Gregor Zinoviev and Arthur MacManus, was declared genuine by the incoming Tory government but is now universally taken to be a forgery. Finally, let us not forget a much earlier incident, the Bad Ems despatch sent by Bismarck on 13 July 1870.

In discussions of suspect documentation pertaining to the Easter Rising, pride of place has been given to the so-called Black Diaries of Roger Casement. The controversy, launched by W.J. Maloney in 1936, deserves historical reflection on its merits, even if, since the forensic examinations of 2002, it is generally accepted that all the diaries held in the National Archives at Kew are genuine (McCormack 2002). However, the question is not monopolised by Casement, as an account of 'Secret Orders' can reveal.

The document as catalyst?

If one turns to well-received accounts of Easter 1916, a fluctuating interest can be traced. London-born Desmond Ryan (1893–1964) published *The Rising, the complete story of Easter Week* in 1949. Its fifth chapter, 'A most opportune document', by teasing successive references, admits that the object now under consideration was a forgery, concluding with a reference to Seán MacDermott on the eve of his execution. Asked about the truth behind the 'Castle Document', he smiled and said, 'that is a secret that is buried in Joseph Plunkett's grave – a secret that I and Plunkett will keep' (Ryan 1949, 75). Ryan was a partisan, who had studied in Saint Edna's school under Pearse and served under him in the General Post Office.

The half-centennial year brought a flurry of commemorations, most of which were openly celebratory. Twenty years after Ryan's book, the Northern Troubles had broken out, and, in a relatively autonomous development, 'revisionist' history was getting to grips with the events generally taken to have brought independence to southern Ireland. Dublin's leading lights of the Irish historical profession – Dudley Edwards (1909–88) and T.W. Moody (1907–84) – were both children of the period to be commemorated. It fell to a younger historian, Maureen Wall (1918–72), to deal in passing with the 'Secret Orders' in the two lengthy chapters she contributed to *The making of 1916: studies in the history of the Rising*, published in 1969. Referring to 'the famous "Castle Document"' (Wall 1969a, 185), she proceeds to evaluate how its alarming contents were designed to justify the 'defensive war' which the Volunteer leaders (notably MacNeill and Hobson) regarded as their only reasonable option. 'If the Military Council manufactured the "Castle Document" (which threatened suppression and disarming of the Volunteers) with the hope of bringing about this situation they were eminently successful for a brief period' (Wall 1969b, 203).

Among the many books about the Rising which have appeared in this century, Charles Townshend's *Easter 1916, the Irish Rebellion* deserves consideration in this context for several distinct reasons. First, it is written by an English military historian; second, he devotes sufficient time to the 'Secret Orders' to allow consideration of arguments against its being a forgery *tout court*. In effect, though not in so many words, he distinguishes between the contents and the material form, allowing that an 'original' may indeed have been smuggled out of Dublin Castle by an official sympathetic to the advanced party among the Volunteers. Joseph Plunkett, as Townsend puts it, then 'sexed up the document'. However, where Wall had regarded the IRB ploy as 'eminently successful' in the short run, Townshend lists it with Casement's doomed adventure and MacNeill's countermand as events which 'came together to derail and almost destroy the Rising' (Townshend 2005, 133, 125).

Despite these divergences of interpretation, it is legitimate to regard the 'Secret Orders' as a catalyst in the experiment of rebellion or rising. A dictionary definition of the term as used in twentieth-century chemistry would emphasise the material as setting off changes in various chemicals while remaining itself unchanged. The word's apparent first use in this sense dates from 1902. But its familiarity today derives from a literary, not a scientific, source: T.S. Eliot, in his 1919 essay 'Tradition and the individual talent' in exploration of his theory of impersonality (Kermode 1975, 37–44). This is not a theme to be pursued here, except to note certain points for further investigation. There is a powerful connection between the Easter Rising and contemporary literature, French, English and Irish. There was a significant component of activists in and behind that event who were not the renowned poets (Pearse and MacDonagh, notably) but others whose training was scientific or technological. Many of these were associated with University College Dublin. In its cryptic brevity and its avoidance of all personal names, the 'Secret Orders' as a material object embodies these antinomies (authoritative contradictions).

'Secret Orders': production and distribution

And so, back to Dublin and Holy Week, 1916. Around 15 April, the Castle Document was printed on a Columbia hand press, owned by Joseph Mary Plunkett and located at Larkfield, near Kimmage, south of Dublin. It consisted of a single small sheet of off-white to yellow lightweight paper, printed on one side, with 37 or 38 lines of text. Those said to have carried out the printing operation included Joe Plunkett, his younger brother George, his even younger brother John (aged 18 or 19), Colm Ó Lochlainn and Rory O'Connor (all former public school boys). The quality of typesetting was quite high, the design rudimentary. The text was said to have been supplied by Eugene Smyth, a telegraphist in Dublin Castle. It is undated. There is an extended version of this account worth quoting at length:

> Eugene Smith [*sic*] had access to a document from General Friend to the Chief Secretary, Augustine Birrell, in London. Smith believed the document was a response to questions about the actions of the armed forces when conscription was introduced. The document was lengthy but as he dealt with it himself, he had enough time. He was 'deeply interested in the political situation in Ireland and in the threat of conscription to Ireland.' He decided to give the document to those whom it would affect and, having memorised it, he wrote it out and gave it, complete, to one of his contacts – he wasn't sure which – but probably one of Seán MacDiarmada's agents – he dealt with several. It is likely that Smith's contact passed the document to MacDiarmada who put it into a 'cipher', a simple mixture of shorthand and word contractions. The IRB could not risk a document like this if the carrier were arrested. The document was delivered to Plunkett in the nursing home where he 'de-coded' it

with Grace sitting on his bed and writing the contents down. Plunkett then brought it to Larkfield, where there was a meeting of the Military Council, and George Plunkett, Rory O'Connor, and Colm O'Lochlainn were told to print it on Plunkett's small handpress. Colm left after a while, but the other two carried on. They had no experience of printing, and found it slow and difficult, passing the time singing ballads and God Save the King. They ran out of punctuation and capital letters almost immediately, but continued anyway. They found that the wrong name *'Ara Coeli'* had been given to Archbishop House and sent Jack Plunkett across to Joe, who was now back in Mountjoy Square and Joe told them to change it to Archbishop House. As tiredness grew, a tray of ready type was knocked over and they had to start again, but at last it was done and on the orders of Plunkett and the Military Council copies were sent to all the papers on 15 and 16 April, and to many prominent people. (O Brolchain 2012, 364–5)

This account provides additional information and attendant puzzles in equal proportion. About Smith or Smyth, we learn that he memorised and copied a lengthy document which he had access to in the course of his work. On several levels, the printed 'Secret Orders' does not fit – it is strikingly brief (*c.*360 words) and presents itself as something beyond the normal reach of a telegraphist in its confidentiality. Smyth dealt with several agents reporting to Seán MacDermott of the IRB and the secret Military Council controlled within the Volunteers by the IRB, though little or nothing is known of any other work he did in the nationalist or separatist cause. MacDermott transcribed the material into shorthand and word contractions, hardly a 'cypher' of any complexity. This was then delivered to Plunkett at his Mountjoy Square nursing home, where he deciphered it while Grace Gifford wrote down his dictated text. This detail effectively presents Gifford as a confidante of the Military Council. The Council's blasé approach in these proceedings is underlined by the presence of Rory O'Connor, Colm Ó Lochlainn and George Plunkett (and perhaps teenage Jack) if not *at* the Larkfield meeting then on hand outside the door. Up to this point, the O Brolchain account provides no indication of the lengths of time intervening between Smyth's delivering his copy to the agent to MacDermott's 'encyphering' of it, to Plunkett and Gifford's production of a third stage copy, the Larkfield meeting and the commencement of typesetting by Ó Lochlainn and the others. It reads like a breathless, dramatic evening's adventure but, on the other hand, days or even weeks may have intervened between Smyth's initiative and the Military Council's instructing the amateur printers. In a later recollection of the affair, Ó Lochlainn (1954, 58) wrote of printing 500 copies of 'Secret Orders' with

George Plunkett (no reference to anyone else) about ten days before the insurrection, a quantity which would have facilitated its distribution by Bulmer Hobson, a stern opponent of the Military Council (Townshend 2005, 135).

The quality of typesetting would certainly argue against the statement that the team 'had no experience of printing'. Plunkett owned the press and had issued several brief items for personal use. Ó Lochlainn was the son of a professional Dublin printer – and later a printer-publisher of great distinction. That they 'ran out of punctuation and capital letters' is manifestly untrue, for almost four lines of text occurring low on the page are set entirely in capitals, presumably to highlight target addresses to be seized by the authorities. The statement that 'Colm left after a while but the other two carried on' suggests a continuous period of activity, the ballad singing an absence of urgency in crisis. And why did Ó Lochlainn leave this highly secretive operation? Was he meeting his mother at Arnott's to buy shoes? Or had he decided that the 'Secret Orders' project was suspect (to say the least) and treacherous to the Volunteer leadership?

The dropping of type in a tray, and resumed typesetting, might explain the coexistence of the '3-dot' and '5-dot' versions, except that no printing could have commenced until the entire text had been locked and the press put to work. The confusion of the distinctively named Ara Coeli (the residence of the archbishop in Armagh) with William Walsh's nameless palace in Dublin is puzzling in many regards, not least the revelation that young Jack Plunkett was also present during typesetting at the direction of the IRB (Larkfield, admittedly, was a Plunkett family stronghold). While it is not impossible that the military or the Irish Office were confused on Catholic minutiae, Plunkett's instruction to alter underlines to the point of uniformity that the supposed 'Secret Orders' were concerned solely and exclusively with Dublin.

Following the organisers' failure over the weekend to have the document published in any newspaper, on Spy Wednesday, 19 April, Alderman Tom Kelly read it to a meeting of Dublin Corporation. He had learned of it earlier in the day from Arthur Griffith, and may have obtained a copy from the pacifist Frank Sheehy-Skeffington who feared it would provoke bloodshed if left unchallenged. In essence, the 'Secret Orders' outlined plans for a martial law regime to arrest numerous leaders of nationalist organisations, seize their buildings, and generally stamp out all political activity unsupportive of government and the war effort. From the outset, there were divided views about the document's authenticity.

It is tempting to assume that this latter issue could be resolved to the unambiguous yes or no. Indeed, the implications of its dissemination over a week or ten-day period (including the first stages of the Rising itself) are so extensive that the present moment is not long enough to deal with them adequately. So, if only by default, we should concentrate on the question, what is forgery? – with specific reference to the 'Secret Orders'.

Let us begin with the heading, and the following two lines of print. 'Secret Orders issued [*sic*] to Military Officers' might be taken as the title, part of the text, though the implication that orders have already been issued would argue to the contrary. Then comes an explanation that 'the cipher from which this document is copied does not indicate punctuation or capitals'. This implies that the original was in cipher, whereas the temporary and simplistic ciphering was introduced by MacDermott and removed by Plunkett.

What follows as the body of the text amounts to 35/36 lines divided visually into two parts by an ellipsis (...) of three or five dots. Conventionally, an ellipsis was used by printers to indicate the omission of some material from a text being quoted. If we take the dots in this sense, then the printed document is not a full copy. At this point, the court of enquiry might hear from Otto von Bismarck. In July 1870, the King of Prussia was confronted at Ems, a spa resort, by the French ambassador to Berlin, and a political discussion resulted. The King's secretary wrote up a report sent later in the day to the Iron Chancellor with approval for release. Bismarck edited the report, removing phrases which indicated the King's conciliatory tone, and generally sharpening the import of the exchange. Once released, the Ems telegram provoked Napoleon III to declare war on Prussia, with calamitous results for France, and world-historic ones for Germany. Was the victorious Bismarck's communication a forgery?

There are two witnesses to be heard, both recording their views years after the incident. Eugene Smyth claimed that 'he was in a position to know, at first hand, the entire contents of the suggested plan of operations, and I can definitely confirm the truth of the contents of the document' (Caden 2007, 99, quoting Labhras Breathnach). He also stated that the contents had been *abstracted* from Castle files, suggesting a lengthy source or more than one source and, consequently, indicating that the 'Secret Orders' was not a single unitary text. The second witness was Grace Gifford, who married Plunkett on the eve of his execution. In a later statement, she recorded that she had watched and heard her fiancé decode some of the material. This first-hand evidence is, by the same token, compromised. Plunkett was a show-off, and Grace was no super intellect: her statement vindicates her late husband, loyally, that is all. Others more closely involved in the printing of 'Secret Orders' deserve consideration. George Plunkett, aged 21, was his brother's no less loyal shadow. At Larkfield, Rory O'Connor was busy making bombs, and unlikely to do more than pull the Columbia's lever when the others tired. Colm Ó Lochlainn presents a very different case.

Aged 23 at the time of the Rising, Ó Lochlainn had graduated in Celtic Studies at University College Dublin under the guidance of Eoin MacNeill. He had joined the IRB in 1913 and was a founding member of the Irish Volunteers. In the wake of Alderman Kelly's public reading of the document, and the various responses of Sheehy-Skeffington, MacNeill and others, Ó Lochlainn aligned himself with MacNeill, deploring the efforts of Pearse, Plunkett and Clarke to rise without further thought. Later, he concluded that the document he had helped to print was a forgery perpetrated by Joe Plunkett.

This judgement of course raises the problem of definition. If Eugene Smyth had delivered intelligence from the Castle, and if Plunkett edited this (in the Bismarckian manner), was the result a forgery? Charles Townshend, usually a stern critic of 'street-savvy' language, has declared that Plunkett had 'sexed-up' the data, which, nevertheless, was no forgery in the professor's eyes. The question now shifts to one of intention. What did Plunkett and his cohorts intend when they printed and distributed 'Secret Orders'?

After months of Volunteer demonstrations, deportations by the authorities, threats of conscription and inflammatory rhetoric from Carson, Connolly, Kitchener, Pearse and others, it was reasonable for all to assume that Dublin Castle had contingency plans to suppress opposition whenever it deemed drastic action necessary. Plunkett's document was undated, and so impacted on the public as an immediate threat. It was also unconditional and comprehensive: no mention of specific circumstances which would trigger the drastic action, no limit to the number of individuals to be rounded up. The result could be calculated to stampede moderate nationalist opinion and its leadership. Bernard Shaw (1985, 397–8), writing to H. W. Massingham from Weymouth before the month was out, was in no doubt about the document's status and intent:

> it purports to be an official military set of instructions for the capture of the Sinn Féin barracks throughout Dublin & the disarmament of the S. F. Volunteers. Just the thing to take the poor devils in and manufacture a rebellion. It is much too clever to be German: only an Irishman could be at once clever enough and scoundrel enough (or bigot enough) to have planted such a trap.

A week later, in the *New Statesman*, he claimed to have 'a copy of the fabricated document' and also a letter from Sheehy-Skeffington to the London press warning of a defensive-offensive response by Sinn Féin. Shaw regarded the minor pre-Easter crisis as romantic folly, which 'made those unfortunate Sinn Féiners mistake a piece of hopeless mischief for a patriotic stroke for freedom' (Shaw 1962, 109–10).

This public argument, less forthright than private denunciation of scoundrel forgers, curiously if ironically echoes Charles Maurras's defence of Joseph-Hubert Henry's conduct at a late stage in the Dreyfus Affair. Some detail is unavoidable. Colonel Henry had fabricated a handwritten document, seemingly exchanged between German and Italian diplomats, by taking pieces of two letters which had been torn into fragments, and constructing a third incorporating parts of the original two. The actual (or material) forger was named Lemercier-Picard. Thus assembled, the document compounded Dreyfus' apparent treason. Unfortunately for Henry, the apparently identical paper in both differed slightly in colour when scrutinised in subdued light. Though Henry confessed to the deception in 1898 (and committed suicide), some fellow anti-Dreyfusards regarded him as a virtual hero. For Charles Maurras, royalist, anti-Semite and ultra-conservative, this was 'patriotic forgery'. Was the Castle Document also a patriotic forgery, circulated with the intention of justifying in advance the Rising led by the forger and others?

The details of Colonel Henry's activities are helpful in one important regard: they concentrate attention on the materiality of certain kinds of fabrication. Minute differences of paper colour and of handwriting led to the exposure of a complex dossier of falsification of which Alfred Dreyfus was the victim. Nearer home, a textual detail, Pigott's inability to spell the word 'hesitancy', led to his exposure as forger of the letters approving violence. This latter instance, though less material than the Henry case, is still closer to the physics and chemistry of classic forgery than Bismarck's edited telegram or Plunkett's pale yellow flier. The technology of print, whether the state machinery generating telegrams or the privately owned hand press used most often for verse, complicates judgement about forgery.

William Blackstone's *Commentaries on the laws of England* (1765–9) offers a workable definition – 'the fraudulent making or alteration of a writing to the prejudice of another man's right' (4:287) – though it doesn't distinguish between manuscript and printed material, and doesn't anticipate the telegram or computer. It may, however, despatch Professor Townshend's finesse to the margins of historical debate, provided it can be shown that 'Secret Orders issued to Military Officers' prejudiced some person's right. To this end, let us glance at the method of distribution adopted.

The first individuals to hear of the Castle Document included Griffith, Sheehy-Skeffington and Thomas Kelly. The last stated that he got his copy from P.J. Little. None of these was a member of the Volunteers, the Citizen Army or the IRB, though Griffith and Little were members of Sinn Féin. In the evening of 25 April, the first full day of the Rising, Diarmid Coffey (a Volunteer who did not take part) was given a copy by Douglas Hyde which is now preserved in Trinity College Library. In his diary, he referred to 'the supposed orders of General Friend which may have been the spark which fired the whole business.'[2] Thomas MacDonagh (IRB and Volunteers) claimed the document was genuine, and that it had been put into his hands by friends in Dublin Castle, a remark which may simply restate the account of Eugene Smyth's providing the originals, MacDonagh having been close to the Plunketts. From this, one might conclude that distribution was aimed at initiating public discussion through individuals *not* identified with the advanced separatist position, people whose independence of mind would be acknowledged, notably Kelly who was called 'Honest Tom' even by his opponents. In addition to the alderman, Little publicised the document through *New Ireland*, a weekly paper of which he was editor. Some might claim that these tactics amounted to a clever manipulation of public opinion at a time when opinion was firmly policed through censorship. More specifically, however, it prejudiced the authority of Eoin MacNeill on two distinct but successive occasions. The first occurred when he accepted the document as genuine, and advised the Volunteers to ready themselves against suppression. The second occurred when he was obliged to countermand orders, having decided that it had been forged by his subordinates.

Other deceptions had taken place. The seven-man secret Military Council of IRB men manipulated the Volunteers and Citizen Army rank and file; indeed, the Castle Document was only part of that larger betrayal of the Volunteer leadership, connived at by the Citizen Army leadership in the person of Connolly. Pearse lied to MacNeill when visiting his home. These are the men who, as deceivers or deceived, issued the Proclamation with others on Easter Monday. In this explosion, the 'Secret Orders' had acted as a catalyst would in a chemical reaction. Three years later, when Eliot published 'Tradition and the individual talent' (Kermode 1975, 40–1), he wrote:

> There remains to refine this process of depersonalization and its relation to the sense of tradition. It is in this depersonalization that art may be said to approach the condition of science. I therefore invite you to consider, as a suggestive analogy, the action which takes place when a bit of finely filiated platinum is introduced into a chamber containing oxygen and sulphur dioxide ... the newly formed acid contains no trace of platinum, and the platinum itself is apparently unaffected.

Eliot in 1916 had been lecturing on Georges Sorel and writers of the French cultural Right Wing, cautiously approaching the doctrines of conservative revolution which he later expounded more directly. Like the argument in his

2 See cataloguer's notes attached to the Trinity College Dublin copy of 'Secret Orders'.

essay of 1919, the republican Proclamation of Easter 1916 sought to restore a living understanding of the dead generations and 'old tradition' (for a fuller discussion, see McCormack 2012). W.B. Yeats spent much of April and May in London, with access only to censored news from home. On 30 April, he wrote to the younger of his sisters, 'the whole thing bewilders me for Connolly is an able man & Thomas MacDonagh [*sic*] both able & cultivated. Pearce [*sic*] I have long looked upon as a man made dangerous by the Vertigo of self sacrifice' (Yeats 1992, accession no. 2,935). Later in the year, when he began to compose 'Easter 1916', he found it necessary to characterise or symbolise that element which, unchanging in itself, results in 'all changed, changed utterly'. The catalyst in his poetic account was a stone in the midst of all (Yeats 1990, 228–30).

6

The 'aftermath' of the Rising in cinema newsreels

Ciara Chambers

The events of Easter 1916 have been revised, mythologised and utilised to define, condone and condemn the subsequent struggle within Irish politics. The contemporary media (press and newsreels) had a large part to play in reporting and commenting on the unfolding of the rebellion, the subsequent executions and their legacy. This case study will explore the problematic nature of cinema newsreel coverage of the Rising.

The cinema newsreel: form and content

In 1909, Charles Pathé, founder of the French Pathé company, issued the first specially edited news film and it did not take long for several core companies to grow and develop a genre which became, internationally, a significant part of public viewing until the advent of widespread television news broadcasts in the 1950s. Often dismissed as a meaningless add-on to the cinema programme, the importance of what the newsreels tell us about how events were visually depicted for contemporary audiences is underestimated.

By 1916, the newsreel industry was still in its infancy, but newsreels were already a popular and well-established part of the standard cinema programme. The newsreels were necessarily delayed due to the mechanics of production, so by the time they arrived in the cinemas they provided the pictures to illustrate stories which had already been reported in the press or discussed by audiences through word of mouth. Accordingly, they 'did not make the news – they could only reflect it' (McKernan 1992, 68). They covered a range of stories about international and local events, personalities, sport and fashion, usually with a light touch and upbeat tone.

Ireland was part of the British newsreel distribution circuit and because of a lack of sustained indigenous production Irish audiences watched mostly

British newsreels from 1910 through to the 1950s when the newsreel industry began to decline. Given that the newsreel era coincided with a particularly unsettled period of Irish history, editors faced unique challenges when dealing with Irish events and catering for Irish audiences with a diverse and shifting range of political sensibilities. The newsreels' relationship with Ireland during this turbulent era would prove problematic given the controversial nature of many of the unfolding events and the practical difficulties for British companies attempting to film in conflict-ridden zones. Their motivation was always to support the establishment and, in coverage of Irish events, often violent attacks or disturbances were simply ignored by editors in preference for the usual staple of personalities, sporting events and royal visits. The newsreels particularly sought to avoid controversy given the fact that they were screened in places of entertainment: cinema exhibitors were keen to ensure audiences were not offended or upset during their leisure time. Furthermore, in wartime it was felt that audiences should be rallied in the cinema as any dip in morale could filter through to troops at the front through letters from home. The newsreels sought to remain positive and consistently strove to construct war news in particular optimistically, even in the face of great losses.

The Dublin rebellion

There were only two news films produced directly covering the Easter Rising. The first was for the company Topical Budget and, in typical self-congratulatory style (the newsreels were always trying to 'scoop' their rivals), in its introductory intertitle[1] it boasts 'exclusive pictures of the scene of the fighting in Dublin' accompanied by panning shots of ruined buildings in Sackville Street and along the Quays. Pedestrians are initially depicted in comparative normality at ground level: it is only as the eye rises to the battered skyline that the evidence of destruction becomes clear. Soldiers are shown marching through the streets while civilians stand beside piles of burning debris. The exterior of the General Post Office is shown, followed by interior shots to illustrate the claim in the intertitle that it has been 'completely gutted' after the battle. The footage amply evidences this claim by showing the ransacked shell of the building (Fig. 6.1). Members of the fire brigade are depicted inside as the camera pans up slowly to the open air to reveal the entire roof gone. A third and final intertitle describes 'a street

---

1 Before sound came to the newsreels in 1929, information about the events, locations and personalities onscreen was conveyed through intertitles which were often read aloud in the cinema by literate members of the audience for the benefit of those unable to read.

6.1   Still from Topical Budget's *The Dublin rebellion*.
Courtesy of the Imperial War Museum; IWM/NTB/245/2

barricade, batches of rebels being marched off to the Quay, one of the looted shops, soldiers on guard having their meals in the street'. A close-up of a damaged shop front is followed by shots of a soldier on guard. Again, armed troops are shown marching while civilians stand outside a shop with all its windows shattered. A final shot of soldiers, seated on the pavement, eating and chatting, concludes the item.

Topical Budget operated between 1911 and 1931 and became an official government mouthpiece in 1917 when it became War Office Topical Budget (Reeves 2004, 28). It covered Ireland frequently throughout its years of operation and, interestingly, in his book on the newsreel, Luke McKernan (1992, 134) suggests that Topical Budget was more sensitive in its portrayal of Ireland than Gaumont or Pathé, the other two main newsreel providers of the time. However, this newsreel provides no contextual information on the events of the Rising, nor does it mention the execution of its leaders which had commenced at the time of filming and was well under way by the time audiences began to view the film in the cinema. This newsreel does, however, spend an unusual amount of time covering the Rising: generally

6.2   Still from Topical Budget's *The Dublin rebellion*.
Courtesy of the Imperial War Museum; IWM/NTB/245/2

items were covered over one or two minutes and several items were included in one edition. In this case the coverage of the Rising lasts four minutes and there is only one other item covered. Its inclusion is quite significant as it features the Allies' bands in Paris and the singing of the national anthems of France, Italy and Britain by the French actress Paule Andral, who also poses as the feminine personification of each of the countries (Marianne, Italia Turrita and Britannia) (Fig. 6.2).

   This juxtaposition is interesting given the timing of the newsreel's release (6 May 1916). It was released just after the executions had started, and so it was a moment when the Irish public had not yet been fully exposed to the daily reporting of more executions. This reminder of a larger international war would have been expected particularly to tap into the sympathies of the wives of Irish soldiers who had enlisted in the Allied war effort. They were known as 'separation women' because of the separation allowance paid to them while their husbands were away fighting. They were thus concerned that the rebels' actions put at risk the financial assistance afforded to soldiers' wives. Tim Pat Coogan (2003, 60) reports a comment by prisoner Frank

Thornton: 'if it weren't for the fact that we were so strongly guarded by British troops, we would have been torn asunder by the soldiers' wives in the area'. Clearly, responses to the Rising were varied and complex and this also problematised coverage of the insurrection for newsreel editors keen to please their distributors and audiences.

Another interesting feature of this edition is the inclusion of its only other item: the fact that the newsreel moves from Irish insurgents to 'Britannia' is also characteristic of the newsreels' tendency to jump from stories of conflict to lighter fare, often in what appears to be an insensitive manner. The juxtaposition here, however, does not seem to be coincidental. Ireland is shown as a small and violent nation pitted against everything that 'Britannia' epitomises and, perhaps, by association, there is an attempt to persuade Irish audiences that loyalty, rather than insurrection, is preferable in a time of global war (Chambers 2012, 67). Clearly, Topical Budget also had to incorporate the official government propaganda agenda.

Aftermath of the Easter Rising

A second film, *Aftermath of the Easter Rising*, is currently held in the Imperial War Museum and although it was most likely an official film there are no further details available on its production (IWM/194). The film opens with a shot in the shape of a shamrock of Sackville Street before the rising. The scenes are similar to those in the Topical Budget film except for the fact that all of the buildings are intact. There is a sharp cut to shots of Irish Volunteers in civilian clothes and carrying rifles drilling before the Rising, followed by shots of uniformed Volunteers. In both cases, the Volunteers are openly marching, in some shots in crowded Dublin streets. The film then moves on to scenes of destruction after the Rising, depicting damage done to Liberty Hall, the head office of the Irish Transport and General Workers Union. The camera lingers over the damaged building showing the devastation in minute detail and from every angle (Fig. 6.3). British soldiers are shown outside the Customs House while shots of the interior of a hospital depict three wounded British soldiers in beds being attended by two nurses who chat with the men in a relaxed manner. Again, this serves as a potential reminder of the Irish soldiers who had enlisted in the British army and were off fighting at the front. Subsequent shots show barricades, improvised armoured cars and more damaged buildings. The film concludes with a posed shot of Thomas Clarke (one of the leaders executed on 3 May 1916) with Miss O'Donovan Rossa.

Both films feature smoky shots of burnt out buildings and hazy scenes of the devastation of the Rising's aftermath. This type of footage would become characteristic of the depiction of Irish warfare during both the

6.3   Still from *Aftermath of the Easter Rising*, as listed in Northern Ireland
Screen's Digital Film Archive catalogue.
Courtesy of the Imperial War Museum; IWM/194

War of Independence and the Civil War. The connotations arising from
these representations for both British and Irish audiences are of a country
accepting of violence and willing to follow a path towards self-destruction in
order to further political ideals.

Topical Budget's 17 May edition opens with the trial of Roger Casement,
and two items featuring the inspection of Irish troops are included, probably to
stress the restoration of order in Dublin after the Rising. These are immediately
followed by *German Rifles*, an item showing some of the equipment used by
the rebels. Topical Budget deals with the aftermath of the Rising again three
days later in *Sinn Féin Rebels*, introduced by the intertitle 'disarmed rebels
marching from the military barracks in Dublin to Kingstown for deportation'
and accompanied by shots of rebels under military guard walking past the
camera, and then posed shots of six rebels with close-ups. Topical Budget
was showing its audiences what the rebels looked like at a time when many
of their leaders were being executed day by day. While there is no direct
reference to the executions, it is interesting that a British newsreel included
shots that might have potentially humanised the insurgents for audiences.

A year later, Gaumount Graphic showed the release of many of these same prisoners and their return to a rapturous response in Dublin. The vast crowds shown welcoming prisoners back into their community demonstrated the post-Rising change in Irish attitudes, which has been repeatedly attributed to the British government's drawn-out execution of the rebel leaders.

With the north and south Irish at the front

The War Office, ever conscious of the political power of well-constructed propaganda, attempted to counteract the images of insurgency in Dublin by releasing a film on 1 May 1916 called *With the Irish at the front* dealing with Irish volunteers serving in the war effort. Crucially, the film appeared days before Topical Budget's film covering the Dublin rebellion (which had the standard newsreel delay due to the necessities of editing). The film covered the 16th Division, which was made up largely of nationalist volunteers. This original footage was later re-edited to include material of the 36th Division, comprising mostly members of the Ulster Volunteer Force, the division which was to suffer heavy losses during the Battle of the Somme in July 1916. The final two-reel version of the film was released in 1918 as *With the north and south Irish at the front*. The footage of Irish regiments appearing in the 1916 version was repackaged and juxtaposed with footage of northern soldiers to produce a propaganda film displaying unity amongst Irish soldiers in their support for Britain in the war effort. The film's ultimate goal was clearly to produce propaganda demonstrating camaraderie between soldiers from the north and south of Ireland, thus stressing a unity of support in the war effort despite any prior tensions caused by debates on Home Rule. Its propagandistic comment on Irish politics was clear, particularly at a time when war was coming to an end and the resumption of the Home Rule debate was in sight.

The second part of the compilation begins with the 'ruins of Wytschaete Village, captured by north and south Irishmen fighting side by side'. Wytschaete was taken on 7 June 1917 by the 16th Irish and 36th Ulster Divisions. Northern soldiers are clearly positioned here 'side by side' with their southern counterparts for propaganda purposes: they actually fought on either sides of the bridge in Wystchaete, some distance apart (Chambers 2012, 76). The film also includes scenes of soldiers marching along the streets of Cork with enthusiastic crowds watching and waving from the street and the windows of buildings. It then moves north to Belfast with scenes at Belfast City Hall where large groups of soldiers are depicted in orderly lines while being inspected by the Lord Mayor, demonstrating in a very propagandistic way that soldiers were being welcomed throughout Ireland, a portrayal which was not entirely accurate:

The scenes of the inspections in Belfast juxtaposed with scenes of parades in the south extend the camaraderie of the battlefield to the home front, projecting onto audiences the suggestion of continued good relations between both communities. With the inclusion of footage of Canadian battalions there is a hint at both national and international unity through the process of unified global action in time of war. (Chambers 2012, 78)

The film ends with images of soldiers attending mass in Armagh Cathedral and a plea from Cardinal Logue relayed through an intertitle: 'we are all longing for peace, but it must be a just peace, it must be a stable peace, it must be a permanent peace, and not a halting one'. The final message of the film, Cardinal Logue's plea for peace, transcends international conflict to refer to political instabilities closer to home. The message calls for a measured and permanent solution to the Home Rule conflict – a plea cleverly set up just as war was ending and focus would return to events in Ireland. The fact that the film includes scenes of soldiers eating, washing and during general leisure time (even kissing the Blarney stone) as well as drilling humanises the military, and frequent close-ups of the men's faces further stress that individuals from each community are (apparently) content to interact with one another and unite against the common enemy. This is a British propaganda message to Irish audiences with the agenda of showing that if times are difficult enough, communities can work successfully together for mutual benefit and against a common enemy. As oftentimes occurred in the newsreels, particularly due to a lack of sustained indigenous production, the representation of Irish affairs was overly simplistic and lacking in any nuanced political analysis.

The newsreels – 'All pictures but no politics'[2]

The complexity of the politics behind the Rising does not manifest itself in newsreel coverage. The reporting of the events of 1916 in the two main films to cover the insurrection summarises many of the characteristics of early newsreel portrayals of Ireland. A British, pro-establishment agenda is clear in coverage of all three main companies operating at this stage (Topical, Gaumont, Pathé). Scenes of Ireland are often smoky, conflict ridden, full of the 'aftermath' of destruction – hardly surprising, given the time lag and the practicalities associated with capturing footage at this point in the newsreel industry's development. However, Irish politics are seldom contextualised

---

2 A claim made by Luke McKernan (1992, 64–140) about silent newsreels in the 1920s but certainly applicable also in the 1910s.

or explained. In contrast, the frequent representations of Unionist demonstrations are more easily covered due to the 'stage-managed' nature of the events. These show well-organised displays of British loyalty that tapped into and reflected the general tone of newsreel coverage with its predilection for the political, military and cultural establishment (Chambers 2012, 69).

Beyond the specific case studies examined above, the newsreels operated to normalise British presence through the promotion of repeated images of Britishness in Irish places of entertainment. While propaganda films were essentially about keeping up morale throughout the United Kingdom, in Ireland it was also important that they consolidated Irish unity to garner as much support for the war effort as possible in what were subversive times, particularly after the events of Easter 1916. However, owing to the Rising and the shifting attitudes of the Irish public after the prolonged executions of the insurrection's leaders, it was not possible to be overtly propagandistic, so images of British presence in Ireland, or Irish participation in the war, sought to construct 'British Ireland' as the status quo, the correct order of being, and to instil in the Irish psyche a sense of normality in relation to a continued link with Britain. These images were also exhibited to audiences in Britain, of course, so the process of consolidating and normalising the Britishness of Ireland was as important there as it was in Ireland itself. Despite the fact that the newsreel industry was still in its infancy, a pattern was already set in terms of coverage of Irish affairs, a pattern that would ultimately reveal itself to be 'partitionist' in nature – capitalising on representations of northern, orderly, industrial, Unionist loyalty in comparison with a more backward, rural and inherently violent south.[3]

Newsreels

Aftermath of the Easter Rising. Imperial War Museum, 1916.
The Dublin rebellion. Topical Budget, Issue 245-2, 6 May 1916.
German rifles. Topical Budget, Issue 247-1, 17 May 1916.
Sinn Féin rebels. Topical Budget Issue 247-2, 20 May 1916.
With the north and south Irish at the front. British Topical Committee for War
    Films, 1918.

---

3 Much of the coverage of Ireland can be explored through the British Universities Film
   and Video Council's News on Screen database, which is an almost fully comprehensive
   account of the British newsreel industry, with links to digitized footage and contextual
   production documents: see http://bufvc.ac.uk/newsonscreen.

II The affective bonds of the Rising

Introduction

The contributions to this section address the emotive power of objects. Objects are not only intimately bound up with personal memory – speaking poignantly of moments past – but they create the context in which memory is performed as practice. Objects act as markers of social relationships: the bags and brooches made by male internees for wives, mothers and sisters and discussed here by Brück, for example, work to condense the emotional charge of those relationships in material form, signifying love, loss, hope and fear, and contrasting the disruptive temporalities of internment with material memories of life outside the camp. McAtackney's treatment of a related body of material, the autograph books created by female internees during the Civil War, illustrates how these not only reveal personal links between prisoners but helped to highlight and sustain relationships with the dead – particularly the dead leaders of 1916; in doing so, they sought to identify the women as the true heirs of the ideals of the Rising.

Objects do not simply mark relationships, however, but make them. As Elliott shows, even those who had only oblique connections with the Rising interacted with ephemera such as postcards and newspaper clippings to create intimate links with the dead. Items such as images of the executed leaders were curated and modified – pasted into scrapbooks and made into rudimentary but nonetheless sacred artefacts. Active engagement with ephemera allowed people to make sense of the violent and bewildering events of the Rising and to thread these into the narratives of their own lives. Of course, the power of objects to elicit an emotional response means that they must be viewed as active social agents. Fitzpatrick's discussion of the photographs of the widows and orphans of those who died in the Rising explores the impact these had on public opinion – providing visual evidence of sacrifice that was co-opted to link the 'martyrs' of 1916 to Catholic ideology.

In contrast to the personal and private character of the scrapbooks and other objects described by Elliott, the photographs discussed by Fitzpatrick were deliberately created for public consumption. Fitzpatrick examines how the 'staging' of these studio photographs produced an image of dignified grief and respectability designed to appeal to the emotions of the conservative readership of the *Catholic Bulletin*; at the same time, however, they elided differences in the social backgrounds and circumstances of the fractured families they portrayed. Similarly, Crowley's discussion of Pearse as icon shows how carefully he attempted to frame his image in his own lifetime, and how that image has been co-opted, venerated, vilified and transformed since his death. Pearse's image, he argues, continues to have particular emotive power, yet its use runs the danger of sustaining a reductive and unidimensional figuring of the man himself. Objects (and images-as-objects), as these chapters demonstrate, work not only by evoking particular social and political ideals but by their sensuous appeal to the emotions, their power to conjure memories and their intimate connection with the body.

7

Portraits and propaganda: photographs of the widows and children of the 1916 leaders in the *Catholic Bulletin*

Orla Fitzpatrick

The December 1916 issue of the *Catholic Bulletin* contained 23 photographs showing the widows and children of men who had fought and died in the Easter Rising. Its editor J.J. O'Kelly (1872–1957) collected or commissioned them, knowing that in order to gain sympathy for their cause he needed to convey both their normalcy and respectability. He opens his editorial with the quotation 'suffer little children to come unto me' and immediately shifts focus from the insurgents onto their fatherless and innocent children.[1] The article's power lies in the cumulative effect of images of bereaved families. Generic studio photographs gained a currency and meaning beyond the domestic through their mass-media reproduction, and the repetition of near-identical family groupings creates a photographic typology of grief.

O'Kelly and the *Catholic Bulletin* played an important role in gaining acceptance for the Rising and in recording testimonies and biographies in the months after the event. Historians have acknowledged this although they have not explicitly examined photography's role (Murphy 2005, 225; Nic Dháibhéid 2012, 723; Wills 2009, 110–11). The photographs and O'Kelly's editorial reveal much about gender and class relations and how these were entwined with notions of Catholic martyrdom. The 23 pictures show 70 fatherless children aging from five months to 19 years. 17 were commissioned from a single studio after the Rising. The others were borrowed from families and friends and were taken before 1916. The *Catholic Bulletin* article is illustrated by photographs of the families of three signatories of the Proclamation, Thomas Clarke, Eamonn Ceannt and James Connolly; however, most of the images depict those of lesser-known volunteers and members of the Irish Citizen Army.

---

1 'Events of Easter Week' in the *Catholic Bulletin and Book Review* VI (12), December 1916, 697–711, 697.

This portrayal of Easter Rising widows contrasts with the near invisibility of the more numerous First World War widows. Censorship prohibited the publication of photographs showing European battlefields, which were deemed bad for morale. Newspapers printed casualty lists but they were seldom accompanied by portraits. As conflict was ongoing and conscription had been recently introduced, images of war widows did not serve the imperial power's purposes. Meanwhile, photographs of the Rising widows were used with religious language and notions of martyrdom to elevate the protagonists to near saint-like positions.

These photographs are similar to those from any family album excepting that they have been reproduced using photo-mechanical technologies and circulated to a mass audience. Family photographs are usually viewed within intimate domestic settings; however, O'Kelly has changed their context making them available for public consumption. Photography could also bypass the censors, who hampered the production of the May/June issue. Few could fail to be moved by these images and O'Kelly recognised that photographs of fatherless children would generate donations to the National Aid and Volunteers' Dependents Fund set up to assist them. Indeed, their success in eliciting funds was such that they were reproduced for several years.

The *Bulletin's* publisher M.H. Gill was known for its devotional literature, the market for which peaked during the revolutionary years (Allen and Brown 2011, 702). Kerry-born O'Kelly was its editor between 1911 and 1922. An Irish-language enthusiast, he was a one-time rival of Patrick Pearse for the editorship of *An Claidheamh Soluis*, the Gaelic League's newspaper, an organisation of which O'Kelly was to become president. The *Bulletin* was set up to promote Catholic literature, an activity that O'Kelly relished. In 1912, he issued his list of classified books with a Catholic 'character of absolute reliability' (Murphy 2005, 168). Its audience were Catholic families and clergy and its average circulation was between 10,000 and 15,000 (Murphy 1989, 73). These figures are nowhere near those of daily newspapers but they compare favourably with other literary and political journals (Kennedy 2010, 247). The *Bulletin's* July 1916 issue, profiling the Rising's leaders, sold out and was definitely attuned to the zeitgeist.

The politics of the *Bulletin* has received attention, especially O'Kelly's role in a series of anti-Semitic articles. It is often cited as an example of the narrowness of Irish society (O'Callaghan 1984), although its stance on the Rising was unique amongst religious publications. As Wills (2009, 112) noted, the 'hagiographical sketches brought home to readers – who could buy the *Bulletin* without embarrassment after Mass – that the rebels were not German stooges but Irishmen and Catholics, who had devoted themselves to their nation'.

Discussions of photography and loss have concentrated upon memorial photography such as the images of family members that are placed in altars or memorial cards and photographic objects like Mexican *fotoesculturas* (Batchen 2004). Daguerreotypes sometimes show family members holding photographs of the dead. Along with post-mortem images, these reveal how a photo-portrait can 'stand-in' for the dead. They emphasise the continuation of the familial bond; however, O'Kelly's series shows the families as fractured and fatherless.

Hirsch (1999) explores how the familial gaze changes when domestic photographs are recontextualised for consumption outside the family. This has applications for the 1916 series although only those pre-existing photographs (submitted by families) have undergone a true reappropriation from the domestic to the public. The portraits commissioned for the *Bulletin*, although utilising the mores of family photography, were conceived with mass distribution in mind and are a highly unusual use of the vernacular.

From the 1890s, halftone blocks allowed for the printing of photographic images alongside text. This technique breaks up an image into a series of dots and reproduces the full tone range of a photograph: 'the halftone photograph appeared to offer viewers a direct trace of the individual it depicted. As such, it apparently represented them with an unmatched candour and intimacy' (Beegan 2008, 6). The halftone reproductions in the 1916 issues of the *Bulletin* have an immediacy lacking in earlier commemorative imagery.

Photographs of the leaders of the 1916 Rising appeared with great rapidity: indeed, many at the 'month's mind' masses wore badges featuring photographs of the executed men. Booklets and albums depicting the city centre destruction were also published. All were facilitated by the technological advancement mentioned above. Mass reproduction and dissemination of photographic imagery are aspects of the modernity of the Rising, creating an iconography and adding to the foundation myth required by emerging nation states.

O'Kelly commissioned 17 of the images from Thomas Francis Geoghegan, 2 Essex Street. A photographer since the 1860s, his clients included the National Gallery of Ireland. He was a member of the Royal Society of Antiquaries of Ireland and contributed to the *Capuchin Annual*. His logo appears on the portrait of Kathleen Clarke held in the National Photographic Archive. This is the only extant source image from the December 1916 issue located within a public collection.

By 1916, having one's photograph taken had become an established ritual in the construction of middle-class identity. Studio portraits played a part in the performance of respectability. Photographers evened out social distinctions through the provision of a space replicating middle- or upper-class reception rooms. The nineteenth-century studio used upholstered furniture and elaborate backdrops to give the appearance of respectability. By 1916, these had become more understated, however, so that the space offered a staged neutral setting conferring propriety. It is worth noting that the backgrounds and incomes of those depicted within the *Catholic Bulletin* article were widely divergent. A similar space may not have been available within the homes of the bereaved.

Customers visiting studios adhered to the social contract which having one's photograph entailed. This included wearing one's 'Sunday best' and following the photographer's instructions. Geoghegan posed the families in conventional arrangements facing the camera straight on and surrounded by the usual furniture, thereby complying with the conventions of studio portraiture. It is this very conformity and ordinariness which resonated with readers. The 17 photographs commissioned by O'Kelly constitute a photographic typology of the grieving family. Typologies are a series of similar images which together create patterns allowing for comparative analysis. Photographers such as August Sander and the Bechers employed this type of methodological image-making to explore concepts of nationality, industrialisation and modernity. Geoghegan's portraits comply with the norms of a typological series. Taken from the same angle, with similar backgrounds and lighting, they depict loss and absence. The absence of the father from the group is emphasised. As depictions of loss, these photographs have a strength lacking in the composite family groupings assembled from disparate photographs (Fig 7.1).

O'Kelly (1916, 699) outlined his belief in the centrality of family to Irish identity:

> [It] will help to a truer appreciation of the sacrifices involved in the tragic family severances of Easter week, and proudly faced at what all concerned deemed the call of duty. Whatever the time or clime or circumstances, all, save the dastard, must appreciate the passionate love of freedom which is strong enough to prevail over such sacred parental ties as hallow the Catholic homes of Ireland.

Hirsch (1981, 15) states that family photographs 'describe the family as a state whose ties are rooted in property; the family as a spiritual assembly which is based on moral values; and the family as a bond of feeling which stems from instinct and passion'. However, the *Bulletin* photographs reveal families where the natural bond has been overridden by a passion to secure Ireland's freedom. O'Kelly recognises their propaganda value and uses them to show that only a truly worthy cause would compel someone to endanger his life and leave his children fatherless. The contemporary viewer must take into account the rhetoric of sacrifice which permeated society in relation to both the Rising and the First World War.

7.1   Mrs Patrick Doyle and her children, the *Catholic Bulletin*, December 1916.
Courtesy of the National Library of Ireland

The experience of viewing photographic images within a magazine or journal differs from an encounter with a single print:

> The halftone is essentially multiple, meant to be seen in relation to other images, whether those images are reporting the same story or are juxtaposed with it in the magazine. It becomes a text that potentially speaks to every other image in the publication in which it is printed. (Beegan 2008, 14)

An analysis of the photographic element of the article must also refer to the journal's overall visual identity. In addition to theological and social issues, the *Bulletin* placed an emphasis upon family and included sections directed to mothers, daughters and children. A quaint illustration in the style of Kate Greenaway, known for idyllic portrayals of childhood, was used for the monthly 'children's circle'. The accompanying motto reveals the *Bulletin*'s ethos. Children should aim to become good Irish Catholics: 'Next to God, I love thee, Dear Erin, my native land.' Religion and nationality can be found together within even the children's section.

Decoration derived from Celtic manuscripts was, by 1916, well-established and popular with Irish designers (Sheehy 1980). It could be used to imply nationalist sympathies and it is not surprising that it was adopted here. One cover shows Armagh Cathedral and the Rock of Cashel entwined in neo-Celtic knotwork. This imagery resonated with those for whom Catholicism and nationality were inseparable. Black-and-white fields of neo-Celtic knotwork were also used as framing devices to enclose photographs of the widows and children (Fig. 7.2).

The article's layout mirrors that of domestic photographic albums and utilises design tropes known to the readers from their own albums. The familiarity of such domestic photography assured readers that the bereaved families were like them and countered negative press depictions of the fighters. In contrast to the albums they reference, the pages were not arranged or sequenced by family members; instead, they were collated by an editor.

The accompanying text reflects the rhetoric of sacrifice which permeated much commentary on the Rising. There are many occurrences of words associated with the family and concepts of martyrdom. The following extract relating to George Geoghegan betrays complex notions of sacrifice, duty and patriotism whilst also revealing the mindset through which the men rationalised their decision:

> On receipt of his mobilisation order on his return from early Mass, Easter Sunday morning, George Geoghegan, turning to his wife and children, said: 'Goodbye, dear wife and children. I am off to do my duty, and I ask you not to be uneasy about me. If I am killed you will know I died fighting in a sacred cause, and I trust it will benefit you and the children and the children of every good Irishman in the years to come.'[2]

This concentration upon the piety of the leaders and their identification as Catholic is noted by Wills (2009, 110): '[the] Catholic Church responded swiftly to the popular mood and in effect co-opted the rebels' secular martyrdom for itself. The socialist and republican aspects of the Rising were downplayed; the rebels had died for a Catholic nation.' Reframing secular sacrifice in terms of religion was not confined to Ireland and much of the rhetoric surrounding the First World War referred to glorious redemption in the next life. However, the mixture of Catholic imagery with that of the Rising provided a potent mix and had a particular resonance with the Irish psyche.

O'Kelly wrote to the widows requesting copy to accompany the images; however, the article does not include the women's opinions or feelings.[3]

---

2 'Events of Easter Week', 703-704.
3 National Library of Ireland (NLI) NLI/MS/18, 555, 'Letters to J.J. O'Kelly from relatives etc. of participants in Easter Rising, 1916–1917'.

7.2   Mrs A.J. Byrne and her children; Mrs William MacDowell and her children, the *Catholic Bulletin*, December 1916.
Courtesy of the National Library of Ireland

Instead, he quotes heavily from their husbands' final messages. The omission of the women's voices is telling. Whilst O'Kelly purports to outline their plight he does not reveal their personal attitudes to the Rising.

On 2 August 1916, O'Kelly wrote to Hannah Sheehy-Skeffington, whose picture was included although her husband was a civilian casualty. He cannot quote from her letter as 'I am afraid I'll not be able to say more in the face of limitations under which I am dealing with the whole subject.'[4] During this period she was attempting to secure an investigation into the murder of her husband, and her condemnation of the British forces differed from the other widows, whose responses to O'Kelly did not refer to political matters.

Some women pictured in the December issue were to assume a public role as a result of their loss whilst others had been highly politicised beforehand. Some became household names whilst others faded from view. O'Kelly does not make any distinction between those with prior political affiliations (Clarke, Sheehy-Skeffington) or those with none. All are depicted as grieving widows and mothers. He subsumes their identity within that of their husbands and only Sheehy-Skeffington is captioned with her Christian name. He conceals the complexity of their backgrounds, presenting a uniform picture to readers. This simplification makes it easier to elicit sympathy from his conservative readership. It also prefigures the restrictive interpretation of women's roles adopted by the state after the revolutionary period: a construction of femininity emphasising home and family as the traditional and natural space for women.

The leaders' families usually had higher profiles than those of regular fighters; however, the December issue mainly depicts the families of lesser-known men. Their biographical details reveal a diversity and range of affiliations which was not reflected by O'Kelly. It included labourers, housepainters, silk-weavers and bakers. The O'Rahilly's widow claimed that her income was not changed by his death; however, for most the loss of the breadwinner meant financial ruin (Matthews 2010a, 170). The plight of Philip Clarke's family provides a telling example. In 1911, he lived in Dolphin's Barn with his wife and eight children in two rooms classified as a third-class dwelling.[5]

Obtaining donations for dependants was an integral aim of the *Catholic Bulletin* article. Kathleen Clarke, the widow of Thomas, was a founding member of Cumann na mBan. She played a major role in the formation of the Irish Volunteers Dependants' Fund. The complexities surrounding its

4 NLI/MS/18, 555.
5 Census of Ireland, 1911. Form A for Philip Clarke and family. Available at: www.census. nationalarchives.ie/reels/nai000161538/. Accessed 28 April 2015.

subsequent merger with the National Aid Fund are many and cannot be covered here; suffice to note that the resulting Irish National Aid Association and Volunteer Dependants' Fund (INAAVDF) raised considerable sums and was administered in a competent manner. Nic Dháibhéid (2012, 723) has traced the role played by the committee in the radicalisation of public opinion, recognising how O'Kelly and the *Bulletin* significantly shaped popular memory of the Rising.

Interestingly, with regard to the educational provision for children, it was found necessary only to provide for them in the manner to which they were previously accustomed. Certain children were sent to school at Saint Enda's whilst others went to work. O'Kelly's 1919 report on the aid committee outlines the information requested whilst processing claims.[6] They wished to know the amount considered necessary to enable families to live up to their old standard, the number of children, ages and the provision necessary for their education or the feasibility of starting them in appropriate employment. These questions demonstrate that class-consciousness continued after the Rising. Nic Dháibhéid (2012, 715) remarks upon the varying amounts awarded to the families of executed men and that this hierarchy of victimhood also seems to have operated when it came to the families of the 64 men killed in action. These families received much smaller sums in the form of immediate relief grants, even though in the cases of Richard O'Carroll and Philip Clarke there were seven and eight dependent children, and the final investments or payments made were generally to the tune of £75 or £100.

Commenting upon the plight of mothers of First World War dead, Evans (2007, 5) states that their stories were co-opted by the authorities and their profiles were either raised or lowered depending upon their perceived value for the war effort: 'Mothers bereaved in times of conflict have been remembered and honoured by their communities and their leaders in proportion to the perceived need to support and develop a sense of patriotism and, if necessary, militarism.' This has a resonance with the photographs of the bereaved families in the *Catholic Bulletin*. The following quotation would suggest that the article secured the desired results for O'Kelly, that of gaining sympathy for the fight for Irish independence:

> A monthly journal with a large circulation … which reached the homes of the majority of the people, was a major factor in bringing it home to people that the men who planned the Insurrection … were of their own sort, kindly Irish of the Irish, neither Saxon, Italian nor German. (Murphy 1989, 75)

6 Irish National Aid Association and Volunteer Dependants' Fund papers, National Library of Ireland, MS 24,386 (2).

8

'After I am hanged my portrait will be interesting but not before': ephemera and the construction of personal responses to the Easter Rising

Jack Elliott

In February 1916, Seamus Doyle wrote to Patrick Pearse to ask if he would consent to his image being used on the front cover of a souvenir publication. He wrote back that 'the souvenir is a very good idea, but I think a portrait of Emmet would be better (as well as handsomer) on the cover. After I am hanged my portrait will be interesting but not before.'[1] This brief exchange demonstrates that Pearse understood the value that would come to be posthumously attached to images of those who led the Rising; he was not unique in this awareness. In the weeks prior to Easter 1916, both Con Colbert and Countess Markievicz had photographs of themselves taken in their uniforms.[2] In Markievicz's case she did so in order that the image circulated of her following the Rising would be that of her in military dress and not, as was eventually the case, of her days as a debutante of the ascendancy elite.[3]

In the wake of the Rising, as Pearse predicted, images of the executed leaders, and those whose death sentences were commuted, circulated widely in newspapers and on pieces of mass-produced ephemera. Historical scholarship notes the existence and proliferation of these ephemera (Alter 1987; Laffan 1999). However, with a few notable exceptions, there is an absence of any serious consideration of the significance of this material (Cashman 2008; Jarman 1997; Wills 2009). This case study contends that by paying serious attention to the material culture produced in the aftermath of the Rising, one can begin to explore the ways in which individuals engaged with and began to shape narratives that sought to make sense of the armed insurrection.

---

1 Irish Military Archives, MA/BMH/CD 127/3, letter to Séamus Doyle from Patrick Pearse, 17 February 1916.
2 Dublin City Archive, BOR F02/07, portrait of Con Colbert in military uniform, 17 March 1916. MA/BMH/P7, photograph of Countess Markievicz in the uniform of the Irish Citizen Army.
3 MA/BMH/CD 256/3/7, postcards of the Easter Rising leaders.

Following a brief overview of the mass-produced commemorative material available after the Rising, attention will turn to the ways in which individuals interacted with these ephemera. In particular, a case study of six badges containing newspaper images of leaders of the Rising will demonstrate that the modification of pieces of mass-produced material was integral to the ways in which individual responses to the Rising were mediated. This case study of badges will be contextualised with other examples of modified ephemera. Taken cumulatively, the physical and emotional labour invested in these items highlights a critical engagement with the creation of interpretive frameworks for the Rising.

In the immediate aftermath of the Rising advanced nationalists were extremely active in producing newspapers, journals, handbills, postcards and assorted ephemera that emphasised the chivalry, camaraderie and sacrifice of those who fought (Elliott 2012, 184; Githens-Mazer 2006, 142–3). These items simultaneously sought to present a sympathetic and intelligible narrative of Easter Week 1916 to the public, and to claim ownership of the legacy and symbols of the Rising. However, companies motivated by commercial opportunity were also quick to produce 'souvenirs' of the Rising. Questions raised by MPs in the Westminster Parliament indicate that souvenirs were available to the public by June 1916.[4] The sale of the souvenirs was being advertised to the public by August 1916.[5]

Information about the quantity in which such items were produced and sold is hard, if not impossible, to ascertain given the nature of ephemeral commodities, especially those considered seditious. However, from the various references in reports to the Chief Secretary of Ireland, and surviving items within archives, it appears that postcards and souvenir publications were the most prominent examples of mass-produced Rising ephemera.[6] These items focused on two principle themes. First, a great deal of attention was given to republican combatants and their families, specifically the executed leaders. Secondly, the destruction of Dublin city due to the Rising was strongly emphasised. In both cases images were used to familiarise the public with a particular stock of information, presented in each case to form a holistic narrative of the events of Easter Week and the subsequent executions.[7] The

---

4 National Archives of Ireland (NAI), NAI/5620/13271, Chief Secretary's Office Registered Papers (CSORP), 1916.
5 *Leader*, 12 August 1916.
6 NAI/5630/26071, CSORP, 1916.
7 Kilmainham Gaol Museum: KGM/17pD/1A15/5–30, Sinn Féin revolt postcards; KGM/17BK/1J21/12, 'Rebellion album 1916'; KGM/17BK/1J21/13, 'Sinn Féin rebellion album 1916'; KGM/17BK/1J21/14, 'The Sinn Féin revolt illustrated'; KGM/17BK/1J41/13, 'Dublin after six days insurrection'; KGM/17BK/1J41/15, 'Dublin and the Sinn Féin Rising'; KGM/17PC/1A53/28, 'The rebellion in Dublin

factual information and images recorded in these ephemera were, almost without exception, identical. However, differences in the presentation and order of the material, alongside significant differences in the subjective statements that were made by the authors, give a clear indication of the ways in which the public were exposed to numerous different competing interpretations of events.

After the Rising, the authorities tried hard to supress material that might lead to increased support for Sinn Féin.[8] However, a number of enquiries and complaints that passed through the Irish Chief Secretary's office related to the fact that there was inconsistency in what was considered to be prohibited and the enforcement of those prohibitions.[9] Subsequently, the authorities were encouraged to acknowledge that they would have to allow some material, produced for commercial consumption, to flow more freely.[10]

The production and circulation of mass-produced ephemera illustrates a desire to give an interpretive framework to the Rising and the competing interests attempting to do so. However, in limiting our focus to *what* was produced we risk treating the purchasers of the items as passive consumers. An analysis of *how* these items of ephemera were interacted with, and modified by, their owners demonstrates that individuals used them to create a more nuanced and personalised narrative of, and relationship with, the Rising.

Figures 8.1a and 8.1b illustrate six badges each containing an image of one of the leaders of the Rising. Depicted are Thomas Clarke, Edward Daly, Éamon de Valera, Seán McDermott, Patrick Pearse and James Connolly.[11] They are small, cheap and crudely made objects. The casing for the images was made of tin and the images themselves are newspaper clippings affixed to thin cardboard. In their original form the newspaper images that were used to make these badges were not seditious. And yet, the process of modification that transformed the newspaper images into personal pieces of jewellery shows an emotional connection to and support for the rebels that constituted a challenge to the authority and power of British rule in Ireland.

The Leader noted in May 1916 that prior to the Rising many of the leaders were 'absolutely unknown to the public … [and] some of them were

April 1916'; KGM/17PC/1B14/10, 'Sinn Féin revolt 1916: twelve interesting views'; KGM/17PR/1H22/05, '*The Times* history and encyclopedia of the war – Irish Rebellion of April 1916' (1); KGM/17PR/1H22/06, '*The Times* history and encyclopedia of the war – Irish Rebellion of April 1916' (2); KGM/17PR/1K11/03, '*Irish Life* record of 1916 rebellion'.

 8 NAI/5630/26071, CSORP, 1916.
 9 NAI/5617/11840, 5621/13987, 5642/25286, CSORP, 1916.
10 NAI/5621/13867, CSORP, 1916.
11 KGM/17PC/1A44/16.

8.1a   Six small lockets containing newspaper photographs of the 1916 leaders (obverse).
Courtesy of Kilmainham Gaol Museum/Office of Public Works; KGM/17PC/1A44/16

unknown to us even as names'.[12] And yet, the badges demonstrate that, in the aftermath of the Rising, the circulation of the leaders' images meant that they had become recognisable figures. So much so that the producer of these badges identified with the rebels strongly enough to invest physical and emotional labour in the creation of a new object that allowed for mass produced newspaper images to be worn. Despite the lack of monetary value the badges clearly demonstrate that ephemera were 'invested with emotional charge' by individuals (Wills 2009, 105). The unique nature of the badges allowed the individual who owned them to claim an authentic proximity to the Rising and an associational relationship with its leadership

12   *The Leader*, 20 May 1916.

8.1b   Six small lockets containing newspaper photographs of the 1916 leaders (reverse).
Courtesy of Kilmainham Gaol Museum/Office of Public Works; KGM/17PC/1A44/16

even if, in reality, the individual in question had played little or no role in the community of Irish radicals prior to the Rising. The creation of a personal connection to the rebels in this way facilitated the expression of the authenticity of the owner's nationalist and republican identity to the community around them. However, the successful communication of the wearer's republican sympathies relied on the wider public recognising the images of the rebels. Consequently, these badges suggest a reciprocal relationship between mass-produced ephemera and more personalised items. Mass-produced ephemera created a general public awareness of the Rising and a familiarity with the appearance of its leaders. More personalised items, such as these badges, demonstrated sympathy with the Rising and a desire on the part of the individual to be associated with those who fought in Easter

Week, 1916. By wearing modified and personalised ephemera in public, indications of the changing attitudes towards the rebels became increasingly visible. The growing support for the rebels was increasingly reflected in the tone of mass-produced items in the year following the Rising.

The badges are a particularly interesting example of the modification of mass-produced material because they highlight that the widely circulated images of the Risings leaders were being worn in public to communicate support for the rebels. Such indications support wider research that concludes that, in the aftermath of the Rising, individuals used ephemera to create spaces within Dublin to express seditious political beliefs (Elliott 2012). However, it is important to note that it was not uncommon for individuals to procure mass-produced ephemera that, through the application of physical and emotional labour, they transformed into more personalised items. This process of modification allowed individuals to engage critically with the narratives the items contained in their original state, and to challenge, support or embellish the details they provided in order that the narrative more closely reflected that of the owner (Elliott 2012, 223–6). In one souvenir publication, the owner had fully annotated it with statements rejecting the narrative of Easter Week it presented.[13] In another example, the *Irish Life Record of the Irish rebellion of 1916* noted that 'The conduct of the [British] troops under the most trying conditions of fighting, that of street fighting, was beyond all praise, and was enhanced by the fact that the troops in question were to a great extent composed of men who were receiving a baptism of fire'.[14] Beneath this, the owner has added in pencil, 'they were not, however, shelled like Pearse + his men were'.

A particularly notable way in which individuals chose to modify ephemera to negotiate individual reactions to the Rising was to create a scrapbook. For instance, on one double-page spread of his scrapbook, Frank Martin (an Irish Volunteer) arranged Powell-Press postcards of Patrick and William Pearse together, surrounding their images with other assorted ephemera that told the story of their executions. The material he includes emphasises Patrick Pearse's farewell to his mother in which he professes to have died willingly for Ireland. Martin also includes newspaper cuttings that refer to the brothers as 'unconquered and unconquerable: the brothers Pearse and the saving of Ireland's soul'.[15] Finally, he goes on to transcribe a poetic lament entitled *P.H. Pearse*, originally by Seán MacEntee.[16] Like all the

13 KGM/17PR/1H22/05, '*The Times* history and encyclopedia of the war – Irish Rebellion of April 1916' (1).
14 KGM/17PR/1K11/03, '*Irish Life* record of 1916 rebellion'.
15 National Library of Ireland, MS 33,695/1, scrapbook of Frank Martin.
16 KGM/18BK/1B52/01, 'The poems of John Francis MacEntee'.

individuals who compiled scrapbooks, Frank Martin invested emotional and physical labour in its construction. He made active decisions about its layout and presentation that indicate an attempt to present a narrative. To build his narrative, he took existing ephemera and modified them to suit his purposes. In the particular example described above, Martin supplemented the Powell Press postcards of the brothers Pearse to strengthen and reiterate the message that they, and Patrick in particular, had willingly made a knowing sacrifice in the name of Ireland and, what is more, that it was their mother who would bear the burden of grief knowing that her sons had died for an independent Republic.

Similarly, Elsie Mahaffy, the daughter of the Provost of Trinity College Dublin, wrote in her scrapbook about the exhaustive efforts she made to collect all the Rising ephemera she could.[17] She placed the material she gathered alongside her written narrative about her experiences and reflections on the events of Easter Week and the year that followed it. Again, images of the leaders were crucial to constructing a narrative of the Rising and to creating personal familiarity with the event. Whilst Mahaffy included handbills of Pearse's poetry and took the time to transcribe his last letter to his mother, it was two images of Pearse that she included in her scrapbook that she felt helped her 'to realise this man'. Mahaffy did not support the rebels. However, the seismic effect the Rising had on the physical and political landscape of Dublin meant that she sought to make sense of the event and situate her personal response within a wider narrative. Ephemera provided her the means by which to achieve this.

The scrapbooks of Martin and Mahaffy are representative of other examples. The care that went into the creation of these items, the placement of each item and the annotations that so often surround each object communicates an individual narrative and an emotive relationship to the political events they describe. When talking about individual mediations and emotive responses to objects it is possible only to ascertain so much. The slivers of insight that have been left to us by the owners of the objects are often expressed through their treatment of the object rather than any explicit pronouncement about its worth. However, what is clear from the material now preserved is that ephemera were prevalent in the immediate aftermath of the Rising. Moreover, individuals purchased, engaged with, and preserved this material. They placed sufficient worth on the items to pass them on, either to an archive or a relative. Consequently, in seeking to make sense of the sea change of public opinion towards the Easter Rising, and advanced nationalism more generally, between 1916 and 1917, we must take seriously

---

17 Trinity College Dublin Archives, MS 2074, 'Ireland in 1916: an account of the Rising in Dublin, illustrated with printed items and photographs', by Elsie Mahaffy.

the role that material culture played in shaping narratives and emotional reactions to the events of Easter 1916.

In sum, mass-produced ephemera were created with the intention of presenting a self-contained narrative of the Rising. It has been demonstrated that this was manufactured by groups and companies with a variety of different reasons for doing so ranging from profit to political conviction. What is more, these goods circulated under the watchful eye of the authorities whose anxieties around the production and distribution of potentially seditious material belied an awareness of the significant role ephemera played in mediating public opinion toward the Rising. However, more significant is the argument that the consumption of mass-produced ephemera was an active process whereby owners modified, preserved and used the items such as postcards and newspaper clippings to create a didactic relationship between the creation and appropriation of the narratives and symbols of the Rising.

9

Nationalism, gender and memory: internment camp craftwork, 1916–1923

Joanna Brück

The years from 1916 to 1923 were marked by several episodes of mass internment, most famously at Frongoch in north Wales in the immediate aftermath of the Rising but also at camps such as Ballykinlar, Tintown and Hare Park during the War of Independence (1919–21) and subsequent Civil War (1922–3) (O'Mahony 1987; O Duibhir 2013). This case study will explore how the craftwork made by internees allowed them to negotiate the changing social and political conditions of the period and to cope with the psychological challenges of camp life. Over 130 objects from museums and private collections were examined for this research: these included harps and crosses worked in wood and bone, macramé handbags and tea cosies, metal brooches and rings, woolwork mats, and a range of other small, decorative items. Relationships with objects are particularly intense in contexts of material privation, providing a sense of ontological security to those who experience the disruption and trauma of internment (Carr 2011; 2012; cf. Moshenska 2008; Saunders 2003). Craftwork acted as a conduit for feelings of loss and fear, yet at the same time it expressed internees' ongoing engagement with the social world as well as their enduring sense of personal capacity and intellectual freedom (Dusselier 2012).

Crafting the nation

It is no surprise that much of the craftwork created in camps and prisons during this period should engage with political themes. Although internees came from diverse backgrounds and often took ideologically distinct standpoints, the objects they made expressed a strong sense of shared national identity and cultural heritage. Motifs such as harps and round towers were carved onto bone and wood objects (Fig. 9.1), while brooches imitating the

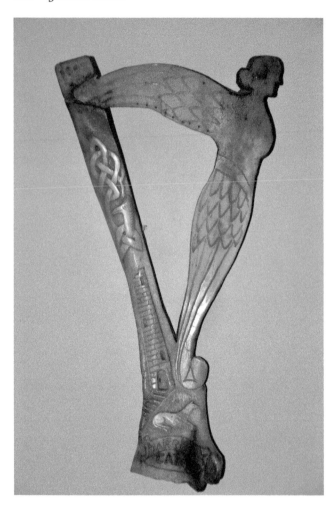

9.1   Bone harp featuring Éire, round tower, greyhound and Celtic interlace, from Hare Park internment camp, Curragh, County Kildare.
Courtesy of Kildare County Council

early medieval 'Tara' brooch were especially popular. Such imagery sought to demonstrate the achievements and sophistication of Gaelic Irish culture prior to the Norman conquest, while their imagined links to early Irish kingship underpinned claims for the legitimacy of self-government. Symbols such as the harp and the wolfhound had long been associated with cultural nationalism (Morris 2005), but by the late nineteenth century their use in contexts as diverse as the badge of the Royal Ulster Constabulary (in this case, the harp was surmounted by a crown) and to promote sentimentalised visions of 'Celtic Ireland' to generations of Victorian and Edwardian tourists meant that they had become so ubiquitous – and even banal – that they had lost some of their political potency (Sheehy 1980). Yet, this fluidity of meaning made them particularly suitable for use by a republican movement that was itself far from unified; at the same time, it allowed the re-imagining of motifs that had been appropriated to imperialist purposes.

Expressions of religious identity are also common in internment camp craftwork. Wooden crosses commemorating hunger strikers or those who had died in combat legitimated violence by linking religious imagery with an ideology of self-sacrifice (cf. Wills 2009). Holy water fonts, chalices and monstrances of wood and bone were decorated with religious symbols such as the Sacred Heart: such items forged a growing ideological link between republicanism and Catholicism despite the long history of Protestant involvement in Irish cultural nationalism and independence movements. In a similar way, an embroidered handkerchief from Hare Park features several decorative elements in orange, but the tricolour itself is worked in green, white and gold – an act that worked to erase Protestantism from this emblem of national identity.[1]

Memory and temporality

A concern with remembrance and commemoration was a leitmotif of late Victorian and early Edwardian society and became particularly marked in European cultural consciousness in the aftermath of the First World War (Saunders 2003). As such, the interest in memory and temporality that is visible in Irish internment camp craftwork of this period is part of a broader cultural trend, but it was also rooted in the particularities of the experience of imprisonment. Almost a third of the objects examined for this project were inscribed with the camp name or date (nearly a quarter had both), creating souvenirs around which memories could be recounted and reworked (cf. Stewart 1993; Wills 2009). Many such objects were brought home by internees on their release: a pair of bone harps from Newbridge Camp are mounted on turned and polished mahogany stands that were clearly not made in the camp itself and it is not hard to imagine these items displayed on a mantelpiece.[2] Objects like these facilitated the production of collective memory (Halbwachs 1992 [1951]): through shared acts of remembrance, such items authenticated the memory of internment.

The marking of time was important for other reasons too. Imprisoned without charge and without trial, internees had no idea how long they would be detained. Inscribing objects with a date demonstrated a commitment to the future and acted as a means of controlling and transcending the uncertain temporalities of internment (Dusselier 2012, 83). Faced with crippling

1 National Museum of Ireland (NMI), NMI/EW.929.
2 Cork Public Museum (CPM), CPM/1972–37; CPM/1972–38.

uncertainty in a profoundly dehumanising environment, it was crucial to maintain a strong sense of personal history and to nurture memories of life beyond the wire (Rachamimov 2012, 293). Objects such as the watch pendant made from a spoon and engraved with the message '*Seosamh ón a Athair*' ('To Joseph from his father')[3] countered disconnection from normal temporal rhythms by evoking enduring structures of sociality that transcended the physical boundaries of confinement.

The challenges of camp life

Inevitably, internees had to be creative in their search for raw materials. Camp-issue objects were frequently repurposed: spoons were made into Tara-style brooches at Tintown and Hare Park (Fig. 9.2), while the women imprisoned in Kilmainham Gaol made skirts and slippers out of blankets.[4] This reworking of camp objects was often viewed as a contentious act of appropriation (cf. Carr 2012). The production of rings and brooches from coins, for example, was banned by camp authorities who viewed it as the deliberate defacing of legal tender (Jim Higgins, personal communication): indeed, a brooch from Spike Island made during the War of Independence has had the king's head carefully cut out and removed.[5] Of course, internees found imaginative ways of obtaining coins for the purpose: Michael O'Brien, interned at Ballykinlar Camp, made a brooch for his wife from a silver half-crown she had hidden inside a cake for him (Myra Heffernan, personal communication). Here, craftwork subtly challenged the authority of the prison guards and disrupted the routines of camp life.

Such subversive acts illuminated the social and ideological division between the prisoners and their guards; doubtless they also helped to generate a sense of camaraderie amongst the internees (Carr 2011; 2012). Yet the difficulties of camp life were such that the prisoners themselves cannot always be seen as a cohesive group, and here, too, craftwork became a focus for the playing out of interpersonal tensions. In some cases, craftwork was cast in a negative light, epitomising the boredom, tension and frustration of camp life. A poem in an autograph album from Ballykinlar expresses it thus:

> Oh for a cell all to myself
> A clean white floor – a tidy shelf

---

3 NMI/EW.216.
4 University College Dublin Archives (UCD), UCD/P140, memoirs of Maighréad and Siobhán de Paor, 1923.
5 CPM/1988-1.

9.2   Tara brooch fashioned from a spoon by John 'Blimey' O'Connor in Tintown internment camp, Curragh, County Kildare.
Courtesy of Cáit Mhic Ionnraic

A book to pass spare time away
To rise and work at dawn of day
Far from the bloke who hammers rings
Far from the 'can' who *thinks* he sings
Far from this den where rumours dwell
If it *must be jail* – give me a cell.[6]

Gender relationships and concepts of the home

Although some women were imprisoned during this period, the majority of internees were male. In this context, it is interesting to observe that the most common objects made in camps were items associated with women, such as macramé handbags (Fig. 9.3) and bone and metal brooches. These played

6 NMI/EW.2711.

a significant role in ensuring the endurance of affective bonds central to personal identity: sent as gifts to wives, mothers, sisters and female friends in return for parcels of food and other necessities, they constituted an economy of love and remembrance that transcended the boundaries of the camp (cf. Saunders 2003). Often, these were highly personalised: Michael O'Brien engraved the words 'May God above increase our love' on the brooch he made for his wife (see above); later, his daughter wore this special object for her Confirmation. Such items gave material form to enduring relationships, condensing memory and emotion into objects that sustained interpersonal ties in the face of spatial and physical disruption (Saunders 2003).

Many of the objects made for women were worn on the body, recalling the intimacy of relationships that had been abruptly severed by internment. Indeed, written discourse around these items was often distinctly erotic in tone: a letter from a female friend thanking Edward Leonard for some macramé handbags he had sent commented 'of course all the girls are jealous over them I hope you will bring me home as nice a boy' [*sic*].[7] Other internees sent objects closely associated with their own bodies: a female friend writing to thank James Ryan for a button from his uniform, described how, 'When I get rich I am going to get one of them dipped in gold and made into a brooch for myself.'[8] Sexual longing was expressed in the desire for objects, countering disempowerment, disruption and loss with a discourse of enduring sensual connection and sexual potency.

At the same time, however, the experience of internment called into question normative definitions of masculinity. Internees were required to do their own washing, mending, cooking and cleaning – tasks that usually fell to women. This disruption of gender roles appears to have provoked a considerable degree of disquiet that was often addressed through humour. Craftwork contributed to this disconcerting sense of emasculation, as a poem in an autograph book from Ballykinlar demonstrates:

> If you want a young man who can mend his own socks,
> Or your stockings (perhaps), an' 'as cookin';
> An' washin'; an' sewin';
> Who can make fancy furniture out of a box,
> An' macramé bags, that you see in a book,
> In a manner as neat and so knowin';
> Well, you'll find one up here
> Anyday o' the year

7 National Library of Ireland (NLI), NLI/MS/15,353, correspondence of Edward Leonard.
8 UCD/P88/20, papers of Dr James Ryan.

9.3 Macramé lady's handbag made by Pat Moran in Kilmainham Gaol. Courtesy of Kilmainham Gaol Museum/Office of Public Works; KGM/20EF/3L21/07

> In the camp out at Baile Cionn Leóra,
> Where the boys from all parts
> Learn housekeepin' arts
> With the gentle assistance of DORA.[9]

In this context, it is hardly surprising that the ambiguities around the definition and performance of masculinity should be addressed in a variety of ways (cf. Rachamimov 2012), including plays and shows in which men took on female roles to the amusement of their fellow internees. A letter from Harry Boland describing the fancy-dress competition held in Frongoch at Hallowe'en recounts how 'we had three "ladies for a night" who were very much sought after'.[10] In the all-male context of the camp, such performances reinforced yet also challenged the conventions and boundaries of gendered

---

9 NMI/EW.1059; the Defence of the Realm Act (DORA) (1915), allowed prisoners to be detained without charge and suspended the right to trial by jury.
10 UCD/P88/39, papers of Dr James Ryan.

identity. Craftwork was co-opted into these discourses on the troublesome
definition of masculinity: a spoof advertisement in the Ballykinlar Camp
magazine *Barbed Wire* sought a 'Principal boy and other well-shaped ladies
for panto. Send waist measurements to this office. Bring own tights unless
prepared to wear macramé mantle border as substitute'.[11]

Alongside bags, rings and brooches, internees made a variety of objects
associated with the home. Tea cosies, mantle borders and woolwork table
centres expressed a poignant longing for domesticity. Camp conditions were
harsh and uncomfortable yet contemporary photographs and drawings of hut
interiors do not feature such items; instead, they were sent to wives, mothers
and sisters so that the romanticised home of the internee's imagination was
figured as spatially and ontologically distant (Rachamimov 2012, 294). This
lack of desire to transform the camps into a 'home-from-home' acted as
a way of rejecting the spaces of internment and emphasising its transient
nature (cf. Parrott 2005). At the same time, the production of objects for
the home provided male internees with a continued sense of involvement in
domestic life. The experience of internment undermined norms of masculine
authority and fathers were unable to provide for their families. The emotions
experienced under such difficult circumstances are nicely encapsulated by
a set of macramé child's reins from Frongoch.[12] These evoke the sense of
loss and helplessness felt by so many internees, the weaving and knotting of
the thread speaking of the longing for physical proximity to a much-missed
child. At the same time, as technologies of bodily discipline, they expressed
a desire to exert continued paternal authority over family life.

Indeed, perhaps the most significant role of objects such as tea cosies,
brooches and handbags is that they helped sustain particular forms of
gendered identity. They portrayed women as interested only in decorative
trifles: an issue of the Ballykinlar camp magazine describes how, 'We
have made up for the absence of the superior sex here by attempting their
conceits: the making of vanity bags, rings and other knick-knacks is now
all the rage'.[13] At the same time, such objects located women firmly in the
home, conforming to contemporary gender ideologies which legitimated
male power in the public realm by relegating women to the domestic domain
– an ideal which, of course, was contradicted by women's active involvement
in the nationalist and republican movements of the time (e.g., McCoole 2003;
Matthews 2010a).

This depiction of women served a particular political purpose. The
definition of Irish masculinity was especially troublesome in the context of

11 Private collection.
12 NMI/EW.532.
13 Irish Military Archives (MA), MA/BMH/CD/134/4/3.

imperialism (Sisson 2004; Valente 2011). Central to the colonial project was the feminisation of the subject: Irish men were figured as irrational and emotional Celts in need of firm paternalistic guidance. Yet, in the popular imperial imagination, they were also stereotyped as brutish and uncivilised. In this context, by conforming to patriarchal and imperialist ideals of manliness that foregrounded qualities such as self-control, courage, honour and obedience, Irish men could demonstrate a capacity for self-determination that legitimated their political endeavours (Valente 2011). Adherence to the ideology of a martial masculine culture can be seen in the ordering of camp life along military lines (O'Mahony 1987): these men were presenting themselves as soldiers on a par with those in the British army. Set in this context, the production of objects such as handbags and tea cosies was a way of validating the normative conception of manliness by placing it in opposition to an ideal of femininity as passive, superficial and inextricably bound up with the trappings and trivialities of the home. In this way, Irish men could counter the feminising tropes of imperialism and lay claim themselves to the characteristics that epitomised Victorian manliness.

Conclusion

The internment camp craftwork discussed here provides a rich source of evidence for the varied perspectives, ideals and fears of those involved in the nationalist and republican movement during this period. Objects such as these were powerful agents of social change, bound up with emerging concepts of social and national identity. They were memory objects that embodied the struggles of the present and aspirations for the future, and their importance to the families who still cherish these objects today ensures that they continue to play a significant role in the construction of narratives of personal and national identity.

Acknowledgments

I am especially grateful to the many individuals, curators and archivists who made their collections available to me and shared their family stories. Thanks also to Seán O'Mahony, Ann Matthews, Liam O Duibhir, Jim Higgins, Pádaraig O Ruairc and Will Murphy who took the time to discuss their own research with me, and to Niall Bergin of Kilmainham Gaol for arranging permission to reproduce Fig. 9.3.

10

Female prison autograph books: (re)remembering the Easter Rising through the experiences of Irish Civil War imprisonment

Laura McAtackney

This chapter will provide a number of insights into how the Easter Rising of 1916 was actively reutilised in justifying standpoints and maintaining steadfastness and resolve during the Civil War period. The Easter Rising, War of Independence (1919–21) and short but divisive Civil War (1922–3) interconnect in many ways, including through many of the leading military and political figures, the places of conflict and confinement, and how earlier events and ideals were continually reconceived in order to utilise the past as an impetus for present actions and inspiration for the future. In exploring this, the chapter will overtly engage with gender as the primary vector of interpretation in order to present the often forgotten experiences of 'renegade' women (Matthews 2010a). It will reveal how they conceived the promises for equality, as articulated by the executed leaders of the Rising, as a motivation in mobilising their opposition to the compromises of the Free State.

The Irish Civil War was conducted with more bitterness, ruthlessness and duplicity than the previous cross-national military interactions and as such is still considered difficult to commemorate publicly (Dolan 2003). This state of affairs means that as we enter a decade of commemorations in Ireland there is an emphasis on the more comfortable and clear-cut narratives of the Easter Rising and War of Independence than the enduring, bitter memories of the Civil War. Of the many repercussions of this public amnesia two will be explicitly explored in this chapter. First, the sidelining of gendered experiences of the period, particularly experiences of imprisonment, is examined. Secondly, the uses and articulation of the Easter Rising – as materialised in Kilmainham Gaol – by female prisoners provides interesting insights into the self-perception of the women as they publicly proclaimed their place as descendants of the leaders of 1916.

Margaret Ward argues that the Civil War was the first period in Irish history that witnessed the mass imprisonment of women for political reasons. Her argument is supported by the statistics: around 50 women were political prisoners during the War of Independence, whereas at least 400 were imprisoned during the Civil War (Ward 1995, 190). Although these numbers are still small in comparison to the almost 12,000 men who were imprisoned during the same period, they were sufficient to ensure that the state needed to provision for their mass accommodation, held indefinitely as political prisoners for the first time. There continues to exist a number of material legacies of this imprisonment, including large collections of prison craft, huge swathes of graffiti that still cover many of the walls of B (West) Wing in Kilmainham Gaol, and a significant number of extant autograph books that the women held and wrote in during their confinement.

Historical archaeologists have been interested in the materiality of texts almost from the inception of the subdiscipline. They moved swiftly from self-identification as the 'handmaiden of history' (Hume 1964) to problematising the relationship between textual and non-textual forms of material culture (including Hall 2000). Archaeologists have increasingly argued for the need to explore the material nature of texts – explicitly discussing their biographies as things, their transition from the functional sphere to the archival and their shifting values in wider society. Such approaches can provide insights that the text alone will not reveal. This is particularly important when exploring texts that were not official or government sources but were created as personal keepsakes and records by those who experienced events rather than administered them. In this respect, I argue that autograph books are an especially significant source in understanding female imprisonment during the Irish Civil War.

Autograph books were relatively inexpensive, mass-produced volumes of blank paper that were popularly circulated in westernised societies in the late nineteenth to mid-twentieth centuries. They were usually passed between school children to mark transitions and changes in their young lives and were filled with prose, verses, images and collages. Although widely used in popular culture, there are relatively few academic studies of their uses, contexts and meanings, undoubtedly due to their ubiquitous nature and the assumption that their contents were essentially meaningless. However, Hanna Herzog and Rina Shapira examined the contents of teenagers' autograph books in Israel during the 1980s and argue that autograph books were important as 'authentic material not created for the purpose of study' and that the entries – although 'ritualisitic and uniform' – were meaningful in cementing social networks (Herzog and Shapiro 1986, 109–10). Whilst the contents of autograph books surviving from the Civil War do demonstrate strong similarities, careful analysis has the potential to reveal variations and personalised insights. Furthermore, they allow access to the unselfconscious feelings and experiences of the women imprisoned at this time. Owing to these qualities, and to the availability of a number of examples held in the archive at Kilmainham Gaol, this often forgotten source is a valuable means of accessing the women's connection to, and articulation of, the Easter Rising.

Autograph books: survival, access and usage

Autograph books were used widely by both women and men imprisoned during the Civil War and a significant number continue to exist and are accessible for study. A collection of 25 that are held in the Kilmainham Gaol archive are of interest as much for the individual object biographies and their often-circuitous routes to the archive as for their contents. Of the current collection, four are on loan from their original owners and ten are photocopies; most were accessioned to the archive in April 1995 as a direct result of research conducted by Sinéad McCoole (1997; 2003). Only two autograph books located by McCoole were donated in perpetuity; three others were probably acquired during the Kilmainham Gaol Restoration Society era (1960–6), three during the 1970s and three since 1999. The very different timescales and routes that these books took to arrive in the archive reveal various transitions in value in their biographies as material culture of the Civil War. One can only speculate as to the impact that changing emotional, familial, academic, historical and financial values have had on the decisions as to whether they were donated in entirety or as a photocopy or loan. This is particularly the case with the passing of time, as they have transitioned from owner to descendants, from being personal papers to nationally important material culture of revolutionary Ireland. Few donations have been made in this 'decade of commemorations', as these personal mementos are now cultural commodities of economic value. One can only wonder how representative this small sample is of the period.

Despite their under-utilisation, autograph books are both an element of the material culture of 'revolutionary Ireland' and unique textual sources revealing the experiences, feelings and thoughts of the imprisoned women compiling them. They allow us to reconstruct networks and connections between the owner and the writers, as well as to undertake textual analysis. Networks can be reconstructed through examining who is writing and how they are presenting themselves, who is missing (or excluded) and the details of 'memories', including reminiscences about the book owner or times they shared (see also Shapiro and Herzog 1986, 442). Although inclusions and exclusions can often be explained by the circumstances and timing of imprisonment, there were evidently some women who maintained the books in smaller and more select friendship circles than others and there was often a strong geographical bias to the women's friendships. At the most basic level, there was a strong county commonality to many of the friendship groups, and those from less active counties, particular the North and the British deportees, are in relatively small numbers or arrange their names and affiliations communally. There are many readings that can be extracted through analysis of these volumes; this chapter will concentrate on the relationship with the events and symbolic nature of the 1916 Easter Rising.

The Easter Rising, Kilmainham Gaol and the Civil War

The Easter Rising – as a touchstone, reference point and source of inspiration and steadfastness – runs throughout this collection. Places of previous political incarceration, particularly Kilmainham Gaol, were especially important in materialising linear connections between the Rising and the present realities of imprisonment, and no doubt inspired many of the entries referencing 1916. Kilmainham Gaol was intimately connected with the leaders of the Rising. It was first closed by the British forces in 1910 and was only opened sporadically after this time to hold both male and female rebels. Famously, it had been the prison where many of the 1916 leaders spent their last hours and where they had been executed in the gaol yard. Kilmainham therefore represented not only a place of incarceration but a material connection between the women and the leaders of the Easter Rising. The re-imaging of Kilmainham in this way maintains a tradition begun when republican women began holding meetings in the ruins of Sackville Street in the aftermath of the Rising (Clare 2011, 229). Indeed, Patrick Cooke has argued that Kilmainham Gaol 'constitute[s] the spine of the Irish nationalist and Republican tradition' (Cooke n.d., 1) due to its association with nationalist insurrection, particularly the Easter Rising.

These connections were articulated consciously, if selectively, by the women in their autograph books. The focus on the male leaders of the Rising, in particular, linked to their steadfastness of resolve and the injustice of their predicament. In doing so, they presented themselves to be true descendants of 1916, through their current sufferings as well as strong emotional bonds. Prisoner autograph books, as products of this incarceration, bear witness to how the women, in particular, perceived and presented their first period of mass incarceration as a continuation of male, nationalist tradition. This connection of place is articulated in the autograph book of Peg Lawlor Kilmainham (July 1923):

Joseph Mary Plunkett's Cell/1916

God give us men, A time like this demands
Great hearts, Strong minds & willing hands

Men, whom the lust of office will not [keep?]
Men – who possess opinions & a will
Men, who have honour, Men who
will not die

Alice McGrath, Emly. Tipp[1]

In a similar vein, the enduring connection between the imprisoned women of the Civil War and the ideals of the Easter Rising can be found in the unambiguous linking of the two in the autograph of Criss Stafford:

Easter Week 1916 C na mB [i.e., Cumann na mBan] stood by the IRA
Seven Years have passed since then,
But the same old fight goes on
And C na mB are still to the good
By the side of the IRA.[2]

Indeed, this close, even intimate connection with the executed leaders of the Easter Rising is often explicitly made, particularly as many of the female relatives and partners of the executed leaders now found themselves imprisoned. In the autograph book of Frances Casey, there is a poem by Joseph Mary Plunkett, transcribed by his widow Grace Gifford Plunkett (Fig. 10.1).[3] By the time of the Civil War, Grace was established as one of the tragic figures to have emerged from the Rising on account of her marriage to Joseph Plunkett the night before he was executed (O'Neill 2000). A prominent republican before the Civil War, her imprisonment at this time was a difficult proposition for the Free State. Whilst she was an outspoken advocate for the anti-Treaty side (Clare 2011, 230), she was also inextricably linked with the tragic blood sacrifice of the Rising. Therefore, the entry in the autograph book is revealing for a number of reasons. First, the choice of poem, 'Treason! Treason!', was not accidental. Grace read it at the Easter Rising commemoration held by the women in Kilmainham Gaol that year (of which more later) (O'Neill 2000, 72). Furthermore, she signs the poem with her full name in Gaelic and then notes 'North Dublin Union / June 1st 1923: / (late Kilmainham Jail)'. This referencing of previous imprisonment in Kilmainham Gaol is a common feature of the signatures of those women

---

1 Kilmainham Gaol Museum (KGM), KGM/2010/0114, autograph book filled in Kilmainham Gaol, 1923, belonging to Peg Lawlor.

2 KGM/2010/0173, autograph book relating to imprisonment at Kilmainham Gaol and North Dublin Union, April–June 1923, belonging to Nellie Lambert.

3 KGM/20/MS/ID34/01, photocopy of an autograph book relating to imprisonment at Kilmainham Gaol and North Dublin Union, 1923, belonging to Frances Casey.

TREASON! TREASON!
BY JOSEPH PLUNKETT 1913

The night that brave Lord Edward died
The blood ran red in Dublin town
As ebbing from his throbbing side
It might the stain of treason drown.
Their corpses swung upon the air
In England's jail — the martyred three
For hanging is the patriot's share
And felon - setters still are free

And now Clontarf + Batchelor's walk
Have still the bloody purpose shown:
Unless our dreams that purpose balk
A Nation shall be overthrown.
By God! The volunteers shall bear
The banner of our liberty
Though shooting be. the patriot's share
And felon - setters still be free

Sgáinia Kean Beasann uí Pluingcéis
North Dublin Union
June 1ˢᵗ 1923:
(Late Kilmainham Jail:
Arrested Feb 5ᵗ)
HOME ADDRESS . 49 PHILIPSBURG AVE
FAIRVIEW: DUBLIN

10.1 'Treason! Treason!': poem by Joseph Mary Plunkett, transcribed by his widow Grace Gifford Plunkett into Frances Casey's autograph book. Courtesy of Kilmainham Gaol/ Office of Public Works; KGM/20/ MS/ID34/01

who were transferred (many under duress) to the North Dublin Union in April 1923. To continue to reference Kilmainham Gaol reveals the enduring symbolic use of the place as a material connection between 1916 with the bitter reversals of 1923.

The most obvious indication of Kilmainham's transition from place of incarceration to representation of the ideals of the Easter Rising – and also the female prisoners' centrality to remembering publicly those ideals – is revealed in their commemoration of the Rising in 1923. This commemoration coincided with a time when many of the anti-Treaty men and women were either on the run or incarcerated. Therefore, the official commemoration of the Easter Rising for that year was organised and took place within Kilmainham Gaol. This event is recorded in some detail in a number of the extant autograph books. At least three in Kilmainham Gaol archive contain highly ornate and colourful renderings of the programme of commemoration for the day (e.g., Fig. 10.2). These programmes not only highlight the women's claiming ownership of the memory of the event but show how they

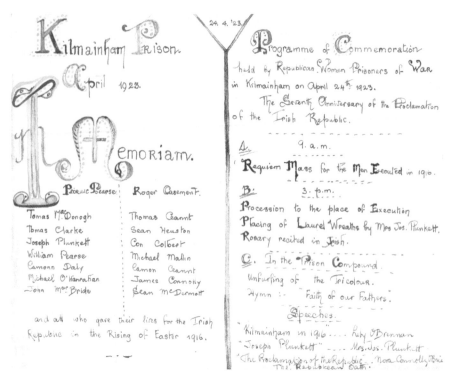

10.2   Programme of events for the commemoration of the Rising in Kilmainham
Gaol, April 1923, from Nellie Fennell's autograph book.
Courtesy of Kilmainham Gaol/Office of Public Works; KGM/2010/0196

used the spatiality and materiality of the prison in doing so. The care evident
in the recording of the day's commemoration in the autograph books makes
them self-conscious, portable memorials to the events of the day.

The programmes reveal the organisation of the women and particularly the hierarchy of involvement in the key structuring elements of the
processions, wreath-laying and speeches. Not unexpectedly, the closest
relatives of those men who had been executed leaders of the rebellion were
most active, with 'Mrs Joseph Plunkett' leading the procession to the prison
yard, laying the wreath, unfurling the tricolour flag and providing a speech
on the subject of her husband. This was complemented by further speeches
on 'Kilmainham in 1916' (by Lily O'Brennan, sister-in-law of Eamonn
Ceannt) and 'The Proclamation of the Republic' (by Nora Connolly O'Brien,
daughter of James Connolly).[4] The events of the day continued into the

---

4 KGM/2010/0196, autograph book relating to imprisonment at Kilmainham Gaol and
   North Dublin Union, 1923, belonging to Nellie Fennell.

10.3 'Patriot to his
motherland': poem by Patrick
Pearse transcribed into Frances
Casey's autograph book.
Courtesy of Kilmainham
Gaol/Office of Public Works;
KGM/20/MS/ID34/01

evening with a concert of carefully selected poems, verse and speeches (the majority written by 1916 leaders) inside the 'A' wing of the gaol. It is telling of the tacit Free State acceptance of the women's claim to the memory of 1916 that they were allowed to complete this full-day programme by the prison authorities.

Further references to 1916 – both explicit and implicit – abound within the autograph books. These often take the form of poems, verses and slogans connected with the leaders or events of the Easter Rising. They include one example where a photographic representation of Patrick Pearse is attached to a page filled with two verses of his poem 'Patriot to his motherland' (Fig. 10.3).[5] More prosaically, 1916 is referenced in dating conventions. A number of the entries replace the year of writing (1923) with 'the 7th year of the Republic'.[6] Therefore, even in the everyday practice of dating, the link between the two events is made – not only in the circumstances of political imprisonment but in justification for enduring defiance and ongoing nationalist struggle.

Conclusion

The autograph books circulated by imprisoned women during the Irish Civil War provide an often overlooked but important insight into the 'claiming' of this event by the anti-Treaty forces. Their entries – which explicitly and implicitly reference the Rising, its leaders and their aims – support Dolan's contention (2003, 138) that the anti-Treaty forces presented themselves, at an early stage, as being the rightful heirs of the Easter Rising. I would argue that this case was most forcefully made by the women who publicly articulated both the irregularity of their incarceration and their familial and marital connections to many of the executed leaders of 1916. Their first period of mass imprisonment, especially at the politically loaded site of Kilmainham Gaol, provided a variety of inspirations and parallels that were often articulated in prose, verse and drawings in their autograph books.

In particular, the placing of the official commemoration of the Easter Rising for 1923 in Kilmainham Gaol (exclusively in the hands of the women) presented them as not only steadfast to the aims of the original rebellion but also selective in their focus on the executed leaders. In concentrating on the poems, prose and proclamations of Pearse and Connolly, the women claimed their links to the higher ideals of the revolution, but in doing so created and perpetuated the myth that the women themselves were not central to its preparation, execution and continuation. Through the utilisation of these autograph books, I hope a small part of that myth can be dispelled.

11

Pearse's profile:
the making of an icon

Brian Crowley

The author Julian Barnes devoted one of the essays in his 2012 collection, *Through the window*, to the nineteenth-century French art critic, Félix Fénéon. Fénéon was painted by several artists throughout his life including Signac, Vuillard, Bonnard and Vallotton. Each artist chose to represent him in profile. Reflecting on this tendency to depict Fénéon from the side, Barnes (2012, 124) writes that 'this profilism was also psychologically and aesthetically accurate: a representation of Fénéon's obliqueness, his decision not to face us directly, either as readers or as examiners of his life. In literary and artistic history he comes down to us in shards, kaleidoscopically'. The side-profile of Patrick Pearse has a similar enigmatic quality. Pearse's image is the best-known of all the 1916 leaders and has become as much a symbol of the Rising as the Proclamation or the burnt-out ruins of the General Post Office. It has been reproduced on stamps, coins, medals, in marble, plaster and stone. And yet, despite the ubiquity of Pearse's image, he remains distant from us, remote and other-worldly. It is an image which was ideally suited to the interpretation of Pearse which emerged from the ruins of the Rising. He looks like a saint-like visionary, utterly devoted to his dream of a free and heroic Ireland. His head is fixed, staring at a destiny only his prophetic soul can decipher.

However, the profile has also contributed to a one-sided, reductive conception of Pearse which has allowed no space for complexity or nuance. Pearse has not so much been elevated as reduced to the status of an icon. When the veneration of Pearse's memory was challenged in the 1960s, this was often done as an act of iconoclasm, without any consideration that this iconic image was just one side of a multifaceted personality. Throughout his life Pearse created and recreated different identities for himself. This tendency often stemmed from his own unease with himself and a need, particularly in the years before his death, to remake himself within a romantic heroic paradigm. His success in projecting this self-created persona, combined with his equally self-cultivated physical image, transformed him into the first and pre-eminent icon of the new Irish state. It was an image which suited both those who sought to appropriate Pearse following the Rising as well as those who sought to undermine that persona in later years.

Ironically, although Pearse remains one of the most enigmatic figures associated with the Rising, his life is better documented than most of his comrades. Pearse even began an autobiography which he left uncompleted. It only covers his early years and is not dated, but it would seem to have been written in the latter part of his life. It is a revealing document, often unintentionally so. He begins describing the circumstances of his birth in 1879 in the backroom of No. 27, Great Brunswick Street (now Pearse Street). The building housed his father's monumental stone-carving business and one of Pearse's earliest memories was the sound of the 'rhythmic tap-tapping' of a chisel on stone which came from his father's workshop – an appropriate beginning for someone whose image was destined to be carved so often in stone. His father, James Pearse, was born in London, grew up in Birmingham and came to Dublin for the first time in the 1850s. Pearse's Irish mother, Margaret Brady, was James's second wife and they married in 1877.

Pearse grew up surrounded by the paraphernalia of his father's business: statues, casts and drawings would have been commonplace in the Pearse household. James Pearse's business expanded and his work was in great demand. This gave him the means to indulge in his passion for books – he was a typical Victorian autodidact and self-educator. Although he had little formal education, he was a committed bibliophile and the Pearse Museum contains an eclectic collection of his books on subjects such as art, architecture, history, religion and geography. Many of the books feature lavish illustrations and the walls of the Pearse household were adorned with fine engravings. They also had a magic lantern projector which Patrick and his father would use to give illustrated talks.

Growing up in this atmosphere, it is not surprising that Pearse developed a sophisticated visual sensibility and appreciation for art. His maternal great aunt, Margaret Brady, was a regular visitor and she would tell him heroic tales of ancient heroes like Cúchulainn and Fionn MacCumhaill as well as modern figures like Napoleon, Robert Emmet and Wolfe Tone. Pearse had an intense and deep reaction to this wealth of imaginative stimuli. He wrote that 'with every book that was read to me, with every picture I saw, with every story or song that I heard; I saw myself daring or suffering all the things that were dared or suffered in the book or story or song or picture' (Pearse n.d.). Later accounts of his childhood describe how Pearse formalised these fantasies as he grew older, and wrote plays in which he, his brother

Willie, sisters Mary Brigid and Margaret, and cousin Mary Kate would perform. Pearse would also disguise himself as an old woman and wander around the streets, knocking on doors and asking after made-up characters. These childhood anecdotes prefigure Pearse's later engagement with theatre but also a fluidity within his own persona and a desire to adopt other identities (Pearse 1934, 55–6).

Growing up in an artistic home, Pearse appears to have enjoyed being the subject of an artistic gaze. In a sensual description, he recounted how he would pose, sometimes naked, in front of the fire for his father's bohemian artist friends:

> Many of these visitors made drawings and paintings of me, sometimes of my head only and sometimes of my whole body without any clothes on. They said I had a thoughtful face and that I was finely shaped. I think what they valued me chiefly for was my faculty of remaining still for a long time. (Pearse n.d.)

Pearse seems to have revelled in this experience, proud of the fact that one of his father's artist friends praised him for being 'the best and quietest little model he had ever had'. This experience of being observed seems to have allowed Pearse to consider himself as an imaginative subject: 'Some of the longest stories I have ever made up about myself were made up while a man was making a picture of me stretched on my face at full length with my chin resting on my hands' (Pearse n.d.).

This theme of self-observation dominates the autobiographical fragment. In the opening paragraph, Pearse writes: 'I am not sure whether it is a good thing for a man to possess so fully as I have possessed it the faculty of getting, as it were, outside of himself and of contemplating himself from a little distance' (Pearse n.d.).

While Pearse may have often been oblivious to how he was perceived by others, he was never free from his deeply self-conscious sense of himself. This may explain not just his insecurity about his appearance, but also his desire to shape his life into a form which lived up to his heroic ideals. The autobiography also reveals an intense self-awareness and his attempts to understand his own life. In his article, *Patrick Pearse: the Victorian Gael*, Pat Cooke (2009, 45) comments on the contrast between its tone and that of Pearse's political writings at the time: 'instead of a prophet uttering adamantine certainties about the destiny of the Gael, we find a man deeply unsure of his identity'.

Cooke concentrates in particular on perhaps one of the best-known passages of the autobiography in which Pearse contemplates his mixed parentage:

For the present I have said enough to indicate that when my father and my mother married there came together two widely remote traditions – English and Puritan and mechanic on the one hand, Gaelic and Catholic and peasant on the other; freedom-loving both, and neither without its strain of poetry and its experience of spiritual and other adventure. And these two traditions worked in me and fused together by a certain fire proper to myself, but nursed by that fostering of which I have spoken made me the strange thing that I am. (Pearse n.d.)

By returning to the original manuscript, Cooke was able to identify that initially Pearse had said his mixed parentage had made him 'an Irish Rebel' (capital I, capital R) but crossed out that phrase and replaced it with 'the strange thing that I am' – a much more troubling yet also more revealing phrase. The manuscript itself is a physical representation of Pearse's intention to set aside, at least for a time, the persona of the heroic rebel and attempt instead to come to some degree of self-knowledge. The manuscript is unfinished and Pearse's inability to continue with it is in itself significant. Just before he abandoned the project, Pearse (n.d.) wrote that 'One must not put all one's secrets into a book.' Cooke (2009, 60) argues that Pearse was unwilling to face 'the prospect of writing about his own adult years, and lingering too long over the cracks in his own fissured identity'. Significantly, Pearse would appear to have abandoned the manuscript and its resultant self-examination around the same time that he committed himself entirely to his public political role and its promise of a clearly defined identity and a clear path of action.

Throughout his life, Pearse had few intimate friends, and people who met him for the first time described him as shy, reserved and somewhat grave. Beatrice Elvery, the illustrator of his short story collection, *Íosagán agus Sgéalta Eile*, described him as a 'bulky, pale, shy young man whose black clothes made him look as if he belonged to some religious order' (Glenavey 1964, 90). Ironically, while he seems to have been awkward in social situations, he blossomed in front of an audience, even going so far as to organise his own debating club, the New Ireland Literary Society, at the age of 16. This need for a public audience may also explain his decision to go on to study law: Pearse was called to the Bar in 1901, the same year he achieved a BA in modern languages from the Royal University. Despite his distaste for the law as an unworthy calling, Pearse was also conscious that qualifying as a barrister was a definitive social milestone for him and his family. The studio photograph of him posing in his barrister's robes was a clear sign that they had left behind their working-class roots forever. While Pearse never pursued a career as a barrister, his frequent and prominent use of the initials 'B.A., B. L.' after his name led to him being cattily nicknamed 'Babble' by his fellow Gaelic Leaguer, Fr. Dineen (Dudley Edwards 1977, 48).

His need overtly to allude to his qualifications was a symptom of Pearse's social anxiety about his newly won middle-class identity. It was also manifested in his early clothing choices when he joined the Gaelic League. Pearse quickly rose within the organisation, becoming a member of the executive council before he was 20. As he found his feet within the organisation, it took him some time to strike the correct sartorial note, particularly on important occasions, such as the annual Oireachtas. As a young man, he wore a formal frock coat and top hat, alienating other members who saw this as a form of British affectation and inappropriate for a Gaelic Leaguer (O'Neill 1935, 220). Despite playing a role in the adoption of the kilt as a distinctively 'Irish-Ireland' form of national dress (Ó Buachalla 1980a, 22–3; Ó Kelly, Chapter 15), it was not something he ever wore himself, and certainly no images survive of him wearing one. He built a traditional thatched cottage in Rosmuc in Connemara and spent time among the Irish-speaking native community there, but he never adopted their forms of dress. His own sense of dignity, and perhaps his fear of looking ridiculous, always took priority.

It is significant that during this period in which Pearse sought to establish a public persona he increasingly adopted the side-profile pose which played such an important part in how he has been remembered. Pearse's need to control how he appeared, particularly in photographs, undoubtedly stemmed from his self-consciousness about a physical deformity in one of his eyes. It has been described as a cast, squint or drooping eyelid and was probably hereditary – photographs of his older sister Margaret suggest that she had a similar defect. Pearse died before the widespread proliferation of cheap portable cameras which allowed people to take spontaneous photographic 'snaps', so having a photo taken was still quite a formal event. This enabled Pearse to have power over how his image was captured. Full-face images of Pearse are rare and seem to have occurred in informal situations or when Pearse was unaware that he was being photographed. One of these is a family photograph taken in a garden when Pearse was in his twenties: in it, Pearse leans nonchalantly against a garden bench in a casual summer suit and straw boater. Perhaps because of the relaxed atmosphere, Pearse forgets to adopt his usual severe side-profile. However, a second image taken on the same occasion sees Pearse take up his usual pose. The straw hat is removed and is clasped to his breast. Pearse now appears distant and disconnected from the rest of the family group, isolated and almost melancholy in his contrived pose (see Figs 11.1 and 11.2).

Allowing for the control that Pearse exercised over how he was photographed, it is still remarkable how many surviving photos show him only in profile. Even images of him speaking at public events, such as the O'Donovan Rossa funeral or at a public meeting in Dolphin's Barn in August 1915, only capture his face from the side. It would seem that

11.1   Pearse family group photograph, with (left to right): Miss Brady (a cousin), P.H. Pearse, Miss Margaret Pearse, Mrs. Pearse, William Pearse, Mary Brigid Pearse.
Courtesy of the Pearse Museum/Office of Public Works

Pearse's self-consciousness about his appearance was not just confined to the photographic studio. According to C.P. Curran (1966, 24), Pearse would hold his head to one side when speaking to people, a gesture Sydney Gifford (1974, 18) also noticed. Mary Colum (1947, 152), who taught in his girls' school, Scoil Idé, felt that his 'slight squint … added to the strangeness of his gaze'. Like Yeats, she felt that Pearse had an 'intense expresssion' and 'mysterious eyes' that looked 'concentratedly and fascinatedly at something the rest of us did not see'. Many of those who met him remarked on the dramatic contrast between the shy private man and the magnetic public orator who could fearlessly command the attention of a public audience. It was something that intrigued Pearse as well. In 1912, he set up a short-lived Irish language political newspaper called *An Barr Buadh*. One of its regular

11.2   Photograph taken on the same occasion as Figure 11.1, but William Pearse has swapped places with his cousin, Alfred McGloughlin, and Patrick has adopted his habitual side profile; left to right: P.H. Pearse, Alfred McGloughlin, Miss Margaret Pearse; front (seated): Mary Brigid Pearse, Mrs Pearse, Miss Brady.
Courtesy of Kilmainham Gaol/Office of Public Works

features was a series of 'open letters' written by Pearse under the name of 'Laegh Mac Riangabhra'. Pearse used this persona to criticise and offer advice to significant figures on the Irish cultural and political scene, including John Redmond, John Dillon and Douglas Hyde. He also demonstrated his faculty for searing and brutal self-analysis when he decided to address an open letter to himself:

> I don't know if I like you or not, Pearse. I don't know if anyone does like you. I know full well many who hate you … Pearse, you are too dark in yourself. You don't make friends with the Gaels. You avoid their company. When you come among them you bring a dark cloud with you that lies heavily on them. Is it your English blood that is the cause of

that, I wonder? However you have the gift of speech. You can make your audience laugh or cry as you please. I suppose there are two Pearses, the sombre and taciturn Pearse and the gay and sunny Pearse. The gay and sunny Pearse is seen too seldom, and generally at public meetings and in Scoil Éanna … I don't like that gloomy Pearse. He gives me the shivers. And the most curious part of the story is that no one knows which is the true Pearse. (quoted in Le Roux 1932, 40–1)

Pearse founded his school, Scoil Éanna (Saint Enda's), in 1908. In the prospectus, he wrote that it offered a 'secondary education distinctly Irish in complexion, bilingual in method and of a high modern type generally' (Ó Buachalla 1980b, 317). Perhaps because of his unease with his own identity, Pearse was also determined that the school would allow his pupils to realise themselves at their 'best and worthiest'. Outlining his educational vision in the school magazine, *An Macaomh*, Pearse said that the 'true teacher' does not attempt to make his pupil into a replica of himself; rather he 'will recognize in each of his pupils an individual human soul, distinct and different from every other human soul … craving, indeed, comradeship and sympathy and pity … demanding to be allowed to live its own life, to be allowed to bring itself to its own perfection' (quoted in Ó Buachalla 1980b, 330). The focus of the school was on the individual pupils and its success was measured by how it facilitated their development. Pearse wanted Scoil Éanna to be a role model for a new and radical approach to education in Ireland, so promoting its work to a wider audience through open days, lectures and public performances was crucial. However, the visual identity of the school did not centre on Pearse himself. Instead, he used images of the school and grounds, photographs of the pupils, the school art collection, sports teams and plays. Pearse felt himself so much a part of the school that reproductions of his own image were unnecessary. Ultimately, all aspects of the school were a manifestation of his vision. Ironically, in creating a space which allowed his pupils to discover their individual identity, Pearse found a community in which he was entirely at ease for the first time.

The foundation of *An Barr Buadh* in 1912 was an indication that Pearse was no longer content to be solely identitified with Scoil Éanna. From that period on his focus shifted to politics and his views became increasingly radical and revolutionary. He was one of the founders of the Irish Volunteers in 1913 and during a fundraising tour of the United States in 1914 he found an audience anxious to hear about his vision for Ireland's future. His emergence as a significant political figure also precipitated a need for a distinct visual identity, and while in New York Pearse had a studio portrait taken in Rockwood Studios. On his return to Ireland, the momentum leading Pearse towards the 1916 Rising seemed unstoppable. In

August 1915, he was chosen to give the speech at the funeral of Jeremiah O'Donovan Rossa, a former Fenian who had lived out his life in exile in the USA. The funeral was orchestrated by Thomas Clarke and the Supreme Council of the IRB and he picked Pearse to deliver the graveside oration which would mark the culmination of the event. Pearse was not only a gifted orator, he was also a devout Catholic, Irish-speaking, university-educated, cultured and respectable. Pearse thus became both the voice and the face of the coming revolution. Pearse knew how important a figurehead could be. He had written a series of articles for the radical republican newspaper *Irish Freedom* between June 1913 and January 1914 entitled 'From a Hermitage'. In the July article, he considered how the ongoing presence of the face of George V on coins and stamps in Ireland was not only a source of shame for Irish people, it was also a significant part of a wider apparatus of control which emasculated the colonial subject and made them complicit in their own subjugation. He also recognised the positive potential of symbols: 'The symbol of a true thing, of a beneficent thing, is worthy of all homage' (Pearse 1952, 149). His role as leader may have been largely symbolic, but he realised that its power would come from its ability to inspire those around him.

It is interesting to consider how Pearse's ability to embrace his symbolic role and 'see himself from a little distance' might have influenced how he approached his involvement in the 1916 Rising. There is an essentially theatrical quality to his actions, and he even went so far as to create a fictionalised imagining of the forthcoming revolution in the form of *The Singer*, his final play written in 1915. It presents an idealised version of an Irish rebellion, transplanted to the rural simplicity and purity of the Irish-speaking west. The play was never performed in Pearse's lifetime; it seems there was a fear that it might alert the authorities to the forthcoming rebellion. However, it can be seen almost as a 'poetic dress rehearsal' in which Pearse was able to work through the meaning of the rebellion in imaginative terms. The chief talent of the play's hero, MacDara, is his ability to inspire others with his words and songs and ultimately he chooses to march into battle unarmed: his willingness to die for others is his great gift. The play concludes with the lines: 'One man can free a people as one Man redeemed the world. I will take no pike. I will go into battle with bare hands. I will stand up before the Gall as Christ hung naked before men on the tree' (quoted in Ní Ghairbhí and McNulty 2013, 228).

With little or no military knowledge or skills, Pearse concentrated on the ceremonial set-piece events when the rebellion came. On Easter Monday morning, he read the Proclamation (which he had largely composed) aloud outside the General Post Office, thus outlining the aim and purpose of the Rising. This was not for the benefit of the small crowd of bemused onlookers, but for those in the future who would try to make sense of the events of that

IRISH REBELLION, MAY 1916.

P. H. PEARSE.
Commandant-General of the Army of the Irish Republic).
Executed May 3rd, 1916.
One of the signatories of the " Irish Republic Proclamation."

11.3   One of a series of souvenir postcards depicting those involved in the 1916 Rising. This image, based on a Lafayette studio portrait, would become the dominant image in the depiction of Pearse after his death. Courtesy of the Pearse Museum/Office of Public Works

week. In the days that followed, he played no major role beyond maintaining morale and writing propaganda, but he came into his own once more at the surrender on Parnell Street. Pearse was freshly shaven with a razor borrowed for him by his brother Willie, and appears to have been in full uniform. He had brought a sword with him to the Rising which he handed to Brigadier-General Lowe. Although defeated, Pearse was determined that his side should not be found lacking when it came to the pageantry of British military etiquette. This occasion also marked the last time that Pearse was to be photographed. The dignified image of Pearse and Nurse O'Farrell facing Lowe and his son John was crucial in ensuring that while the visual record of the surrender might show a defeat, it was not a humiliation.

The final acts of Pearse's 1916 drama took place in his court martial in Richmond Barracks and subsequent execution. In his statement to the court martial, Pearse stated that 'I went down on my knees as a child and told God that I would work all my life to gain the freedom of Ireland' (Barton

2002, 116–17). In an echo of *The Singer* he also asked that the court spare his followers and that he alone be executed. Pearse thus sought to subvert the court by making its verdict the fulfilment of a predetermined fate he had chosen for himself. His final piece of legacy-making came from a series of poems he wrote in his prison cells in Arbour Hill and Kilmainham Gaol. One of these poems in particular, 'A mother speaks', made a connection between the plight of Pearse's mother and that of the Virgin Mary. By extension, Pearse's role found an equivalence with that of the crucified Christ. It was a story with which a pious Catholic population with a strong tradition of Marian devotion could easily identify and quickly manifested itself in the post-execution depictions of Pearse. A contemporaneous print entitled 'Last moments of P.H. Pearse' even showed Pearse in full uniform in his cell as a vision of the Virgin Mary appeared to him.[1]

The photographic images of Pearse reproduced in the aftermath of the Rising had a distinctly religious or at least other-worldly quality. The image of Pearse which appeared in the *Irish Times* and in the series of souvenir postcards depicting the leaders in the immediate aftermath of the Rising appears to be based on a studio photograph taken in Lafayette of Dublin, and it remains the best-known image of Pearse to this day (Fig. 11.3). The side profile is sharply outlined and Pearse stares rigidly, intently focused into the distance. The unusual, overly formal pose makes it stand out from the images of the other 1916 leaders. In the years that followed the Rising, Pearse's image not only stood apart from the other leaders, it would also eventually eclipse them. As the Rising moved from recent history to foundation myth, the factors which had made Pearse the perfect choice to give the O'Donovan Rossa oration and act as figurehead of the Rising – his religious belief, immersion in Irish culture and middle-class values – also made him attractive as the founding father of the conservative new Irish state. James Connolly and his radical socialism would never be acceptable to the Catholic establishment. Thomas Clarke had been one of the prime movers behind the Rising and had a long republican pedigree, but he was a backroom man, unlike the charismatic Pearse. Pearse also left behind a rich legacy of published political writings which contextualised the Rising as both the culmination of a long and glorious struggle for independence and an act of redemption for the soul of the Irish nation. By 1966, one of Pearse's biographers, Hedley McCay, could write that to 'the man in the street since the twenties, Padraic Pearse, and his name alone, has come to mean the 1916 rebellion' (McCay 1966, 5).

The view of Pearse as a political saint and martyr quickly took hold. Louis Le Roux, author of the first full-length biography, quoted from

---

1 Collection of Pearse Museum, PMSTE.2005.0399.

Aodh de Blacam who believed that 'it would not be astonishing if Pearse were canonised some day' (Le Roux 1932, x). Pearse's image was the most reproduced of all the leaders and was hung in Irish homes and classrooms alongside mass-produced images of religious figures. As the Catholic hierarchy began to embrace the new order and its origins, they were keen to appropriate Pearse as an example of religious devotion and Christian self-sacrifice. Pearse may never have been formally canonised but he achieved an apotheosis of a sort in the new Catholic cathedral in Galway which opened in 1965. Its mortuary chapel featured a mosaic of the risen Christ flanked on both sides by roundels depicting the head of Pearse on one side and that of John F. Kennedy on the other.

The simplicity and strength of the Pearse profile which made it so ideally suited to graphic reproduction proved less amenable to conventional portraiture. In the sketch of Pearse by Seán O'Sullivan, part of a series of portraits of the seven signatories, it is clear that O'Sullivan's inspiration came from one of the softer, more intimate photographs of Pearse rather than the ubiquitous Lafayette studio image. This image, along with those of the other six leaders, would later be used on the fiftieth anniversary commemorative stamps in 1966. Appropriately enough for the boy who grew up with the sound of a chisel on stone ringing in his ears, Pearse's image proved much more amenable to sculptors. In 1937, a bronze bust of Pearse by Oliver Sheppard was installed in Leinster House. Sheppard had known Pearse personally; Willie was one of his pupils in the Dublin Metropolitan School of Art and Sheppard had visited Scoil Éanna. He shared Pearse's interest in the ancient Irish past, as evidenced in works like the famous 'Death of Cúchulainn', which now stands as a memorial to the 1916 Rising in the General Post Office. Pearse had written an admiring and perceptive critique of Sheppard's symbolist piece, 'Inis Fáil', in *An Claidheamh Soluis* in 1906 (Turpin 2000, 70–1). Although the bust was sculpted at the behest of the Commissioners of Public Works, Sheppard later indicated that he was 'requested personally' to undertake the work by the then Taoiseach and 1916 veteran, Éamon de Valera. De Valera deliberately cultivated the support of Pearse's mother and older sister Margaret and presented himself as the political heir of Pearse (Moran 2005, 77). In Sheppard's bust, which he completed in 1936, Pearse was draped in a classical toga with a garland of bay-laurel, a symbolic reference to Pearse as a poet and warrior. According to John Turpin (2000, 172) this was a new approach for Sheppard in which he 'reverted to the formula of an antique toga, standard in Neoclassical portraiture, but which had been abandoned since the advent of the naturalistic movement in the late nineteenth century'. It gave a 'timeless heroic quality' (Turpin 2000, 172) to the subject and, along with the addition of a victor's wreath of bay laurel, indicated 'Pearse's victory over death in the realisation of the Republican

11.4   Ten-shilling coin
featuring the head of
Pearse, which was issued
in 1966 to mark the
fiftieth anniversary of the
1916 Rising.
Courtesy of the Pearse
Museum/Office of Public
Works

ideal as espoused by de Valera and other nationalists of the 1930s' (Turpin 2000, 173). While Turpin is correct that its placement in Leinster House 'further emphasised the origins of Dáil Éireann in the revolution which Pearse had commenced' (Turpin 2000, 173), the style chosen also gave a sense of respectability and pedigree to the new state. Despite his intimacy with Pearse and his circle, Sheppard depicted the idealised icon rather than the man he knew. The soft features which can be detected in some images of Pearse are nowhere to be seen; instead there is a muscular nobility. Sheppard has Pearse's head turned to the side, acknowledging his favoured public pose, but did not depict the physical deformity Pearse sought to disguise.

The influence of the Lafayette side profile was obvious in Seamus Murphy's 1936 bas-relief of Pearse. Murphy introduced sharp angles to Pearse's features to give the piece a modernist aesthetic. The piece was chosen to be included in the New York World's Fair in 1939 (Murray and Hennessey 2007, 204–5). It was the first occasion that Ireland participated as an independent nation in an international trade fair. The Pearse bas-relief was in keeping with the government's determination that the Irish Pavilion, designed by Michael Scott, would be both modern and distinctively Irish. The adoption of the Pearse profile as a quasi-state symbol reached its zenith in 1966 and the fiftieth anniversary commemoration of the Rising. On 17 February, the Central Bank announced that a special silver ten-shilling coin would be struck to mark the anniversary of the Rising. Designed by T.H. Paget and produced in the Royal Mint in London, it would feature an image of Oliver Sheppard's Cúchulainn on one side and the head of Pearse on the other (Fig. 11.4).

Although it was a commemorative piece, it was intended to be used and was legal tender, though a run of 20,000 proof issue coins was also produced.[2] This was the first and only time that a human head had appeared on coinage in Ireland since independence. As Pearse had once written that Irish people should feel ashamed that the head of George V appeared on their coinage, there was a particular aptness that the next face to appear on an Irish coin was Pearse's own. The tradition of having a sovereign's side-profile on coinage stretched back to the ancient world, and the ten-shilling coin had a distinctly classical quality to its design. The decision to place Pearse's head on the coin was not just an assertion of independence in the year of the fiftieth anniversary of the birth of the Irish state; it also served as a physical sign that an independent Ireland could muster all the symbols associated with political self-determination. Stylistically, Pearse's profile was a natural choice for the coin. However, for those like Kathleen Clarke, the widow of Thomas Clarke, it must have seemed like further evidence of a deliberate policy by successive Irish governments to portray the Rising as the vision of Pearse alone (Higgins 2009, 124). While the coin was beautifully produced, in practical terms it was large and heavy and proved unpopular for everyday use.[3] Eventually the coin was withdrawn from circulation and the majority of the issue was melted down.

While several busts and bas-reliefs of Pearse exist, efforts to create a full-length statue of Pearse have proved more problematic. A plan to place a statue of Pearse on Nelson's Pillar in 1931 came to nothing, as did a proposal to erect a new column topped by a full-size image of Pearse surrounded by his pupils to mark the centenary of his birth (Whelan 2003, 203 and 235). The ubiquity of the bust reflects the continued dominance of the side profile in how Pearse is imagined, but also an inability to conceive of Pearse in corporeal terms. Pearse has been cast in the role of a thinker, poet, idealist, even fanatic, but rarely as a man with a body of flesh and blood. The 'bulky' young man who visited Beatrice Elvery has been banished from popular memory. Ruth Dudley Edwards's suggestion in her 1977 biography that Pearse may have had homosexual urges, albeit nearly entirely suppressed, caused outrage at a time when Irish society was still deeply homophobic and homosexuality itself was criminalized. However, for some, any association of Pearse with sexuality was unacceptable. The artist Robert Ballagh created a pop art version of the famous Pearse profile with a bold black outline for the 1979 centenary stamp. He combined it with a similarly rendered version of the bare-breasted female figure from Eugene Delacroix's depiction of the July Rebellion of 1831, *July 28: Liberty leading the people*. Although Ballagh clearly

2   *Irish Times*, 18 February 1966.
3   *Irish Times*, 2 February 1967.

intended the female figure to represent the spirit of revolution, her nudity was seen as provocative by some of Pearse's more conservative admirers. One correspondent to the letters page of the *Irish Independent* objected to the stamp as 'an outrageous insult' to Pearse who had died so that Ireland might be 'free, Irish and Christian' (Gilligan 1993, 83). In the year that also marked the centenary of the Knock apparition, she castigated those responsible for looking 'to a foreign country and [choosing] the most pagan of symbols'.

The ubiquity of Pearse's image in the visual language of the new state masked the fact that much of what Pearse stood for was quietly ignored. As Irwin, one of the teachers in Alan Bennett's play *The history boys*, points out, 'there's no better way of forgetting something than by commemorating it' (Bennett 2004, 25). Streets, roads, tower blocks and train stations were named after Pearse, and his writings were placed on the state school curriculum. However, that curriculum continued to serve the kind of exam-focused, 'grinding' education system which Pearse railed against in *The murder machine*. Writing about Pearse in 1945, his former pupil Kenneth Reddin (1945, 251) lamented that Irish education remained 'narrow, stereotyped, uninspired, unenthusiastic, without fervor or imagination. It is Victorian. And so we have the bad legacy of Inspectors, Bonuses, Competitive Examinations and Grants-per-capita. Queen Victoria still reigns in Marlborough Street.' For those in power, the idea of Pearse as a thinker and dreamer whose vision was confined to the aspirational and impossible ideals was preferable to that of a social reformer demanding that practical changes be made in the creation of an equitable education system which would foster and inspire the children in its care. The image of Pearse in profile suited this policy perfectly – as he stared off at some unseen vision, those who had inherited his mantle could pursue their own agendas without the fear of a recriminating stare from beyond the grave.

The appropriation of Pearse's image by the Irish State in 1966 might have led one to believe that any radical potential it may have held had been neutralised. However, with the coming of the Troubles in Northern Ireland in 1969, Pearse's uncompromising injunction that 'Ireland unfree will never be at peace' gained a new currency. For northern republicans, the '"timeless" message of Pearse was used to interpret local and private suffering' (Higgins 2009, 133). The spiritual quality of Pearse's writings gave sustenance to the hunger strikers in 1981. Bobby Sands quoted from the O'Donovan Rossa speech and Pearse's image appeared on placards alongside slogans saying 'Don't let Bobby Sands die.' His image also started to appear in murals on the walls of West Belfast (Rolston 2010b) (Fig. 11.5). Pearse had been revealed to be a figure who could be 'used to stabilize and destabilize Irish politics; his myth, studiously promoted, could not be controlled easily' (Higgins 2009, 134).

11.5   Mural from Belfast in 1982 depicting Pearse and a quote from his
O'Donovan Rossa funeral oration.
© Bill Rolston

The process of questioning the Rising, Pearse and many of the other
sacred cows of Irish republicanism pre-dated the Troubles. For many, it
offered a useful and necessary corrective to the adulation and idealisation
of those who had fought in the Rising. However, the spiralling violence in
Northern Ireland from 1969 onwards gave it a new impetus and urgency.
The motivations and justification of the 1916 Rising were viewed through
the context of current events. The traditional portrayal of Pearse as the
embodiment of the Rising now made him the primary focus for attack.
Xavier Carty's 1978 book, *In bloody protest: the tragedy of Patrick Pearse*,
concluded by saying that Pearse's life was a 'lesson in the errors to be avoided
… a terrible mistake, a tragedy, something that should never have happened'
(Carty 1978, 140). Ruth Dudley Edwards's book, *Patrick Pearse: the triumph
of failure*, offered the first proper academic treatment of Pearse's life when
it was published in 1977 and sought to give a balanced assessment of Pearse,
but much of the debate around it was characterised by heat rather than
light. As Pat Cooke (1986, 2) has pointed out, Pearse's reputation during
this period 'suffered the extremes of blind defence and debunking assault'.
Faced with the centenary of Pearse's birth in 1979, Jack Lynch's government

sought to play down the militant aspect of Pearse's life and concentrate on his work as an educationist and writer. It was in that year that Pearse's school and former home in Rathfarnham opened as the Pearse Museum. A film was commissioned from Louis Marcus concentrating on Pearse's work as a journalist between 1903 and 1908. A pageant organised by Coiste Chomóradh an Phiarsaigh, which was written by Bryan MacMahon and performed in the National Stadium, was also supported and extra funds were provided to cover losses due to disappointing attendances. Despite this, the government was satisfied that the programme offered 'a reasonable range of commemorative activity' and was happy that it had neutralised any attempts by militant republicans to make political capital.[4]

Significantly, the refocusing of Pearse's image in 1979 pre-dated the hunger strikes and the identification with Pearse by Bobby Sands and others. If Pearse was in need of a 'rebranding' in 1979, by the early 1980s his brand had become almost toxic. Plans for a statue of Pearse outside the General Post Office were abandoned and the official commemorations of the seventy-fifth anniversary of the Rising in 1991 were muted and characterised by the government's uncertainty about how to deal with the issue. However, with the coming of peace in Northern Ireland, a new confidence about the commemoration of 1916 emerged with a full military parade being reinstated for the ninetieth anniversary in 2006.

The image of Pearse also made a return to public life in the form of a photograph hanging in the office of Taoiseach Bertie Ahern. It was prominently on show in press and television interviews and became one of the defining emblems of his period of office, something which was frequently commented on by political observers.[5] In his autobiography, Ahern (2009, 194) explains its presence in terms of his childhood – growing up in his family home in Drumcondra where a photograph of Pearse always had pride of place. Ahern's interest in and admiration of Pearse is unquestionable, but the conspicuous presence of Pearse's image was also useful in emphasising a connection with older Irish values at a time of rapid political, social and economic change. Throughout the period of the Good Friday Agreement and the Celtic Tiger, Pearse's image presided over the Taoiseach's office and acted as an assurance that his vision and idealism remained at the centre of government. However, this trust in the power of Pearse's image was severely tested with the financial collapse of 2008 and the loss of economic sovereignty which ensued. For many, this crisis highlighted just how far the nation had strayed from the promise and values of the Proclamation.

4 National Archives of Ireland (NAI), Department of the Taoiseach files, NAI/TSCH/2012/90/397, 21 January 1980.
5 For example *Sunday Independent*, 2 February 2008.

Pearse's image, so carefully cultivated by him in life, has been used, appropriated and reproduced so often since his death that it is easy to dismiss it as a cliché or an empty symbol of the past. For some his faraway glance no longer intrigues because they are no longer interested in what he might be looking to. Since his death, there have been many attempts to create a fixed and timeless image of Pearse – often literally in the medium of bronze or stone. This has resulted in the creation of a figure who seems 'out of time' and irrelevant to modern life. However, by adopting a more fluid, 'kaleidescopic' view and allowing our ideas of Pearse to change and evolve, we may get closer to understanding and learning something from Pearse. As Desmond Ryan (1919, 1) wrote in his memoir of his former teacher and friend, 'Pearse never was a legend, he was a man.'

III Revivalism and the Rising

Introduction

In this section, the authors are concerned with cultures of revival, the deliberate recasting of certain material tropes or acts from the past. The case studies here suggest that revival often works to assert a re-imagining not only of the past, but to enable its active use and resonance in the present day. Revivalism of course suffused the 1916 Rising, and was activated vigorously by Patrick Pearse and many of his comrades in their evocation of an ancient heroic past. This informed the choice of imagery utilised to memorialise 1916 – for example, Oliver Sheppard's 1911 statue of the dying Cúchulainn in the General Post Office.

In her case study of the *The Ford of the Hurdles* first staged by Micheál Mac Liammóir and Hilton Edwards for Dublin Civic Week in 1929, Elaine Sisson examines the literal revivification of Pearse and other historical personages. She demonstrates how the work of theatrical reconstruction produced certain forms of collective memory, and how this asserted a particular understanding of the Rising for those who experienced the pageant. Sisson suggests that the materiality of performance generates a collective meaning, and in the aftermath of the Rising helped to 'smooth' the historical narrative into the realm of myth.

Myth-making was also present in the treatment of visual art and the legacy of 1916 in the *Capuchin Annual*. Róisín Kennedy explores how the presentation of art in the *Annual* was often in the service of asserting a Catholic reading of the Rising and subsequent Irish identity, and yet it also ensured a broad audience for contemporary art.

In the last quarter of the nineteenth century, Celticism came to be a dominant trope in Irish visual and material culture. Forms and decorative motifs derived from ancient and early Christian artefacts were both a source of inspiration to the skilled designers and makers involved with the Irish Arts and Crafts movement and pervaded many everyday objects. Celtic revivalism was the de facto style for many of the objects produced in relation to the Rising, as can be seen elsewhere in this volume, for example, in the objects made in internment camps (see Brück, Chapter 9) or to decorate special editions of the *Catholic Bulletin* (see Fitzpatrick, Chapter 7).

Amongst the aspects of this revival was a renewed interest in 'Gaelic' typefaces; as Mary Ann Bolger explains in her chapter, when the Irish alphabet was officially phased out in 1965, designers explored 'alternative ways of expressing national sentiment through letterforms'. She analyses how the typographer Liam Miller's commemorative editions of the *Easter Proclamation of the Republic, 1916*, conferred the foundational document with a patrimony based on early European letterforms, in keeping not only with the status of the Proclamation but the position of Irish culture within the wider world.

A further aspect of the Celtic Revival was an interest in ancient Irish dress, interpreted from the work of antiquarians such as Eugene O'Curry. Hilary O'Kelly's chapter shows how Irish 'national' dress was a viable sartorial choice for leaders and supporters of the Rising. However, the same clothing that once exemplified revivalism in the 'idealistic hopes of a lost identity' elicited markedly divergent responses after 1916, driving 'some formerly apathetic citizens into national fervour', while turning 'the once impassioned towards a more practical modernity'.

12

Dublin Civic Week and the materialisation of history

Elaine Sisson

Early in 1929, Micheál MacLiammóir and Hilton Edwards, the founders of the newly established Gate Theatre, were invited to devise a drama during Dublin Civic Week. In *All for Hecuba*, MacLiammóir recalls how

> the Government approached [us] with a new plan. We were to provide and produce a pageant of a patriotic description for the annual Civic Week ... I had modestly decided to write a sort of historical epic opening with the Viking invasion and coming down to the Easter Rebellion in 1916. (MacLiammóir 1946, 87)

This 'annual' event was in fact only the second such Civic Week; an inaugural event had been held in the city in 1927. The purpose of the Civic Weeks of 1927 and 1929 was 'to instil civic awareness and pride by propagating a distinctly Irish history and to attract a diasporic audience' (Fitzpatrick 2009, 23). It was a familiar enough endeavour in the early years of the state, and the first Civic Week, scheduled towards the middle of September, was designed to extend the tourist season.

The Mansion House historical pageant was called *The ford of the hurdles* but described by MacLiammóir as a 'masque' in seven episodes. MacLiammóir and Edwards had at their disposal a broad circle of theatre professionals and many regular Gate theatre actors were in the cast: MacLiammóir recalls relying on their expertise in addition to 'fifty oversized civic guards, who were to be Gaels, Vikings, Normans, and Volunteers' (MacLiammóir 1946, 87).[1]

---

1 Stage settings and costumes were designed by MacLiammóir and made by Mrs Bannard Cogley. Stage lighting and design was by Hilton Edwards, with props by Dom Bowe. The programme credits the help of the Gaiety Theatre props department and the Stella Cinema, Rathmines, with special thanks to Anew McMaster for theatrical

Edwards directed and sang one of the laments in the third episode; the eminent Dr John Larchet wrote and directed the music.

The pageant mingled historical events with fictionalised narratives. In each episode the figure of a minstrel (played by MacLiammóir) narrated the opening of each event, suturing each period of time together in a historical continuum. The episodes included the arrival of Strongbow in Ireland, the brutality of the Cromwellian period and the Emmet Rebellion of 1803. The final episode, 'Easter: the city in the dawn', is strange and dislocating. Advance publicity describes this section as 'a tableau of the Insurrection of 1916', which, in the tradition of the masque, 'seeks not to reproduce so much a meticulously accurate photographic representation of the past, but an attempt to deal with the mind of the people in each epoch depicted'.[2] This is the realm of both dramatic theatre and historical re-enactment. The transcripts for this episode suggest the desire to present a dream-like sequence, with voices, shadows and lighting used for dramatic effect. The prophetic minstrel stands in a spotlight asking the people to be patient. Restless voices call from the sides, cries of longing and despair phrased in biblical terms: 'Long have we waited in the darkness / Too long, too long have we waited.' As the voices rise and fall, the stage directions indicate that 'the light of dawn gradually creeps over the stage and shows the modern city sleeping'.[3]

The symbolism is clear: the Irish people are awakening to a new dawn and a new future. Some voices protest: 'we are happier when we can sleep / why should we awake?' Against the silhouette of the city, a figure appears, his shadow looming over the backdrop. The minstrel calls the people to 'wake, wake from your sleep' and to listen to the stranger. Referred to as 'The Strange Voice', the figure in bearing and dress is Patrick Pearse, and this link is made explicit when 'The Strange Voice' quotes directly from Pearse's writings. Meanwhile, the voices rise and fall in both harmony and cacophony; grouped and single voices speak together and across each other, giving the impression of confusion, but also of growing will and determination as the voices mingle and swell. It is a powerful dramatic device and one that Edwards, in particular, knew how to combine with choreographed movements and lighting effects. Lighting was an important part of this episode: the stage directions indicate that 'Flames rise from the dark

curtains. Wigs were by 'Drago of Dublin' and artwork and scenic painting by Harry Kernoff and Art Ó Murnaghan. Twenty-one members of An Garda Síochána, who played 'Heralds, Trumpeters, and Soldiers', are also thanked, underlining establishment support for a cohesive narrative of the state's origins. The pageant was performed on the evenings of 9–14 September.
2 'Civic week: a masque of Dublin', *Irish Independent*, 28 August 1929.
3 National Library of Ireland (NLI), NLI/MS/24/562, Micheál MacLiammóir, *The ford of the hurdles*, 1929.

silhouetted buildings' as shots are fired. The crowds move in orchestrated panicked groups as the city burns dramatically. The flames rise, and the chaos increases. The minstrel calls: 'Your dawn is breaking / do not lose courage, your day is at hand.' A shot rings out and the silhouette of 'The Strange Voice' falls, accompanied by a chorus of voices: '16 men / 16 men who were faithful / What will become of us, what will become of us now?'

The minstrel's response is patterned on the rhythm of Pearse's oratory and writing, which calls on the unborn to redeem the present generation of 'your rags and your shame'; it is a rousing message to the citizens of the new state identifying them as the keepers of 'the newest dawn' and the 'flame of my message'. The dramatic and emotive conclusion of the pageant, drawing on recent events, was bound to please. Praise was unanimous, with the *Irish Times* commending 'the beauty of the play itself, the beauty of the lighting, and the beauty of the incidental music'.[4]

Re-enactment and historical narrative: thinking about 1916 in the 1920s

What are historical re-enactments for and what do they do? *The ford of the hurdles* was funded by Dublin Corporation and provided an uncontested, untroubled nationalist history of Ireland up to 1916. The absence of the Civil War from the historical pageant's timeline (and its fracturing effect within Irish society) meant that the tensions of the recent past were neatly elided.[5] Certainly, the pageant's success found favour with the city fathers and secured MacLiammóir's and Edwards's cultural position within the Free State. In *Staging the Easter Rising: 1916 as theatre* James Moran considers the theatricality of the events of 1916 and suggests that positing the question 'when was 1916?' is not as absurd as it might seem (Moran 2005, 1). His book addresses the retelling and remembering of 1916 in dramatic and fictionalised versions, noting how each rendition returns to the story almost obsessively yet 'never being able to feel that it has been formulated adequately in a final, definitive form' (Moran 2005, 1).

The point of a re-enactment is not to extract a historical event from its moment of occurrence (to do so would be to present something chaotic and disordered) but to smooth the narrative into an ordered, and easily

---

4 'Dublin Civic Week: pageants and exhibitions', *Irish Times*, 14 September 1929.
5 The Civil War is not represented in the pageant but may have been displaced on to the medieval episodes that describe the bitter betrayals in the house of Dervogilla and Diarmuid Mac Murchadha, possibly reframing a more painful, recent history. I am grateful to Nicholas Allen for this insight.

understood, representation of that moment. Sven Lütticken argues that film remakes, for example, do not seek to reproduce the original film, but to translate it for a contemporary audience and in doing so create new contexts for understanding and interpreting both the 'remake' and the original. His suggestion that 'the remake becomes a form of speculative history rather than reprocessed content' has resonance for the historical re-enactment also (Lütticken 2004, 118).

What does it mean to be offered a memory of an event you didn't experience? Alison Landsberg (2004, 2) suggests that modern technologies have produced a new form of public cultural memory. She argues this 'prosthetic memory' emerges 'at the interface between a person and a historical narrative about the past' at 'an experiential site' that may be a cinema, a museum, or a theatre space. It is not just a person's apprehension of the past that creates new forms of memory; it is the resulting 'more deeply felt memory of a past event through which he or she did not live'. Importantly, when we are talking about the creation of national narratives, it has the ability to 'shape [a] person's subjectivity and politics' (Landsberg 2004, 2) by enabling them to 'suture' themselves into a larger history.

Theatre, of course, is by its nature concerned with the prosthetic: it draws attention to its own artifice. In this regard, MacLiammóir's knowledge of stage design and visual effect was critical to his manipulation of the dramatic power of history. As the minstrel, stitching each episode together, he presents the past as a narrative of progression: Ireland's manifest destiny. Furthermore, through the technologies of modernity – lighting effects, publicity photography, souvenirs, programmes, mass media, film projection – the organisation of the past into a collectively shared 'prosthetic memory' takes hold more easily and, importantly in Landsberg's argument (2004, 4), is a key strategy in the formation of new group identities. For political, civic and business interests struggling to consolidate the State, the production of collective memories are a way of increasing civic legitimacy as 'the act of publicising a group's memory increases its chances of attaining social and political recognition' (Landsberg 2004, 11).

The actor as revenant

Staging the past theatrically has an effect upon our understanding of history, and performance, argues Freddie Rokem; it has the ability to reveal 'complex ideological issues concerning deeply rooted national identities and subjectivities and power structures' (Rokem 2002, 3). The presence of live actors on the stage as past historical figures creates a particular kind of theatrical energy because they appear both as themselves and as dead people. What the actor 'does', rather than which character he performs, is critical to the credibility, emotion and energy of a performance, but this very communicative power is often overlooked. Rokem suggests that in theatre studies the actor 'often simply appear[s] as the central ligament around which discourses of the theatre have … been organized' (Rokem 2002, 188). Or, that acting is understood as a more sophisticated form of 'pretending'. Acting works best when it is not merely impersonation or a representation (this is what mediocre actors do): it is a particular form of embodiment, and when it succeeds it demands a type of cognitive dissonance from the audience – that they are seeing both the dead and the living materialised in the same body.

The cognitive dissonance involved in looking at the actor's body creates a flattening of time. By collapsing the past into the present, it sees the past as a collective flashback but one that is also immediately accessible. Raphael Samuel (1994, 197) observes how 'the controlled reconstruction of the past' shows neither respect for the historical record nor for the historical event. This is the realm of memory, not history: *prosthetic memory*. Moreover, this conflation of history and memory produces what Slavoj Žižek has called 'a unique suspension of temporality', where the realities of the present and the uncertainty of the future are put aside. 'The utopian future is neither simply fully realised, present, nor simply evoked as a distant promise', he says, but 'in a unique suspension of temporality, the short circuit between the present and the future, we are … briefly allowed to act as *if* the utopian future is (not yet fully here, but) already at hand, there to be seized' (Žižek 2002, 259). As Hilton Edwards's programme note to the 1929 pageant says, the production 'shows how the vestal flame of hope, that was kindled when the first fair stranger planted his pennon in the soil of Dublin, has been carried down through the years until it sprang into an imperishable flame in the light of which could be seen peace and the fulfillment of dreams' (Edwards 1929, 47). History has arrived: the future has been delivered and the absence of radical social voices and the fractured state of Irish society may be carefully set aside.

MacLiammóir, as the minstrel, appears in every episode of *The ford of the hurdles*. He is the ghost of Ireland past, future and present. No wonder contemporary wags renamed the pageant 'MacLiammóir through the Ages' (Ó hAodha 1990, 76). The communicative power of the actor cannot be overlooked, either by us or by the contemporary audience. The fact that it was MacLiammóir playing the minstrel in a pageant that also featured Robert Emmet *was* relevant to a contemporary audience. For those in the know, MacLiammóir had, earlier in 1929, appeared as Emmet in the Gate's production of Denis Johnston's *The old lady says 'No!'* that had established the Gate as a serious rival to the Abbey. In Johnston's play, Robert Emmet wakes up in 1920s Ireland, meeting thinly disguised public figures, and finds a society populated by whores, thieves and charlatans. The play is irreverent, caustic, and experimental in its expressionist staging. It is about as far as it is possible to go in dramatic intention from the seamless corporate narrative that *The ford of the hurdles* offers.

Leo Braudy suggests the actor is a palimpsest: the more familiar he becomes, the less able he is to reinvent himself each time he appears, because each previous role is faintly legible to the audience (Braudy 1999, 419–25). In MacLiammóir's case, it is the role of Robert Emmet which inflects his appearances in the historic pageants, although in fact MacLiammóir did *not* play Emmet in the 1929 pageant: that was a role played by Paul Farrell. However, MacLiammóir played Emmet in all subsequent restagings, presumably in his dashing Regency costume from *The old lady says 'No!'* that was also revived a number of times during the 1930s. Yet the connection between MacLiammóir and Emmet became so popularly secured that most commentators assume that MacLiammóir played Emmet in the original production of *The ford of the hurdles*.

The response to the 1929 pageant was sufficiently successful to ensure a revival of Episode 7, 'Easter', in 1930. In 1932, it was produced in the Gate Theatre as part of a triple bill with Anatole France's *The man who married a dumb wife* and Patrick Pearse's *The singer* with MacLiammóir playing the part of Pearse's messianic revolutionary hero MacDara. *The singer* had not been performed in Pearse's lifetime; written in 1915, it is a play whose central character, the passionate, self-sacrificing MacDara, has been closely identified with Pearse (Sisson 2004, 69). Staging *The singer* alongside the repackaged Easter 1916 section of the pageant confirmed a public perception of Pearse as the central figure of the Rising. The *Irish Times* saw the plays existing within a continuum, noting that they 'hang together as the introduction and climax of a beautiful story for which a line of Pearse's provides the theme: one man can save a nation, as one Man redeemed the world'.[6] The main interest of *The singer*, according to the paper, lay in the restless, tormented MacDara, into whose personality Pearse has managed to breathe his complete soul.[7] Importantly, though, the role, in turn, was understood by the audience (and reviewers) to be an autobiographical portrait of Pearse. MacLiammóir's identification with Pearse was reinforced, of course, by his role as 'The Strange Voice' in *Easter 1916* where he speaks the words of Pearse.

Performed together, *The singer* and *Easter 1916* provided a prologue and an epilogue for a revolutionary moment. The dramatic and emotive conclusion of the pageant, drawing on recent memory and appealing to

---

6 'Triple Bill at the Gate', *Irish Times*, 29 March 1932.
7 'Triple Bill at the Gate', *Irish Times*, 29 March 1932.

everybody's higher nature, was a success. Maud Gonne MacBride praised the production as 'a worthy Easter commemoration'.[8] Her imprimatur was not to be underestimated; her disapproval over Seán O'Casey's *The plough and the stars*, in which a Pearse-like character appears off-stage as 'The Figure', had created enormous public controversy some years earlier. The performances of *The singer* and *Easter 1916* contributed to the continued elevated status of Pearse within the new State. To the 1932 audience, Pearse became more than a figure from the recent past; his death is prefigured in *The singer* and his place in history is secured in *Easter 1916*: he now transcends history. This is the realm of myth, not history: *prosthetic memory.*

The ford of the hurdles was restaged in its entirety at the Gate in 1933 and a reworked version at Soldier Field in Chicago as part of the World's Fair in 1934.[9] During the 1950s, MacLiammóir recorded a selection of 'greatest hits of the revolutionary movement' including Pearse's *Oration over the grave of O'Donovan Rossa*, *The Proclamation of the Irish Republic*, *The fool* as well as Emmet's *Speech before his execution.*[10]

Conclusion

Pearse and MacLiammóir shared an understanding of the power of history: MacLiammóir after all was a man who had rewritten his own past, and, like Pearse, he understood the theatre as a conduit for the temporal (Sisson 2004).

In *Irish times: temporalities of modernity*, David Lloyd urges us to remember 'the work of history is not a therapeutic forgetting' (Lloyd 2008, 7). Yet this is precisely the function of *The ford of the hurdles*: combing the snags of history into a smooth, collective memory. It is incumbent upon us as scholars of the past to, in Benjamin's words, 'brush history against the grain' (Benjamin 1968, 257) and to draw our attention again and again to what Lloyd calls to account: to pay attention to 'the shards and remnants of spent lives and ways of living that the on-going process of progress … has consigned to the rubbish heap' (Lloyd 2008, 7).

Performance, the study of the temporal relationship between space, bodies, objects and narrative, may be useful to the historian in drawing attention

---

8   Maud Gonne MacBride, *An Phoblacht*, 27 April 1933.
9   MacLiammóir and Edwards co-produced and staged a number of events, including *The pageant of the Celt* in Chicago's Soldier Field, as part of the Irish Village celebrations at the World's Fair in 1934 (McLaughlin 2002, 87–9). They were also involved in two versions of *The pageant of St Patrick* staged for the second and third An Tóstal Festivals in 1953 and 1954 (see McMaster 1953 and the programme: An Tóstal May 8th–29th Pageant of St Patrick, Croke Park, issued in 1954).
10 Micheál MacLiammóir, *Revolutionary speeches*. US/UK: Argo Records, 1959.

to the 'smoothness' of memory. Performance's emphasis on the temporal, ghostly and mutable is the antithesis of the fixed and documented historical text. By thinking about MacLiammóir's pageant and the complexity of how it was staged and understood during Dublin Civic Week and afterwards, it asks us to consider re-enactments not as histories of events but as an *experiential* index: by understanding a performance as a material event, we may contextualise its collectively generated meaning in its own time, and in ours.

13

Redesigning the Rising:
typographic commemorations of 1916

Mary Ann Bolger

Ireland's most influential twentieth-century typographer, Liam Miller of the Dolmen Press, printed in pamphlet form three editions of the *Easter Proclamation of the Republic, 1916* – in 1960, 1975 and 1982. Looking at the distinct visual differences between the first and subsequent publications, and in particular at Miller's typographic choices, allows an examination of the changing meaning of the 1916 Rising and of republicanism itself at a time when the Irish state was engaged in a project of wholesale modernisation.

In order to investigate the typographic decisions made in the documents we need first to acknowledge that the shape that printed words take is not arbitrary: it depends on conscious design decisions and the circumstances of production. In everyday reading we look through – not at – letters. The typographic historian Beatrice Warde famously described the printed word as a 'crystal goblet' (Warde 1999 [1932]) which simply presents, rather than interprets, written content. The transparency assumed for the visual form of printed letters is an example of what Roland Barthes (1993 [1957]) termed the 'falsely obvious': as such it provides the perfect conduit for mythological and ideological constructions.

The circumstances of the printing of the original Proclamation of the Irish Republic (Fig. 13.1) on Easter weekend 1916 have been well documented (O'Connor 1999; King 2001; Mosley 2010a) and a summary may suffice here. The Proclamation was composed and printed in great haste and secrecy over Easter weekend of 1916 on the Wharfdale Press in Liberty Hall used by James Connolly to print the *Workers' Republic* newspaper. The text was set in a roman type, identified by Mosley (2010a) as a nineteenth-century typeface commonly used in posters, 'Antique No. 8 of the typefounders Miller & Richard of Edinburgh'. Where there was not enough of the No. 8, the compositors improvised by utilising letters from other fonts of type (especially for the letter 'e'). This gives the text its familiar uneven texture

POBLACHT NA H EIREANN.

THE PROVISIONAL GOVERNMENT
OF THE
IRISH REPUBLIC
TO THE PEOPLE OF IRELAND.

IRISHMEN AND IRISHWOMEN: In the name of God and of the dead generations from which she receives her old tradition of nationhood, Ireland, through us, summons her children to her flag and strikes for her freedom.

Having organised and trained her manhood through her secret revolutionary organisation, the Irish Republican Brotherhood, and through her open military organisations, the Irish Volunteers and the Irish Citizen Army, having patiently perfected her discipline, having resolutely waited for the right moment to reveal itself, she now seizes that moment, and, supported by her exiled children in America and by gallant allies in Europe, but relying in the first on her own strength, she strikes in full confidence of victory.

We declare the right of the people of Ireland to the ownership of Ireland, and to the unfettered control of Irish destinies, to be sovereign and indefeasible. The long usurpation of that right by a foreign people and government has not extinguished the right, nor can it ever be extinguished except by the destruction of the Irish people. In every generation the Irish people have asserted their right to national freedom and sovereignty: six times during the past three hundred years they have asserted it in arms. Standing on that fundamental right and again asserting it in arms in the face of the world, we hereby proclaim the Irish Republic as a Sovereign Independent State, and we pledge our lives and the lives of our comrades-in-arms to the cause of its freedom, of its welfare, and of its exaltation among the nations.

The Irish Republic is entitled to, and hereby claims, the allegiance of every Irishman and Irishwoman. The Republic guarantees religious and civil liberty, equal rights and equal opportunities to all its citizens, and declares its resolve to pursue the happiness and prosperity of the whole nation and of all its parts, cherishing all the children of the nation equally, and oblivious of the differences carefully fostered by an alien government, which have divided a minority from the majority in the past.

Until our arms have brought the opportune moment for the establishment of a permanent National Government, representative of the whole people of Ireland and elected by the suffrages of all her men and women, the Provisional Government, hereby constituted, will administer the civil and military affairs of the Republic in trust for the people.

We place the cause of the Irish Republic under the protection of the Most High God, Whose blessing we invoke upon our arms, and we pray that no one who serves that cause will dishonour it by cowardice, inhumanity, or rapine. In this supreme hour the Irish nation must, by its valour and discipline and by the readiness of its children to sacrifice themselves for the common good, prove itself worthy of the august destiny to which it is called.

Signed on behalf of the Provisional Government,

THOMAS J. CLARKE,
SEAN Mac DIARMADA.   THOMAS MacDONAGH.
P. H. PEARSE.   EAMONN CEANNT.
JAMES CONNOLLY.   JOSEPH PLUNKETT.

13.1   The Proclamation of the Irish Republic, 1916.
Courtesy of the National Library of Ireland

that, together with the damaged types used to print the heading, provides the distinctive typographic 'shape' of the Proclamation (King 2001). Mosley (2010a) writes: 'the evident technical imperfections make one all the more aware how risky the whole enterprise was'. Therefore, we can suggest that, independent of reading the content, one can read the form of the document.

Despite the haste, secrecy and danger surrounding its production, some attempts were made to add typographic variety, but aesthetic considerations were not of primary importance. The heading 'POBLACHT NA H EIREANN' was printed in a simple sans serif type. A second, more ornamental display face with bent arms and curved serifs was used in the next lines. Further variation was provided by the alternation of size and length of line in the headings. If we assume that the compositors were applying what is referred to in printing as a 'hierarchy of information', where the layout follows the meaning and importance of the text, then the most important phrase must be 'IRISH REPUBLIC'. These are the largest words on the sheet, and again use a bold sans serif. Liam de Paor noted that the words in Irish in the original Proclamation are printed in a roman rather than a gaelic face (de Paor 1997, 31). Despite having a distinctive 'national dress' in the form of the so-called 'Gaelic' alphabet, it was not uncommon to find the Irish language printed in roman faces at the beginning of the twentieth century, usually for reasons of economy or, as was probably the case here, availability of type. Throughout the twentieth century, arguments about the correct form of letter in which to write or print the Irish language would occupy typographers, linguists and civil servants and would give material form to broader debates about Irish modernisation. In order to understand how typography could develop such political valency, it is necessary to address briefly the history of the 'Irish' alphabet.

By the end of the ninth century there were two manuscript hands in use in Ireland which historian E.W. Lynam distinguished simply as 'round' and 'pointed' (Lynam 1969, 1). The first was a continuation of the early Christian, and originally Roman, semi-uncial, while the 'pointed' Irish minuscule was a demotic variation. The latter is more angular and with a vertical emphasis and was primarily used for writing in the Irish language. Its form became standardised with the development of printing in Irish in the seventeenth century, particularly as part of Counter-Reformation propaganda in Irish centres on the continent. It was thus associated with the Irish language, Catholicism and nationalism.

There was very little variation in the design of the Irish type, and by the late nineteenth century and the Gaelic Revival there were still only a handful of different typefaces commonly available in the Irish alphabet (see McGuinne 1992). Notwithstanding nineteenth-century antiquarian revivals of a more rounded semi-uncial form, it was the minuscule form that predominated. To some extent, this was because the boundaries between language, letterform and alphabet had become blurred in the mythology of the nationalist cause – but there were also economic reasons. Given the relatively low numbers of consumers of Irish type at any time, there was little incentive for the major foundries to create new typefaces. In the early part of the twentieth century, the main providers all offered effectively the same face, called 'Gaelic'. This seems to have led to a situation whereby the idiosyncrasies of the typeface were comprehended as characteristics of the alphabet and any variation viewed as deviant.

In the mid-twentieth century, economic factors combined with ideological ones in a campaign to romanise Irish printing. This was part of a wider movement towards the 'modernisation' of the Irish language that saw the distinctiveness of the Irish alphabet and orthography as a bar to popularising the language (see, for example, the essays in Ó Cuiv 1969). The Irish alphabet was officially phased out in the 1965 Government White Paper *Athbheochan na Gaeilge. The restoration of the Irish language* (Baile Átha Cliath: Oifig an tSoláthair, January 1965).

Inspired by debates about romanisation, designers in Ireland began to explore alternative ways of expressing national sentiment through letterforms. Among the most influential and prolific were the typographer Liam Miller (founder of the Dolmen Press) and his friend and collaborator, the stone-carver Michael Biggs. Various public commemorations of the Easter Rising provided opportunities for each of these men to promote the 'uncial' form as a modern compromise between ancient and modern, national and international. In 1954, a 'private obsession with Ireland's heritage of lettering' led Miller to approach Biggs to cut an alphabet of the eighteen letters used in Irish (Miller 1976, 31). This was later published with an essay by Miller as a Dolmen Chapbook (Miller 1960). In this essay, Miller subtly argued against orthodoxy in the choice of typefaces in the Irish character. His historical acuity meant that he was able to cut through the romantic rhetoric that imagined 'remote and improbable' origins for the Irish characters. 'In fact', he wrote, 'these letterforms have their origins in the roman alphabet adapted by the scribes to a national mode, based on their own tools and materials' (Miller 1960, unpaginated).

Miller's argument endorsed the modernisation of the alphabet (rather than its replacement by the roman form) in line with modern tools and materials. He complained that symbolic associations of the letterform were favoured over legibility or typographical aesthetic, the forms being based on 'weak originals … only the Petrie type in Dublin University approaches a satisfying solution of the typographical problem' (Miller 1960). However, the Dublin University type did not conform to the conventions of nationalist hegemony, being based on the rounded semi-uncial, rather than the pointed minuscule. Miller praised Colm Ó Lochlainn's 'fine Columcille face, which has uncial characteristics, has a full range of characters for printing both in Irish and in English, and is the only Gaelic face to have a related italic' (Miller 1960). More radically, he endorsed two modern European uncials, S.H. de Roos's Libra (1930) and Victor Hammer's Uncial (1923 and 1945) (Miller 1960).

While preparing his essay on Irish letters, Miller was working on another 'private obsession', a commemorative edition of the *Easter Proclamation of the Republic, 1916*. Unlike other commemorative reproductions of the text (see Mosley 2010a), Miller chose not to echo the layout, hierarchy or typography of the original document. Instead, it seems, he wished to give the text a typographic patrimony worthy of its status as a founding statement of the Irish Republic. The 1960 edition situates the Proclamation in a suitably historical past: the style points to the earliest of printed books,

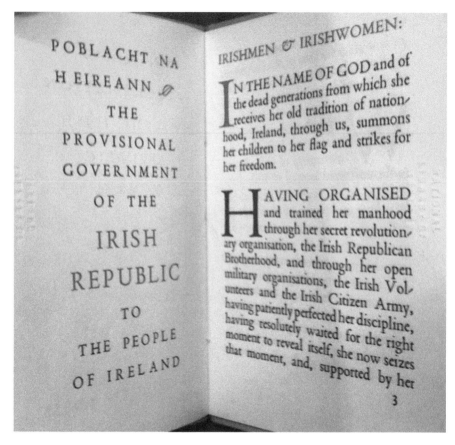

13.2   *The Easter Proclamation of the Irish Republic, 1916.* Dolmen Press, 1960.
Courtesy of the National Library of Ireland

Renaissance incunabula (Fig. 13.2). The text was presented as a small (6 inches × 4 inches) eight-page booklet, bound in fawn, paper-covered boards, perhaps suggesting vellum. The body text was printed in black, with blue and red titling and initials, in 16-point Poliphilus type. This typeface was a revival of a Renaissance type cut by Francesco Griffo for Aldus Manutius in the 1490s.

Inside, the typographic hierarchy was significantly different from the original setting of the Proclamation. In common with its source, the 1960 edition makes the words 'Irish Republic' the most important text. In the original, this was done through size and weight; Miller's version used size and colour, setting the words in red. In an important departure, the addressees of the Proclamation, 'Irishmen & Irishwomen', were given a much greater status in Miller's version, the words printed in red as a heading on the first

easter 1916

poblacht na h eireann
THE PROVISIONAL GOVERNMENT
OF THE IRISH REPUBLIC
TO THE PEOPLE OF IRELAND
IRISHMEN AND IRISHWOMEN:

IN THE NAME OF GOD and of the
dead generations from which
she receives her old tradition of
nationhood/Ireland/through us/
summons her children to her flag and
strikes for her freedom.

HAVING organised and trained
her manhood through her secret revolutionary organisation/the
Irish Republican Brotherhood/and
through her open military organi-
sations/the Irish Volunteers and the
Irish Citizen Army/having patiently
perfected her discipline/having resolutely waited for the right moment
to reveal itself/she now seizes that
moment/and/supported by her exiled
children in America and by gallant
3

13.3   *The Easter Proclamation of the Irish Republic, 1916.* Dolmen Press, 1975.
Courtesy of the National Library of Ireland

facing page. Perhaps this records the transformation of the Proclamation from functional document, announcing the Republic, to historical record, testifying to a historical declaration from which independence could be dated. Using red for these two key phrases creates a link between them and draws attention to the national character of the Proclamation, highlighting through colour the three instances of 'Irish' in its opening lines.

Between 1960 and Miller's second setting of the Proclamation in 1975 (Fig. 13.3), Michael Biggs had been at work defining the typographic form of commemorative lettering in Dublin. Among many other examples, he designed and carved the lettering for the Garden of Remembrance (1966), the plinth of the statue of Thomas Davis (1966) and the plaques commemo-rating 1916 in the General Post Office (1961). All of these use variations on the uncial he explored in the Dolmen Chapbook.

Biggs's innovation was not always well received – Myles na gCopaleen wrote of the General Post Office plaque: 'It is hard not to comment on the Gaelic script, but the M looks like a ram coming straight at the reader with his horns down, while the N seems to be in the last stages of polio'.[1] What is significant about so many of these examples is that they are in English, rather than Irish. The uncial form, unlike the Gaelic, was flexible enough to accommodate both languages comfortably. Indeed, the use of uncial seems to have the effect of 'translating' English into Irish, an idea which Miller used to good effect in his 1975 edition of the Proclamation. This was set entirely in Hammer Uncial and at first glance seems an even more emphatic attempt to fix the text as both ancient and Irish. The hierarchy of information echoed that of the 1960 edition, with a few significant differences. Apart from the change of tone signalled by the use of uncial, the Irish language was given prominence, 'Poblacht na hEireann' usurping 'Irish Republic'. The typographic semantics of this document could suggest a desire to historicise securely the sentiments of 1916, perhaps in contrast to contemporary expressions of republicanism then playing out in the North of Ireland.

But Miller was a typophile. For him, Hammer's Uncial was contemporary, not ancient. In 1975, he was planning a collected edition of the writings of Victor Hammer and must have known Hammer's 'manifesto' for his uncial face, written in 1943:

> With this uncial typeface I am aiming at a letterform which eventually may fuse roman and black letter, those two national letter forms, into a new unity … An uncial hand acquired by copying Latin manuscripts of the sixth & seventh centuries, will never do in writing modern English or German text. (Hammer 1987, 13)

In the pamphlet issued to promote the 1975 edition, Miller effectively incorporated Hammer's typeface into the Irish tradition:

> In our presentation of this historic text as a booklet we have sought to echo the traditions of the earlier golden age when our island was the treasury of Europe's cultural heritage. The text of the Proclamation is set by hand in Victor Hammer's uncial type, in itself a reflection of our nation's contribution to letter design. (Miller 1975, unpaginated)

Millers' statement of Ireland's centrality to Europe's cultural heritage finds echoes in Biggs's design, also in 1975, for the decimal five-punt note. The

---

1   Myles na Gopaleen, 'Look at this!', *Irish Times*, 3 May 1961.

design was criticised by Liam de Paor in 1976 for its 'backwards look' and for being inauthentically Irish. De Paor noted that:

> Its motifs are from the Psalter of Ricemarch (a Welsh manuscript), backgrounds of text from the Book of Durrow (quite likely written and illuminated in Northumbria …) and the Book of Kells (… possibly produced in Scotland) and a 'portrait of Eriguenga, the Irish philosopher at the court of Charles the Bald'.[2]

De Paor failed to grasp the central point: two years after Ireland joined the EEC, Biggs situated Irish heritage as central to European experience rather than peripheral. Likewise, Miller's reminder of the Irish origins of the international, modern, roman alphabet allowed the 1975 setting of the Proclamation to link past and future in a new, optimistic, construction of nationalism.

It is clear that Miller held the original Proclamation in high esteem. In the 1975 promotional pamphlet he wrote: 'The Proclamation of the Republic made at Easter 1916 is Ireland's Declaration of Independence, setting down the principles which guided the founders of our modern state' (Miller 1975, unpaginated). In addition to the three reproductions of the text discussed above, in 1965, Dolmen also published *Yeats and the Easter Rising* by Edward Mallins. This included an image of a version of the 1916 Proclamation. As Mosley (2010a) has noted, this could not have been a photographic reproduction of the original Proclamation of 1916, as the heading is set in Monotype's Gill Sans Extra Bold, a typeface only produced from 1931. The same 'Gill Sans' version is reproduced in the 1975 and 1982 Dolmen Pamphlets. Given Miller's evident typographic nous, this is quite surprising. However, it may reveal his commitment to 'good' (rather than 'authentic') typography.[3] He preferred to honour the document with an improved and repaired facsimile, just as he sought to exalt the text by clothing it in suitably dignified typographic garb in his three pamphlet editions.

---

2 Liam De Paor, 'A look at the new fiver', *Irish Times*, 19 October 1976.
3 The origin of this 'Gill Sans version' has not been identified. In fact, in a later post on his blog *Typefoundry*, Mosely notes that 'it has been suggested to me that it is not impossible that Liam Miller himself, a great admirer of Eric Gill, might have had some involvement in its production. This may seem on the face of it to be one of the wilder guesses – but who knows?' (Mosley 2010b).

14

The *Capuchin Annual*: visual art and the legacy of 1916, one generation on

Róisín Kennedy

Described as 'the leading Catholic publication on Irish art and culture' (Arnold 1998, 320), the *Capuchin Annual* had a circulation of 25,000 and was distributed as far afield as Australia, New Zealand, North America, South Africa and Britain. Launched in 1930, the highpoint of the *Annual* was from the late 1930s through the next decade when the sheer volume of the publication regularly ran to over 500 pages. Its high level of production was unique in Irish periodicals of the period. The editor and founder of the *Annual* was the enigmatic Father Senan (Perkins 2013), known as Friar Tuck (Kiely 1991), a networker and socialite with close connections to Fianna Fáil and more radical republicans, most notably Maud Gonne. One of his closest friends during the 1940s was fellow Kerryman Thomas MacGreevy who became the major contributor on art and architecture in the journal in the Emergency (Coulter and Kennedy 2013, 53). As later correspondence suggests, the critic influenced Senan's deployment of fine art in the journal.[1] Senan's departure from the *Annual* in 1954, partly the result of financial difficulties incurred in its running (Perkins 2013), had a palpable impact, with a noticeable reduction in its range of content.

While at heart a missionary journal, proclaiming the role and achievements of the Franciscan Orders to both Ireland-based readers and the diaspora, a crucial aim of the *Capuchin Annual* under Senan's guidance was cultural. It was intended to be 'an inspiration to and expression of everything which is intrinsically Irish in the fields of literature and art' and to nurture public appreciation of Irish artists and writers, 'not of the clique or the few, but of the people everywhere and in all walks of life' (*Capuchin Annual* 1945, 383). Perkins (2013) notes that in the 1930s Senan replaced Franciscan contributors with creative writers, many of whom were taken up by more

1 Trinity College Dublin (TCD), TCD/MS/8137, papers of Thomas MacGreevy.

intellectually-minded publications such as *Ireland Today* and the *Bell*, whose readers the *Annual* outnumbered five to one.

In addition to reporting on the missions and Irish life and culture, a distinguishing feature of the *Capuchin Annual* is its constant reference to the revolutionary period in Ireland, with special sections devoted to commemorations and anniversaries, most notably the twentieth, twenty-fifth and fiftieth anniversaries of the Rising, in the *Annuals* of 1936, 1942 and 1966 respectively. In this regard, the use of photography and personal reminiscences of the Rising, and above all the pious tone of the coverage, is reminiscent of the *Catholic Bulletin* (Wills 2009, 158). The resulting combination of art, republican politics and organised religion make the *Annual* strangely anachronistic and deeply disconcerting to the contemporary reader. What makes it unique is the way in which visual art actively contributes in its pages to the creation of a sealed reading of Irish life in which the events surrounding 1916 and its aftermath remain of central significance.

The Capuchin Order had played a major role in the Rising. Its friars liaised in the surrender and acted as confessors to the executed leaders, and the *Annual* regularly published accounts of this involvement. In 1942, for the edition dedicated to the twenty-fifth anniversary of 1916, Fr. Aloysius's chronicle of his experience of the Rising appeared (Aloysius 1942). It tells of how, on the eve of Patrick Pearse's execution, Fr. Aloysius looked through the light-filled spy hole of the rebel's cell and saw Pearse kneeling and clasping a crucifix. Such reminiscences reinforced the Capuchin Order's centrality to the Rising as well as prolonging the pious image of Pearse for the benefit of a younger generation. Other recurring accounts include that of Fr. Dominic O'Connor who was the chaplain to the dying Terence MacSwiney, as well as the memories of Fr. Albert, another confessor to the 1916 leaders. The close allegiance of Frs Dominic and Albert to the republican cause lead to their being transferred to America in 1922 (González Corona 2009, 52). The humility and seditiousness of the Capuchins provide a fascinating undercurrent to the *Annual*, one that contrasts with the journal's prevailing note of triumphalism.

Visual art was a cornerstone of the cultural agenda of the *Annual*. A collection of important modern Irish art, which included work by Jack Yeats, Patrick Tuohy, Walter Osborne and Nathaniel Hone, was housed in the Capuchin Periodicals Office at 2 Capel Street during the Emergency. It was open to the public during the afternoons (*Irish Art Handbook* 1943, 139). The Capuchin publications, which included the *Father Mathew Record*, an illustrated monthly magazine, were unusual in Irish terms in their high ratio of visual content. From 1932, the artist Richard King was permanently employed by the company to produce a wide range of illustrations including elaborate religious images. Father Gerald, a Capuchin friar, provided humorous illustrations and cartoons that brought the diverse contents of the *Annual* together in a homely manner.

The *Annual's* reproduction of artworks contributed enormously to the public dissemination of art at a time when there were few, if any, illustrated publications on art in Ireland. Full-page colour reproductions of works from the Capuchin collection or from Irish museums featured as frontispieces. A preference for artworks depicting political images became more marked during the Emergency. Patrick Tuohy's *Portrait of an Irish Volunteer* (1917, location unknown) was used in 1940. John Lavery's veneration of pomp and ceremony and particularly his juxtaposition of Catholicism and nationalism suited the journal's agenda. *Blessing of the colours* (1922, Dublin City Gallery), a depiction of a bishop blessing the tricolour, was used as the frontispiece in 1943 (*Capuchin Annual* 1943). Paintings were also blended into photographic essays, increasing their renown amongst readers while levelling their status as high art. Lavery's *Michael Collins, love of Ireland* (1922, Dublin City Gallery) was included along with documentary photographs of the hero in an extensive photographic essay 'From the Ulster Covenant of 1912', part of a supplement 'The Struggle for Independence, 1916–21' (*Capuchin Annual* 1942).

A photo-essay on Laurence Campbell sculpting the statue of Seán Heuston for Islandbridge gave readers an insight into the physical production of a memorial monument (Campbell 1946) (Fig. 14.1). The development of the work from a rough block of stone to the finished sculpture is portrayed in a series of unfolding images as a heroic process in itself. The section, completely without text, endows the process of artmaking with special qualities. It promotes the idea that the artist is not only a craftsman, but a creator in the commemoration process.

Visual reference is made to Michelangelo's legendary method of carving in which he is said to have released the figure from the slab of marble (Bull 1987, 153). Readers of the Capuchin publications were familiar with Michelangelo through MacGreevy's essay on the sculptor in which he described him as 'among the most tragic figures of the history of art' (MacGreevy 1945a, 3). The emotional bias of his work was, according to this, the result of the profound impact of contemporary political and social unrest in Florence on the sculptor's psyche. Details of the hands of the Heuston sculpture draw inevitable comparison with Michelangelo's iconic sculpture of the adolescent *David* (1503, Galleria dell' Accademia, Florence), a work in which limbs and head are disproportionately large. Thus the parallels between Seán Heuston, brave defender of the First Battalion of Volunteers, and the youngest of the rebels to be executed after the Rising, and David, the boy who succeeded in slaying Goliath, become evident.

Heuston's connection with the Capuchins had been outlined in the most heart-rending fashion in the *Annual* in an account by the late Father

14.1 Lawrence
Campbell at work
on his statue of
Seán Heuston,
Capuchin Annual
1946, 351.
Courtesy of the
National Library of
Ireland

Albert. It concludes with the familiar emphasis on martyrdom: 'I scarcely
had moved away a few yards when a volley went off, and this noble soldier of
Irish Freedom fell dead. I rushed over to anoint him. His whole face seemed
transformed, and lit up with grandeur and brightness that I have never
before noticed' (Albert 1935, 163; 1942, 343).

One of the most significant uses of visual art to commemorate 1916
was Thomas MacGreevy's essay *Three historical paintings by Jack B. Yeats*
(1942). This appeared in the issue devoted to the twenty-fifth anniversary
of the Rising with detailed accounts of the events of the time and a major
photographic supplement covering 1914–21. It focuses on three paintings,
reproduced in full colour, that were made in the revolutionary era. One of the
works, *Communicating with prisoners* (1924, The Model, Sligo), had never been
exhibited before, while *Funeral of Harry Boland* (1922, The Model, Sligo)
and *Bachelor's Walk – in memory* (1915, private collection, long-term loan to

BACHELOR'S WALK — IN MEMORY

14.2   Bachelor's
Walk: in memory,
Capuchin Annual
1942, inserted
after page 240.
Courtesy of the
National Library
of Ireland

National Gallery of Ireland) (Fig. 14.2) had not been seen in public for over
20 years (the last had featured on the front cover of the *Father Mathew Record*
in December 1941). They were part of the collection housed in the *Capuchin
Annual* offices. It is likely that MacGreevy advised Senan on acquiring the
works as he had drawn attention to their significance in the text of his book
Jack B. Yeats: an appreciation and an interpretation, written in London in
1937–8 but not published until 1945 (MacGreevy 1945b, 3–4, 25–6).

The three works encapsulated MacGreevy's belief that in Yeats, Ireland
had found a national painter of great originality and compassion who was
concerned with representing key moments in the history of the Irish people
in his painting. *Bachelor's Walk – in memory* depicts a flower girl placing
carnations at the site where three people had been shot dead by troops in the
aftermath of the Howth gun-running in 1914. Yeats visited the scene in the
days following the massacre and recorded it in his sketchbook. His painting

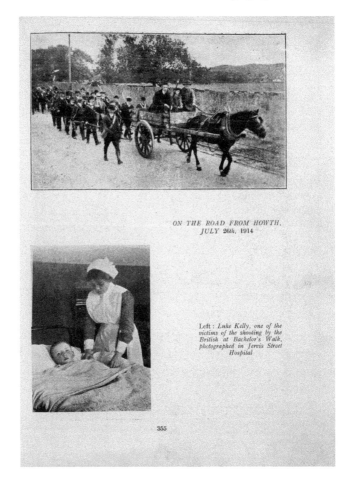

ON THE ROAD FROM HOWTH,
JULY 26th, 1914

Left : *Luke Kelly, one of the
victims of the shooting by the
British at Bachelor's Walk,
photographed in Jervis Street
Hospital*

355

14.3   Luke Kelly,
one of the victims
of the shooting
by the British at
Bachelor's Walk,
Capuchin Annual
1942, 355.
Courtesy of the
National Library
of Ireland

condenses the emotion of the experience into the silhouetted form of a flower girl whose graceful pose recalls classical portrayals of mourning. MacGreevy describes the figure as 'like some Hellenic maiden at an altar, perhaps a Chrysothemis bearing offerings from her half-crazed sister, to the tomb of her murdered father' (MacGreevy 1942, 249).

In his description of the work, MacGreevy pays close attention to the minutiae of the city that surround the woman. Such details as the young boy and the cart racing along the quays act as 'incidentals', stressing the significance of the central historical event. The veracity of the setting places the scene, according to the essay, both topographically and historically. MacGreevy identifies Christ Church Cathedral and the Church of Saints Augustine and John in particular (MacGreevy 1942, 249). In fact, these are barely visible in the painting, but in the pages of the *Capuchin Annual* they add an appropriately religious note.

Yeats's distillation of the public grief aroused by the Bachelor's Walk massacre is reinforced by a very different sort of imagery elsewhere in the *Annual*. A contemporary photograph of one of the children wounded in the shooting, Luke Kelly, is included in an extensive supplement of images titled 'The Struggle for Independence 1916–21' (Fig. 14.3). Shown in bed in Jervis Street Hospital, being tended by a nurse, the child looks remarkably like the urchin that appears in Yeats's painting. This juxtaposition of fine art with photojournalism places Irish art at the centre of a shared remembrance of national history.

The essay devotes close attention to the *Funeral of Harry Boland* (1922, The Model, Sligo), a work that MacGreevy (1942, 250) considers, 'a masterly restatement in terms of modern Irish life of the great European tradition of historical painting'. The painting had been exhibited at the Royal Hibernian Academy (RHA) in 1923 under the less controversial title *A funeral* but it is not mentioned in contemporary reviews of the exhibition. It is in the pages of the *Annual* that it is first brought to public attention. Boland's death in August 1922 was a pivotal moment in the escalation of the Civil War. Yeats's painting shows the burial scene at Glasnevin Cemetery, with the O'Connell Monument dominating the background. While the earth from the freshly dug grave is evident in its bluish colour, the focus is on the crowd rather than the coffin or the body of Boland.

MacGreevy (1942, 249) presents Boland, like the leaders of 1916, in terms of martyrdom and self-sacrifice: 'He was carrying no arms at the time of his arrest and before he died he said simply, "I forgive everybody."' He then goes on to explain to readers what each of the elements of Yeats's painting represents:

> soldiers of the Irish Republican Army attended and fired a salute of three volleys to the memory of the dead. In Jack Yeats's picture they are seen beyond the heaped-up flowers with hands resting on their rifles. To the right of the pictures stands the Republican who was in charge of the proceedings ... he is the only one whose head is unbowed. All around are the members of Cumann na mBan carrying wreaths.[2] (MacGreevy 1942, 250)

The attention that MacGreevy devotes to the group of priests who stand by the graveside is out of proportion to the prominence accorded to them in the work:

> On the left stands a group of faithful priests. Earlier they had assisted

---

2   The republican in charge has subsequently been widely misinterpreted as Harry Boland.

at the Requiem Mass celebrated by Dr. Patrick Browne of Maynooth at the Carmelite Church in Whitefriars Street. Refusing to surrender to despair, with heartbreaking confidence, they sang the Canticle of Zachary from the Gospel of St Luke: *Benedictus Dominue Deus Israel.* (MacGreevy 1942, 249)

The final painting that MacGreevy's essay considers is *Communicating with prisoners* (1924, The Model, Sligo), a contrast to the masculine, militaristic image of the *Funeral*. It depicts a group of women calling up to female republican prisoners incarcerated in Kilmainham Gaol. Referring to the role of women in the revolutionary period, MacGreevy notes that they did everything except get executed. He summarises and trivialises the gender divisions in the republican movement, 'And as women have always tended to do, they showed a magnificent lack of respect for the silliness of many man-made rules' (MacGreevy 1942, 250). Yeats stresses the individuality of the women through their clothing with each wearing fashionable contemporary coats and hats. As MacGreevy puts it, the 'effortlessly differentiated members of the group of listening women are one of Jack Yeats's loveliest discoveries' (MacGreevy 1942, 251).

MacGreevy takes liberties in his accounts of these paintings. His prioritising of subject matter over the treatment of colour and form (Brown 2013, 210) suggests that the artworks are direct representations of particular experiences in the artist's life and by extension that of the nation or at least the readers of the *Annual*. When presented in such terms, art merely replicates the use of photography and illustration found elsewhere in the *Annual*, the ostensible function of which is to record contemporary events as accurately as possible for posterity. More worrying is MacGreevy's need to stress the significance of specific individuals and buildings that have a connection to the Catholic Church. This is most evident in the account of the *Funeral of Harry Boland* and it is at odds with Yeats's rejection of a hierarchical view of society. Arguably, one of the most disturbing aspects of this painting is the way in which the bystanders have become segmented and divided by political events. Yeats's egalitarian views and his corresponding representation of the impact of political violence are at odds with the paternalistic attitude of the *Capuchin Annual* and its presentation of 1916 and of contemporary Ireland. For example, in the same annual as the article on Yeats appears, a photographic section devoted to 'Religious Orders of Men in Ireland' features portraits of leading clerics. While familiar to readers of the *Annual*, it is almost shocking in how it unintentionally reveals the conservative and elitist nature of Irish society in the 1940s.

Following on from the publication of MacGreevy's essay, the *Capuchin Annual* was closely involved in the *Jack B. Yeats National Loan Exhibition*

An Taoiseach with the Artist and Mrs. Yeats   Irish Independent

The Artist with Officers of the Committee   Irish Independent

115

14.4   An Taoiseach
with the artist
and Mrs Yeats,
National Loan
Exhibition
Capuchin Annual
1945–6, 115.
Courtesy of the
National Library of
Ireland

in 1945. Attended by 20,000 visitors, it received extensive coverage in the Irish media, with a special photographic section in the *Annual* of 1945–6. Fr. Senan was instigator of the exhibition and chairman of its impressive organising committee, which comprised over 50 individuals, bringing together republicanism, Catholicism and the international art world. The committee included prominent members of the government, all eminent republicans. The catalogue essay was written by the veteran of the War of Independence and the Civil War, Ernie O'Malley. In addition, the committee also comprised several prominent international curators and directors of art museums.

The exhibition brought art, revolution and party politics together. The opening speech was made by Fr. Pádraig de Brún, who had played such a central role in the *Funeral of Harry Boland*. A photograph of the Taoiseach, Éamon de Valera, with Yeats and his wife, featured prominently in the pages of the *Annual* (Fig. 14.4). Dev, not widely known for his interest in visual art, is shown absorbed in Yeats's painting *Communicating with prisoners*, sharing the experience and memory of a traumatic moment in Irish history. The photograph uses the neutral environment of an art exhibition to consign the divisions of the past to the past.

The prominent inclusion of Yeats's work in the *Capuchin Annual* had a fundamental impact on its meaning. Usually displayed and considered within the narrow context of the gallery, the work became part of a wider non-art agenda. It was enlisted as a public monument to the War of Independence and the Civil War. While Yeats seems to have been willing to let this happen, this treatment of his work permanently damaged MacGreevy's close friendship with Samuel Beckett, who despaired of his overbearing Catholicism in his writings for the *Annual* (Kennedy 2013). Rather than offering a critique of political divisiveness, Yeats's paintings were co-opted into an official narrative of Irish history.

The *Jack B. Yeats National Loan Exhibition* has been forgotten in later accounts of Irish art and culture. The linking of Yeats's art to the framework of 1916 and nationalist politics was seen by later critics as limiting the values and meanings of his work (Kennedy 2008). Equally, the narrow direction of art history in subsequent decades relished more the consideration of the artist within an international art rather than a national historical context.

However, through the pages of the *Capuchin Annual*, the work of Jack B. Yeats and other Irish artists moved into the public sphere. While they were used to validate a Catholic and conservative establishment's view of its past and its present, their prominent inclusion in the *Annual* reveal a genuine curiosity about visual art, and recognition that it has a role to play in enriching an understanding of both the past and the present beyond the narrow confines of the art world.

15

Dressing rebellion:
national revival dress and 1916

Hilary O'Kelly

In Irish–English relations, dress has always been significant to the expression and suppression of identity and power. As early as 1537 the Irish mantle, a culturally distinctive item of clothing materially embodying an 'alien' way of life, was outlawed by Henry VIII. This warm, weatherproof, wool garment had helped its wearers survive outdoors, while its capacity to serve as both clothing and shelter facilitated rapid relocation in times of conflict and, in combat, could even deflect blows with its dense pile weave acting as armour (Dunlevy 1989, 42). Almost 500 years later, in 1976, republican prisoners demanding political status in Northern Ireland refused to wear prison-issue dress, adopting instead a blanket to serve as clothing, uniform and even body armour in riot situations (Ash 2010, 126). But by then the history and memory of the Irish mantle was so far buried that no connection was drawn between these two attires, despite the ancient mantle having served as inspiration as recently as 1916. In the intervening centuries, dress and textiles had been shaped by, while simultaneously giving shape to, changing political, social and economic realities.

This chapter considers how dress was used to encapsulate conflicting perspectives on history and culture, both before and after the Rising, as well as rival visions for a future Ireland. What it suggests is that the visual and material culture of dress and textiles acts simultaneously as a sign and agent of change and a carrier of tradition, not only politically but at the interface of gender, status, tradition and modernity. But, before examining the relationship between Celtic Revival dress and 1916, it should first be noted that while the clothes to be discussed were publicly visible and understandable to most, they were worn by a minority. Images of O'Donovan Rossa's funeral in 1915, for example, confirm a modernity of attire in Dublin, consistent with any city in the Western world. An expanding fashion system diminished difference among city peoples, leading to an increasing similarity in human appearance in the urban spaces of the modern world. Advances in the technology of production, in the standardising of body measurements, and the widening reach of fashion information and fashion merchandise, fed into a shared experience of modernity in everyday life. *Vogue*, for example, established in America in the 1890s, was launched in Britain in 1916. The importance of this accelerated communication was perhaps reflected in the Irish revolutionaries' choice of the General Post Office as the primary site of insurrection.

In the decades leading up to the Easter Rising, nationalism in Ireland had been reflected in a concerted campaign of cultural resurgence primarily aimed, in Douglas Hyde's words, at the 'necessity for de-anglicising Ireland' (the title of his speech to the National Literary Society, Dublin, 25 November 1892). The Irish language, music, games and names (to Hyde, all casualties of centuries of British rule) were rediscovered and promoted. Distinctive forms of Irish dress had also been extinguished at an early date, and by explicit policy (Dunlevy 1989, 47). In the re-imagining of Irishness that flourished up to 1916, Celtic Revival dress played a visible and significant role in embodying idealistic hopes of a lost identity (O'Kelly 1986). Difficult at any time, clothing the individual in the raiments of the national dream would become only more challenging as citizens of the post-revolution period grappled with the reality of creating a viable state in the modern era (Fig. 15.1).

The challenge of embodying disparate aspirations was already evident in the aftermath of the Great Famine when government authorities focused on economic regeneration, while attempting to subdue any attendant nationalist fervour. Official campaigns by the Congested Districts Board aimed to alleviate poverty by fostering cottage industries from fishing to lacemaking. In parallel, private patrician support was expressed by socially prominent women, led by the Viceroy's wife, Lady Aberdeen. In 1893, to encourage American markets, she patronised the Irish Village at the Chicago World's Fair, where among the craft and heritage exhibits was an Irish weaver's cottage, staged as a humble domestic setting, with weavers dressed accordingly. Their clothing appears somewhat staged as most contemporary images suggest that, when dressing for public engagement, even the impoverished achieved a higher level of grooming.[1] Lady Aberdeen herself presented a polished appearance for the occasion, in a belle époque, aesthetic dress, decorated at the hem with Celtic embroidery and a toytown shawl across her shoulders. This distinctly contrasting attire proclaimed a genteel, civilising role for her own position and by extension that of the Ascendency in Ireland. A similar

1 See, for example, the photograph of a group gathered for an open-air mass, 1867, Co. Donegal (Irish Folklore Commission), illustrated in Moody and Martin 1967, 225.

15.1
Broadsheet
published
in Dublin
after the
1916 Rising,
showing
16 portraits
of those who
were executed
or sentenced
to death.
Courtesy of
the Imperial
War Museum;
IWM/Q/70583

sartorial and cultural distance had been conveyed at an earlier Viceregal garden party to which guests were invited to attend in the peasant dress of the nations: suggested attire for an Irish woman was a costume suitable for a porcelain shepherdess, adorned with shamrock-shaped bunching – her male counterpart, a redeemed Paddy from *Punch*.[2]

2   *Irish Textile Journal*, 15 April 1886. For illustrations see O'Kelly (1992).

Such constructs of Ireland and its people were, of course, contested. A celebration of the Ireland of myth and legend appealed to other and growing interests. Around this alternative cultural vision, built on the nationalist energies stranded after the fall of Charles Stewart Parnell, were the revivalist collectives of the Gaelic Athletic Association (founded 1884), the Irish National Literary Society (founded 1892) and the Gaelic League (founded 1893). The ambition of the Gaelic League founder, Douglas Hyde, articulated in 'The necessity for de-anglicising Ireland' speech, was that this process should start with the language and proceed to the manners and customs of daily life, including dress. Irish dress for Hyde was interpreted as straightforward contemporary fashion, made up of local tweed. For many Gaelic League women, a declaration of Irishness might extend to adorning equally fashionable dress with a Tara brooch or other conspicuously Celtic jewellery. In concluding his speech, Hyde appealed to everyone whether Unionist or Nationalist to do his best to help the Irish race to develop in future upon Irish lines, even at the risk of encouraging national aspirations, and 'to set his face against this constant running to England for our books, literature, music, games, fashion and ideas'. His entreaty, he said, was addressed at 'everyone whatever his politics – for this', he declared, 'is no political matter' (Duffy, Sigerson and Hyde 1973, 161; see also www.gaeilge.org/deanglicising.html).

But, of course, dress is political, as Henry VIII had well understood, both in the construction of his own self-image and the suppression of that of others. The dress he outlawed in 1537 included women's 'kirtles or coats embroidered or garnished with silk' as well as the characteristically Irish *brat* and *léine*, the woollen mantle and the long linen shirt, the latter garment commonly said to have been dyed saffron in colour (Hayward 2009, 28). In Derricke's map of Ireland, drawn 50 years after this edict in the 1580s, the women illustrated retain distinctive Irish mantles, while the Irish chieftain wears cloth, tailored to fit the body. The art of tailoring had developed in Europe over the previous century and introduced a clear hierarchy in the dress of peoples of the early modern world: the draped and the tailored – drapery becoming synonomous with worldly grace and gentility, and tailoring with social and physical power. The cultural opposition that women are draped and men tailored soon became fixed.

Henry VIII's explicit suppression of the *brat* and *léine* gives clear evidence of their contemporary centrality to Irish identity, and this is precisely what contributed to their appeal as badges of a restored Irishness to the revivalists at the turn of the century. But, how for a trimly tailored Gaelic Leaguer like Thomas Ashe, for example, were the *brat* and *léine* to be interpreted in the early twentieth century? Before settling on the attire in which he is best remembered he evidently engaged in a degree of research, deliberation and design.

15.2   Thomas Ashe in piper's costume. Courtesy of the National Library of Ireland; NLI/KE/5

For Gaelic revivalists at the turn of the nineteenth and twentieth centuries, the bible of sources had become Eugene O'Curry's *Handbook of manners and customs of the ancient Irish* (1873). Here, the *brat* and *léine* were identified as ancient Irish dress and translated as the Irish mantle and the Irish shirt – or, in an alternative spelling, *léinidh* – as the Irish kilt. That the kilt was worn by the ancient Irish was reiterated in 1906 by P.W. Joyce, President of the Royal Irish Academy (Joyce 1906, 389–90). Revivalists could therefore, with sound authority, adopt the kilt as the basis of a renewed Irish identity in dress. Ashe's design, however, was not achieved before experimenting with more esoteric essays in medieval troubadour costume, seen in marching formation with the Black Raven Pipe Band he founded, or alternatively as artistic–athletic costume, with the kilt fully pleated all around as described in the ancient annals (Fig. 15.2).

In the now-canonical image of Thomas Ashe as hero-piper of the Rising, his ensemble has coalesced in a combination of ancient Ireland (in vestigial *brat* and *léine* – translated as a kilt and now with a flat front like that of the Scots) and contemporary gentleman (in the tailored jacket and starched shirt and tie of the urban male), all given a military air with the addition of shiny buttons. This resolved composition was only one of a great variety of arrangements that emerged and were evident, for instance,

15.3   Gaelic League gathering, *c.*1912.
Copy in author's collection

at gatherings of the Gaelic League, where the attire of those present ranged from mainstream western dress, through Scottish plaid and sporran, to the noble 'Celtic hero' (Fig. 15.3).

In Dublin and the other cities and towns of Ireland, the diverse manifestations of Gaelic League *brat* and *léine* will have stood out against the early twentieth-century homogeneity of the dark tailoring of urban masculinity, and acted as a sign of the group's identity and an assertion of their shared traditions. While it was generally accepted that *brat* and *léine* were the true Irish historic dress, there was no corresponding agreement as to how they might be incorporated or adapted to the present. Indeed, the very terminology used to describe the revivalist attire illustrates the divergent perspectives and depths of commitment of its wearers. To some it offered an occasional opportunity to remember Celtic dress of the past, to others a model of everyday Irish clothing for the future. To some it was a form of light-hearted fancy-dress, to others a serious national costume. To some it represented dress for protest, to others dress for theatre. In exploring these diverse visions some analysis of the terminology might prove helpful.

'Clothing' is among the most generic terms relating to attire and simply refers to articles of dress that cover the body. The term was little employed in this revivalist discourse, nor was the word 'fashion', which suggests uncharted novelty. The word 'dress' is a general reference to a person's appearance, which, when practised with art and artifice, reads as fashion. In the modern era, both dress and fashion include two essential character-istics, the first being that they are understood to communicate aspects of a person's identity, the second that this communication is ambivalent (Wilson 1985; Davis 1992, particularly ch. 2). Among the more prominent ambiva-lences underlying fashion's instabilities are the subjective tensions of youth versus age, masculinity versus femininity, androgyny versus singularity, inclusiveness versus exclusiveness, work versus play, domesticity versus worldliness, revelation versus concealment, licence versus restraint, and conformity versus rebellion (Davis 1992, 18).

For William Gibson, known as Liam Mac Giolla Bhríde (1868–1942), the *brat* and *léine* constituted his dress. Having been privately educated in England and at Trinity College Dublin, in later life he wore the *brat* and kilt every day on all occasions. Heir to the title Lord Ashbourne, his nationalist leanings resulted in his being financially disinherited, but he did succeed to the title, only to insist on addressing the House of Lords in Irish. He was, according to the writer Mary Colum, one of the Celtophiles who refused to speak the English language and confined himself in conversation to Irish and French (Colum 1947, 106). For anyone who wished to assert a Gaelic family and cultural inheritance, dress was a signifcant cultural tool. Sir Shane Leslie (1885–1971) was born John Randolph Leslie and educated at Eton and Cambridge. He later adopted an Irish form of his name, along with the kilt as daily wear. For others, a less dramatic, yet significant declaration was the reintroduction to the family name of the prefixes *O* and *Mac*. For a person claiming status over an entire clan, a designation as 'The O'Rahilly' or 'The O'Mahoney', for example, was accompanied by Celtic dress as expression of that lineage.

While most dress involves an element of performance, the act of dressing-up exaggerates this dimension. Among the artistic of the Celtic Revival these two practices appear to have elided. According to Mary Colum, her friend Moirín Fox 'never wore anything' other than the sort of garb she donned for performance at the Abbey. She would appear:

> in gorgeous purple and gold, a torc on her forehead, a Tara Brooch fastening her brath, and various other accoutrements of the ancient Irish, including the inevitable amber. The rest of us only occasionally appeared in Gaelic costume, which, of course, had to be of Irish manufactured material. For dressy wear I had a white garment with blue and green embroidery, a blue brath, copper broaches [*sic*], and other archaeo-logical adornments. For more ordinary wear, I had the Irish costume in blue green, a brath of the same colour with embroideries out of the

Book of Kells. These, as I remember, were chiefly of snakes eating one another's tails. With this went a blue stone necklace, a little silver harp fastening the brath, a silver Claddagh ring, and a silver snake bracelet which I'm afraid was early Victorian rather than early Celtic.

This 'get-up', as Mary Colum describes it (for illustration, see Pyle 2005):

> was all right for the Abbey Theatre or Gaelic League dances, but once myself and a friend Siav Trench, in a similar get-up and more striking colour scheme, walked together down a street where the fishmongers were selling their fish. We were openly derided. The fishmongers called out, 'Will yez look at the Irishers trying to look like stained glass windows … them Irishers are going daft!' We were not too sensitive to ridicule, but we did not again wear such garments in parts of the city where anything out of the ordinary was mocked at so vociferously. (Colum 1947, 107)

Such dress, it seems, was normally worn as 'costume', a word deriving from the same Latin word as custom (*consuetudo*); hence costume is popularly understood as an outfit embodying the customs of a people. It emphasises group identity while temporarily hiding or cancelling that of the individual.

If, for some, these sallies out in Irish dress could be recollected as entertainment, for others they were part of the serious business of attaining independence. The determination to declare a separate tradition saw Irish dress incorporated into the national uniform of *Na Fianna Éireann*, the military boy scout organisation led by Constance Markievicz and Bulmer Hobson, as a patriotic riposte to its English model. Here nascent ideals of Irishness could be projected onto and through children and youths, hosts to adult aspirations.

Within the lexicon of dress, 'uniform' is a prescribed outfit that imposes an explicit identity on the wearer, effectively controlling their actions. The ambiguity inherent in dress in modern urban society is cancelled in a uniform. Thus Con Colbert's wearing of the uniform of *Na Fianna* throughout the country, in his forays as recruiting officer for the Volunteers, was read as a call to arms. This message was reinforced at Saint Enda's School, where Colbert led the boys in physical training. The kilt was part of the wider ethos of educating boys in the ways of ancient virtue, healthy vigour and patriotic duty. It was, as Frank O'Connor observed, an object of sartorial envy as 'no one could doubt the loyalty of a boy in a kilt' (Sisson 2004, 124).

Values instilled in youth through school or scouting codes make a lasting impression, but none more so than those disseminated within the home. A family's articles of belief, though unwritten, are passed on all the more effectively in lore, custom, dress and personal imagery (Taylor 2002,

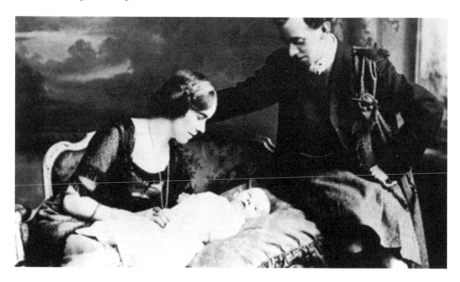

15.4   The MacDonagh Family in 1913.
Courtesy of the National Library of Ireland; NPA/TMD/52

163). This is a practice evidenced in family albums of nationalists of the period. Thomas MacDonagh, writer, teacher and leader of the 1916 Rising, is recorded in a carefully posed photograph leaning, with poetic intensity, over the cradle of his newborn son, Donagh, dressed in *brat* and *léine* and accompanied by his fashionably dressed wife Muriel (Fig. 15.4). His costume was loaned to the National Museum in 1932 (HE:EW.1(loan)), the physical garments highlighting the advantages of supplementing the visual record with material evidence. It had been a mystery how the tunic top of such an outfit worked – no closing mechanism being visible in photographs. The preserved museum garment supplies the answer, which is that the vest is designed to open with buttons along the side or at the shoulder; the garment, then, worn beneath a jacket, reads more heroically as a saffron breast-plate than as the gentlemanly accessory of a waistcoat.

For other nationalists, outside the aesthetic patriotism of MacDonagh, Joseph Plunkett and Patrick Pearse, national sentiment is more often recorded in the dress of their young sons rather than themselves. This is seen, for example, in photographs of Cork Mayor and hunger striker Terence MacSwiney. It is also seen in photographs of Peader Kearney, who fought alongside MacDonagh in 1916, and whose 1907 lyrics were later adopted as the Irish national anthem (1926). Both men are portrayed with their young sons attired in 'national dress'.

As dress, costume or uniform, though not as fancy dress, many of the men and women of 1916 wore some version of national dress – as much a proclamation of separateness as that posted up on a pillar of the General Post Office in Easter Week. But meaning in dress is more fleeting and more fugitive than in words, and the passage of time would only make distant and strange the dress of the rebels, while by contrast their words have rung clearer with time. Already within weeks of the executions, sixteen of the leaders were commemorated wearing mainstream military garb or respectable middle-class dress (Fig. 15.1), with any reference to Celtic 'drapery' surviving only in the dress of two: Thomas Ashe's kilt and Constance Markievicz's lace, that is, in the dress of the musician and the 'lady'. With the War of Independence, Civil War and the new state, all the undefined, idealistic hopes for a new Ireland, it seems, were reduced to concrete facts, as poetry turned to prose.

The fall-out of the Rising on civilian attitudes to Irish dress was notably divergent, galvanising some formerly apathetic citizens into national fervour, while turning the once impassioned towards a more practical modernity. One stand-out instance, indeed almost Pauline conversion, was that of the Ryan family of Cork city, who in response to the executions of the leaders of the Rising were prompted to question 'the point of men dying for Ireland with an English fag in their mouths and an English cap on their heads'.[3] In response, Mr Ryan expanded his 'Blackthorn House' business in umbrellas to incorporate the manufacture of 'Irish Costume', becoming himself a champion and daily wearer from 1918 until his death in 1925. Advocating the adoption of Irish dress in schools around Cork, he had outfits of *brat* and *léine* made in green and saffron from the Dripsey Woollen Mills, sewn by outworkers around the country, thus creating demand for Irish wool, work for Irish men and women, and inculcating patriotic values in the future generations.

A contrary response was that of Mary Butler, a stalwart of the Gaelic League, who wrote in the weightily entitled 'The Ethics of dress' article in the *Irish Monthly* of April 1917:

> But dearly as every lover of National chacteristics, and every admirer of womanly decorum must wish to see these distinctive costumes preserved, we must face facts. In the pressure of modern life, especially in urban districts, it is impossible to secure the general wearing of these picturesque costumes. The most we can hope for is that on gala occasions the daughters of the women who once wore National costume will produce their traditonal treasures. The memory of the romance and beauty will thus be kept alive. (Butler 1917, 222–8)

3 Interview by the author with Mr. Ryan, son of the late Mr M.A. Ryan, proprietor of Blackthorn House, Patrick Street, Cork. Arbutus Lodge, Cork, 1986.

15.5   Michael Collins
in uniform at Portobello
Barracks, *c.*1922.
Courtesy of the National
Library of Ireland; NLI/
INDH/403

There is, of course, very little difference in the practicality of the fashions of 1917 and the clothing sold by Mr Ryan. There was, however, a great distinction in meaning. It is notable that, in the aftermath of 1916, it was a woman who articulated the need for distance from the national costume, even as the mantle was passing to women for its survival. This responsibility appears to persist, as in the National Museum display of Celtic Revival dress at the time of writing, which presents the woman's 'Celtic costume' alongside a man's suit of mainstream metropolitan cut made in Irish tweed. Across cultures, the female remains the repository for tradition, acting as a sign of authenticity in the face of imperialism – but often at the price of being excluded from modernity.

Attitudes to Revival dress for males in the aftermath of the Rising may be expressed in the now famous and arresting image of Michael Collins in military uniform (Fig. 15.5). Behind the striding figure of Collins follows a beaming young admirer dressed in *brat* and kilt. Perhaps the image might be read as suggesting that from the chrysalis of a youthful Celtic dream will emerge a modern international maturity. Certainly, the image of republican Dan Breen, with Luger pistol on his lap, accompanied by his bride in Celtic dress, emphasises a masculine engagement with more cinematic models of heroism and daring (Breen 1981, fig. 23). So too does the famous image of Irish Volunteers swaggering down Grafton Street in 1922.[4]

With the range of dress available to Irish men by 1929, the sartorial choice made by Taoiseach W.T. Cosgrave for the ceremonial reopening of the General Post Office might strike some as surprising, even shocking. As the central figure charged with turning the key of the great hall door, Cosgrave wore top hat and tails. Certainly, Fianna Fáil, 'the Republican Party', vowed never to wear this attire, and condemned the Fine Gael opposition as aping British lackeys for doing so.

The leaders of early independent Ireland might well have felt liberated from any overt personal expression of national identity by virtue of institutional support for cultural instruments like Conradh na Gaeilge and the Feis Cheoil, alongside government policy of replacing imported English clothing with Irish manufacture. Furthermore, they could console themselves with the ghostly survival of national dress among dancers, musicians and children. Thus safely corralled, the aspiration towards Irish dress was indeed being supported and achieved, leaving the national political leaders at liberty to express modern masculinity suitable to the running of a mature independent state aiming to take its place among the modern nations.

4 See http://hdl.handle.net/10599/10043. Accessed 8 May 2015.

IV   Remembering the Rising

Introduction

In this section, contributors are largely concerned with the centrality of visual and material culture in the ways the Rising was remembered and forgotten. Official and institutional responses are of particular significance, their attitude to the objects of the revolutionary past varying over time and space. Initially, the imperative to collect 'relics' of 1916 was felt more keenly by those close to the action, whether due to personal involvement, a sense of historical significance or familial ties. For some, everyday objects were imbued with significance due to their association with the Rising, but their supposed importance could jar with institutional self-image, as was the case with the National Museum of Ireland under Alfred Mahr. As Lar Joye and Brenda Malone's piece on the development of the museum's 1916 collection recounts, the director initially felt the museum should not house 'patriotic relics', although its 'Easter Week Collection' and iterations of its display came to be deeply important in purveying a particular narrative of the Rising.

Curatorial strategies are also of concern to Elizabeth Crooke, who traces how there was an almost total absence of artefacts relating to the Rising in museums in Northern Ireland, but that in a 'post-conflict' situation this is being redressed somewhat. This is within the context of new museological approaches that draw on community narratives and social memory as much as collecting significant objects.

Alongside the potency of even very ordinary-seeming objects in evoking the events of the past, certain places can be deeply resonant. As Pat Cooke discusses in relation to Kilmainham Gaol, the potency of sites sacred to a national past can trouble its creative reinterpretation. He explains particular projects undertaken in Kilmainham that managed to do just that, especially through collaborations with artists. But not all important sites have been treated with reverence. Damian Shiels focuses on a number of instances where the fabric of landscapes of revolutionary conflict has been neglected and even destroyed. He posits an intriguing thesis on the way the materiality of such sites has become less important in relation to rituals of remembering, for example, through gravesite memorials.

As explored elsewhere in this volume, and in Cooke's chapter in this section, remembrance of the Rising often materialised around heroic individuals. One key figure who was less easily valorised than others was Roger Casement. In Catherine Marshall's analysis of Sir John Lavery's painting of Casement's trial, she demonstrates how this controversial subject was shunted off-stage, the painting hanging out of public view in an office in the Court of Criminal Appeal until the Lord Chancellor gave it on indefinite loan to the King's Inn Benchers in Dublin.

In the early years of the Free State, official memorialisation itself was deeply fraught. In the concluding chapter in this section, Lisa Godson explores this through examining the ceremonial cultures that developed around Arbour Hill, the final burial place of the majority of the executed leaders of the Rising. Such were post-war enmities that many of the relatives of those interred there never visited their graves, controlled as the place was by those who the families felt had betrayed the ideals of the Rising. So, too, Justin Carville's analysis of photography and commemoration notes that the politics of commemoration continues to form 'new uncertainties' in the interpretation of events in Irish history.

16

Displaying the nation: the 1916 Exhibition at the National Museum of Ireland, 1932–1991

Lar Joye and Brenda Malone

This chapter examines the creation of the Easter Week Collection and the development of the 1916 exhibition at the National Museum of Ireland over 60 years. The museum was established as the Museum of Science and Art, Dublin, in 1877 by Act of British Parliament, this decision partly arising from requests by the Royal Dublin Society to have their collections transferred to state ownership. The transfer of other notable collections such as the Tara brooch and Ardagh chalice from the Royal Irish Academy (RIA) and ethnographic collections from Trinity College Dublin further enhanced these holdings (Monaghan 2000, 400).

The Royal Dublin Society museum on the Merrion Street side of Leinster House was devoted to natural history and had opened in 1857. This is the classic Victorian cabinet-style museum and is frequently described as a 'museum of a museum'. A new museum was eventually opened on Kildare Street in 1890 designed by Thomas Newenham Deane, the building one of the best surviving examples of Irish decorative stonework, woodcarving and ceramic tiling. The museum worked closely with counterparts in London and Edinburgh and the new exhibitions highlighted the expanding British Empire, particularly through the decorative arts of Japan and China. Museums in the early part of the twentieth century were established to educate new audiences and the Dublin museum's ethos echoed that of the Great Exhibition of 1851 – 'to increase the means of industrial education and extend the influence of science and art upon productive industry' (Candon 2012, 176). The museum had three divisions: Natural History, Art and Industry, and Antiquities. The last was dominated by the RIA collection, although the Irish antiquities of the RIA collection did not play a significant role in the museum; it was displayed in a less-than-prominent space, in a room on the first floor (Crooke 2000, 125). Under the directorship of Valentine Ball (1883–95) and later Colonel Plunkett (1895–1907), the museum expanded, published catalogues and had a popular circulation collection which visited schools. The museum changed its name to the National Museum of Science and Art in 1908 (Candon 2012, 176).

The 1916 Rising and the new Irish State

During the 1916 Rising the museum was closed when Liam Gogan (1891–1979), a junior curator in the Irish Antiquities Department, hung a notice on the front gate with the words (in Irish) 'National Museum Closed by Order, L.G. Gogan'. British authorities investigating the incident afterwards suspected Gogan, a prominent member of the Irish Volunteers from 1913, acted on the order of the newly declared Irish Provisional Government, and Gogan was fired from the museum for his actions.[1] Count George Noble Plunkett had been appointed director of the National Museum in 1907. He was fired from his post and deported to England due to the fact that his three sons fought in the Rising, in particular his son Joseph Mary Plunkett who was a signatory of the 1916 Proclamation and one of the leaders based in the General Post Office. He was later executed for his role. Count Plunkett was eventually to return to Ireland illegally and win the Roscommon North by-election in January 1917 (O'Connor Lysaght 2009). However, he was to spend most of his time until 1923 interned.

The emergence of the Irish Free State in 1922 had a dramatic impact on this Victorian institution. The museum immediately lost space to the new Dáil, which moved into Leinster House, as the RDS moved to its new premises in Ballsbridge and was closed to visitors. Greater emphasis was now placed on the Irish Antiquities collection while the organisation's name was changed to the 'National Museum of Ireland'. The museum faced many problems: the 'loss in space and facilities was matched by ever expanding collections and a decline in resources as a new state struggled to fund other priorities' (Monaghan 2000, 404). The problems of chronic shortages of staff, storage and exhibition space applied for most of the twentieth century. G.A. Hayes-McCoy, former curator of Military History at the museum and later Professor of History in University College Galway, felt that the new governance had badly impacted the museum, writing in 1970 that 'the system on which the National Museum has operated is not a good one. If it was a good system, we should have a better museum' (Hayes-McCoy 1970, 135).

The 1927 Lithberg Report set out a reorganisation plan for the new National Museum. A new Keeper of Archeology, Adolf Mahr (1887–1951), from Germany, was appointed on the death of Walther Bremer in 1927, and

1   National Museum of Ireland Directors' Archive, File 820/A/1916.

became the director of the museum from January 1934 until 1939. Mahr has become more famous recently as 'Dublin Nazi No. 1' (Mullins 2007, 75), which has overshadowed his career as an archaeologist. His selection as the new keeper was not popular among staff; Liam Gogan went so far as to make an official complaint.[2] The greatest change for the museum in the 1930s was the increased focus on the Irish Antiquities collections, which now moved from upstairs to take up the ground floor of the museum. There was no specific Irish history collection in the museum prior to the 1930s; the Antiquities Division was seen as containing collections that expressed the identity of modern Ireland. However, this did not stop the expansion of the Art and Industry Division collections or the creation of new displays such as the Albert Bender exhibition. The reality for the museum, as Elizabeth Crooke has suggested, is that 'it was important only to have it reorganised into a useful national symbol and certain artefacts prominently displayed' (Crooke 2000, 125).

Building the Easter Week Collection

Despite the National Museum's pedigree regarding the involvement of some of its staff in the 1916 Rising, the first real attempt to collect and display artefacts related to the insurrection did not come from within the institution itself. Helen Ruth, or 'Nellie', Gifford-Donnelly (1880–1971), through her work with the 1916 Club (a 1916 veterans' association), was the primary force behind both the first 1916 exhibition and the building of the Easter Week Collection, as it became known.

Gifford-Donnelly, active in the nationalist and feminist movements, was one of the well-known Gifford sisters, and the only one to participate in the Rising. She was also a supporter of the Labour movement; during the 1913 Lockout, it was she who accompanied the disguised Jim Larkin into the Imperial Hotel, from where he gave the speech that precipitated the Bloody Sunday baton charge (Clare 2011, 100). She became a member of the Irish Citizen Army and served in the St Stephen's Green Garrison in 1916. For her part in the fighting, she was interned in Kilmainham and Mountjoy gaols until June of that year, after which she toured America lecturing on the events of Easter Week. During the 1920s, she had contacted the National Museum to suggest the collection of items relating to the revolutionary period (Clare 2011, 251), though there is no evidence that the museum ever acted upon this advice.

In 1932, Gifford-Donnelly, in her role as secretary of the 1916 Club,

---

2 National Archives of Ireland (NAI), NAI/S9336, 'Liam Gogan, alleged victimisation'.

16.1   Adolf Mahr (1887–1951),
Director of the National
Museum of Ireland, 1934–9.
Courtesy of the National
Museum of Ireland

began new correspondence with the Department of Education and the National Museum, now under Dr Adolf Mahr (Fig. 16.1). Her intention was to mount an exhibition of 1916 relics and souvenirs to coincide with the influx of visitors for the 31st International Eucharistic Congress in June of that year, and she requested space in the Kildare Street museum for the display. In a letter to the department dated 19 May 1932, the 1916 Club requested that the museum host the exhibition, and house the collection as the basis of a future Irish history collection which would encompass the eighteenth- and nineteenth-century uprisings.[3] This suggestion was later realised in the 1940s with the establishing of the Historical Collection and a series of history exhibitions curated by Hayes-McCoy.

The department wrote to Mahr to inform him of the Minister's approval of the proposal, and received a strong response from the director outlining his objections.[4] While in principle he was in favour of the concept of a history museum in Dublin, he was adamant that the National Museum should play no role, on a number of grounds: that what he terms 'a patriotic relic' is 'neither scientific nor artistic nor illustrating antiquity or industry', the

3   National Museum of Ireland archives (NMI), NMI/AI/098/006, '1916 Club exhibition and other EW loans'.
4   NMI/AI/098/006.

lack of space at the Kildare Street building, and financial concerns that he expressed in the following terms:

> if a settled policy of acquisition is adopted it means at least some expenditure as a good many objects of this particular kind belong to poor people who want compensation, and although the expenditure may be small it would mean another drain of our purchasing grant which is already far from being sufficient to provide for the normal wants of the Museum.[5]

On 4 May, Gifford-Donnelly responded to Mahr, assuring him that the museum would be put to no expense and staff would not need to undertake any work. The exhibition was installed in the museum, and remained there for over a year, proving to be remarkably popular with the public. While no detailed exhibition list survives, we know that the display incorporated weapons, including a Howth rifle and baton, 'relics' of the executed leaders, including Pearse's barrister wig and gown, and items significant in the action of the Rising, including the watch given by Nellie Gifford-Donnelly to Countess Markievicz and used by her to time the despatches from the Royal College of Surgeons during Easter Week.

In November 1933, the Department of Education wrote to Mahr informing him of the 1916 Club's offer of the artefacts for permanent display, and their intention to speak to the President on the matter.[6] Mahr again objected to the proposal on the grounds that the objects were of neither archaeological nor folk interest or value; but despite much debate on the future home of the artefacts they remained in the National Museum (for a full account of the dispute over the housing and curatorship of the Easter Week Collection, see Clare 2011, ch. 25). It should be noted there is no exhibition list for this first exhibition.

Due to her involvement in the nationalist movement from an early stage, and her personal connections with other participants, Gifford-Donnelly was ideally positioned to collect artefacts with a strong provenance relating to the Rising. For example, Christopher Brady, one of the printers of the 1916 Proclamation, gave her the brass shooter from the printing press from Liberty Hall for display; this object remains in the collections.[7] Though the Easter Week Collection remained with the National Museum and continued to grow there, Gifford-Donnelly was not to work on the collection after 1933.

---

5 NMI/AI/098/006.
6 The President referred to here is the President of the Executive Council, which at the time was Éamon de Valera.
7 National Museum of Ireland register (NMI), NMI/EW.114 (loan), acquired from Christopher Brady.

Collecting the objects of Independence

In the years following the 1932 Exhibition, the National Museum of Ireland began officially to collect objects relating to the Rising. In 1935, the museum established what is known as the 'Easter Week Collection' recording objects' entry with a separate set of register books. This was the first collection in the Art and Industry Division to be registered as an distinct entity (since the Division's establishment in the late nineteenth century all objects had been recorded in a set of general registers and, though curated as collections divided by material or type such as glass, textiles, coins and medals, separate registers for each of these collections did not come about until 1948). The Easter Week Collection, comprising materials and object types bound together only by their association with a historic event, was therefore the first thematic collection in the National Museum.

However, representation of the event in the museum did not come about solely through active and deliberate collecting by the National Museum of Ireland. For some years previously, members of the public had spontaneously passed in objects to the museum collections. An example includes an Óglaigh na hÉireann instruction sheet (Manual No. 4) on the handling of chemicals and explosives, found on the West Road, North Strand area of Dublin, on 30 July 1922, after the explosion at the Four Courts, and donated to the museum in 1926.[8] In 1931, a rusted rifle with '1916' cut into the butt, which had been dug from a ditch in Phibsborough, Dublin, was purchased and registered as possibly an Italian rifle, one of those landed at Howth in 1914.[9] Given that the Division's Arms and Armour collection primarily focused on collecting examples of manufacture, it is clear that this rifle was acquired as a representation of the Howth gunrunning.

Irish Volunteers tunic

One striking early acquisition was an Irish Volunteer tunic, donated to the National Museum of Ireland by Sir J.G. Putting in 1917.[10] The Irish Volunteers were formed in November 1913, but it was not until early 1914 that a uniform subcommittee was established to agree a pattern for the new national army. It commissioned the Murrogh Brothers at the Douglas Woollen Mills in Cork to manufacture the cloth, and eventually awarded a contract to the Limerick Clothing Factory of Lower Bridge Street, Dublin, for the provision of 300

8   NMI/HE/1926.108, acquired from F.J. Roland.
9   NMI/HE/1931.49, purchase.
10   NMI/HE/1917.109, acquired from Sir J.G. Putting.

uniforms made to the agreed design, with the idea that the Volunteers would purchase their uniforms through the committee.[11] However, the delay in finding a tailoring company to make the uniforms led Murrogh Brothers to dispose of some of the cloth commissioned by the committee to other traders who started making uniforms of various designs. Bulmer Hobson reported in August 1914 that only 150 orders for uniforms of the agreed pattern had been received by the committee,[12] as many Volunteers could not afford to purchase the official uniform, and others had uniform tunics made themselves, leading to a variety of tunic patterns.

The museum's tunic is of a grey-green cloth, with a rolled down collar and four pockets, the upper two being patch pockets with a box pleat. It is buttoned down the front with five brass buttons with the symbol of the Irish harp (though this example is without the I.V. lettering). Smaller versions of these buttons are also present on the patch pockets and the shoulder straps. The cuff facings and shoulder straps are dark blue (the colour of the facings was decided at regimental level and therefore varied). The sides of the back have two hooks to hold a leather belt in place, though this is not present. The tunic pattern matches that agreed by the Irish Volunteers uniform subcommittee in early 1914, making it a very early example of an Irish Volunteer uniform. The information recorded at the time of acquisition was that it was worn by an Irish Volunteer in Easter Week, 1916, and found afterwards in Jacob's Biscuit Factory, which had been occupied by the Volunteers.[13] The tunic's acquisition in 1917, one year after the insurrection, is a rare example of contemporary collecting by the National Museum, and it was possibly the first object relating to the 1916 Rising to enter a national collection.

Collecting: the first ten years

Table 16.1 shows the rate of acquisition of objects in the ten years following 1935, the first year of official collecting and the year of the first 1916 exhibition curated by the National Museum. It can be seen that the pattern of acquisition closely follows the National Museum's public activity on the history of the Rising, i.e. the act of exhibiting. The years 1935 and 1941 saw the greatest number of acquisitions per year, with a steady influx in

---

11 National Library of Ireland (NLI) NLI/MS/13174 (1), Bulmer Hobson Papers.
12 NLI/MS/13174 (1).
13 NMI/HE/1917.109, information received from Sir J.G. Putting at point of acquisition, and entered into register books.

Table 16.1   Rate of acquisition of museum objects by the National Museum of Ireland in the ten years following 1935

Year of collecting	Total	Gift	Loan	Purchase
1935 (first official year of collecting) 1916 Exhibition	943	760	182	1
1936	205	141	25	39 (2 transactions, including a collection of 38 watercolours by Countess Markievicz)
1937	383	215	152	16 (5 transactions)
1938	106	55	24	27 (4 transactions: 3 new acquisitions, and 24 objects previously loaned to the National Museum of Ireland now acquired by purchase)
1939	304	281	16	7 (4 transactions)
1940	332	301	16	15 (2 transactions)
1941 (Twenty-Fifth Anniversary Exhibition)	1,004	754	241	9 (1 transaction: the purchase of 9 objects previously loaned to the National Museum of Ireland now acquired by purchase)
1942	457	301	7	149 (4 transactions, including the Joseph Cashman collection of 144 photographs)
1943	178	174	3	1 (the purchase of an original 1916 Proclamation)
1944	179	149	2	28 (5 transactions)
1945	184	181	3	0

the intervening years of donations, loans and purchases.[14] Despite Mahr's assertion that objects relating to the revolutionary period of the early twentieth century would need to be purchased, only a small proportion of objects were paid for. The National Museum of Ireland's collection grew

14 The large influx of objects to the National Museum of Ireland in 1935 can be partly explained by the press appeal in January of that year (see Cooke, Chapter 18). In 1941, the *Irish Press* and various regional newspapers published articles announcing the opening of the Easter Week twenty-fifth anniversary exhibition on Easter Saturday, 12 April, which stimulated an influx of acquisitions.

primarily as a result of the interest and generosity of the public. As of early 2014, the Easter Week Collection stood at a total of 15,262 objects, with the collection continuing to grow. Of this total, 1,825 objects were purchased by the museum, just under 12 per cent, and a substantial proportion of this figure are purchases of large collections, or purchases of important objects from auction houses.

The experimental mortar, 1920

While it could be said that the building of the National Museum of Ireland's Easter Week Collection was as a result of outside influences and a strong public interest, the act of exhibiting by a museum can in itself stimulate donations. An example of this is the gift of the experimental mortar, or 'big gun', to the National Museum of Ireland by Padraig O Huigin and Seán Connell on 16 January 1937.[15] This fragment of metal tube, mounted on a trestle stand, is described as the only piece of artillery used during the War of Independence.[16] It was made by Peadar Clancy and Dick McKee of the Dublin Brigade IRA Headquarters staff. The *Irish Press* reported the story behind the mortar:

> It was tried out by Captain Mat Furlong of the Dublin Brigade at Lustown, Batterstown, Co. Meath. On the fifth shell being fired, it exploded and fatally wounded Captain Furlong. After the accident the gun was searched for by the Black and Tans, but it had been hidden in the River Tolka by Mr John Connell of Lustown. After some years, when Connell was released from Arbour Hill Prison, he recovered the mortar and was instrumental in having it deposited with the 1916 Collection in the National Museum of Ireland. With it were several of the hand-made shells used in the experiments, made of cast iron, fitted with a detonation cap, and that had a range of 185 yards.[17]

The mortar tells us some important details of the technical aspects of guerrilla warfare in Ireland during the revolutionary years: the difficulties encountered in obtaining arms equivalent to British armaments, the attempts to overcome those difficulties, the organisation and roles of

---

15   NMI/EWT.401, acquired from Padraig O Huigin and Seán Connell, 1937.
16   'An IRA big gun', *Irish Press*, 18 January 1937.
17   'An I.R.A. big gun'. For more information on this incident see Irish Military Archives, Bureau of Military History, MA/BMH/WS664. Witness: Patrick McHugh, Lieutenant IV, Dundalk, 1916; Officer (Munitions) IRA, Dublin, 1921.

different sections of the Irish Republican Army and the dangers faced by its members. It remains our only known example of an Irish 'big gun' from the period, and may have remained unknown if the owners had not been prompted by the National Museum of Ireland's exhibition to donate it to the museum.

The development of the Easter Week Collection

Since the establishment of the 'Relics of the fight for freedom' exhibition,[18] curated by the museum in April 1935, there has been a 1916 exhibition at the National Museum of Ireland, and the Easter Week Collection continued to be developed. It was not without problems, however. G.A. Hayes-McCoy (1970, 133) said of the process:

> This, particularly at the start, was as much a patriotic exercise as an ordinary piece of museum work. The collection of items thought suitable was hasty, the staff which was available to deal with such a sudden influx of material of varied kinds ... was inadequate, and exhibition space could be obtained only by withdrawing older material, yet in the end a worthwhile collection, a collection which is now part of Irish heritage, was assembled.

Having been acquired in the 1930s and 1940s (representing a fine example of contemporary collecting), this collection includes official documents issued by the Irish Volunteers and Irish Republican Army, contemporary publications and newsletters, three original 1916 Proclamations and a large collection of prisoner of war items. The collection, founded by Gifford-Donnelly, was developed by Liam Gogan, now back in the museum as Keeper of the Art and Industry Division. On 24 April 1936, the twentieth anniversary of the Rising, the Fianna Fáil government presented the Roll of Honour of 1916 to Gogan. This document consists of 46 pages, divided according to the original 1916 Rising garrisons, with 1,104 signatures of the then survivors, although there are omissions (Joye and Malone 2006).

Within the Easter Week Collection there is a wealth of largely paper-based items which relate specifically to the events of the week of the Rising, 24–30 April. The material includes the last letters of the 15 executed 1916 leaders and a set of ten death certificates for Thomas Clarke, Cornelius Colbert, Edmund Kent, Patrick Pearse, William Pearse, Michael O'Hanrahan, Edward Daly, Joseph Plunkett, John McDermott and John McBride, which give their cause

---

18 *Irish Press*, 'Relics of fight for freedom', 16 April 1935.

16.2   1916 Twenty-Fifth Anniversary Exhibition, National Museum of Ireland, 1941. Courtesy of the National Museum of Ireland

16.3   1916 Twenty-Fifth Anniversary Exhibition, National Museum of Ireland, 1941. Courtesy of the National Museum of Ireland

of death as 'shooting by order of Field General Court Martial'.[19] Among the material relating to Patrick Pearse is his last letter to his mother and his unconditional surrender of the republican forces to General Maxwell. On embossed Crown paper dated 29 April 1916, the surrender document reads:

> In order to prevent the further slaughter of unarmed people, and in the hope of saving the lives of our followers now surrounded and hopelessly outnumbered, the members of the Provisional Government present at Headquarters have agreed to an unconditional surrender, and the commanders of all units of the Republican forces will order their followers to lay down their arms.[20]

Also among the collection are over 600 rare photographs, including the important Cashman Collection. Joseph Cashman (1881–1969) was a photographer for the *Freeman's Journal* from 1912 to 1924, when the newspaper closed down. He recorded the Irish revolutionary period and clearly had a good relationship with all sides. From 1931 to 1942, he was in charge of the photographic department of the *Irish Press* and sold part of his collection to the National Museum in 1941. This collection forms an important visual record of the period.

It was G.A. Hayes McCoy (curator at the museum from 1939 to 1952) who was instrumental in creating the 1916 exhibition for the twenty-fifth anniversary of the Rising in 1941. For this, the existing 1916 exhibition was expanded and moved into the central gallery of the museum, normally the preserve of the Irish Antiquities Division, but was then returned to its original, less prominent room (Figs 16.2 and 16.3).[21]

In 1966, a new revamped exhibition entitled 'The Historical Exhibition Commemorative of the Rising of 1916' (Fig. 16.4) was curated by Oliver Snoddy, Assistant Keeper in the Art and Industry Division. A new addition to this exhibition was the Irish Republic flag recently returned from the Imperial War Museum in London. The topics covered in this exhibition were a very traditional treatment of Irish history and can broken down into two parts – a chronological history of the period from 1858 to 1921 and leading personalities of the 1916 period. Sighle Bhreathnach-Lynch has described this exhibition as 'markedly subdued in its approach, which may seem surprising in view of the triumphalist tone of that year's celebrations' (Bhreathnach-Lynch 2007, 248).

---

19 NMI/EW.796, acquired from Mícheál O'Dunlairge, 1938.
20 NMI/EW.848, acquired from Earl of Granard, (K.P.), 1938.
21 It should be noted there are no details about this exhibition or object list in the museum's archives except for a limited number of photographs.

16.4 1916 Exhibition, National Museum of Ireland, 1966.
Courtesy of the National Museum of Ireland

This exhibition was replaced on the seventy-fifth anniversary of the Rising in 1991 with the 'Road to Independence' exhibition, curated by Michael Kenny, an Assistant Keeper in the Art and Industry Division. The 1966 Exhibition had been taken down in 1988 as it was overcrowded and starting to show its age. The 'Road to Independence' made greater use of graphic panels and interactives. However, the museum was now under the remit of the Department of the Taoiseach and there was more civil service involvement, especially with the title – the original suggestions of 'Struggle for Independence' and 'Path to Independence' became 'Road to Independence', and the large number of weapons on display was questioned. There was further criticism of this exhibition, in particular that there was too much documentary material (Bhreathnach-Lynch 2007, 247). The component relating to the Rising was, fundamentally, the same as the 1966 exhibition, but it was significant as the first exhibition in which the First World War (1914–18) and the Irish Civil War (1922–3) were discussed.

In conclusion, the National Museum of Ireland began life as a nineteenth-century British museum and tried with some difficulty to adapt to the twentieth and twenty-first centuries, limited by funds and lack of staff but also by a lack of a unified and purposeful vision. In the 1930s, there was initial opposition to the Easter Week Collection from within the museum. This is an argument that happens in most museums between the connoisseur and those interested in telling a story. In the end, a permanent 1916 exhibition and the Historical Collections were created, but the focus was a simple narrative of the 1916 Rising and executed leaders. The complicated story of Irish men following nationalist politicians into the British Army was overlooked and the Irish Civil War not discussed until 1991. All the exhibitions from 1932 to 1966 suffered from the fact that they focused on one part of Irish history from 1848 to 1916, and not the period from the 1590s, or the economic or social history which would fully tell Ireland's history.

17

A story of absence and recovery: the Easter Rising in museums in Northern Ireland

Elizabeth Crooke

In Northern Ireland, the narrative of the 1916 Easter Rising is complicated by the different ways it can be interpreted: on the one hand, it can be valued as a republican insurrection, that is still unresolved; but, on the other, it can be regarded as an opportunistic rebellion when Irish soldiers were serving in the Great War.[1] The commemorative landscape in Northern Ireland puts the Rising firmly in the republican tradition – within this canon it was a period that was 'idolized' with its heroes 'sanctified' (Rolston 2010a, 287). Beyond this, efforts (or the lack of) to research, remember and represent the Rising have been shaped by its association with the Northern Ireland conflict (1968–98).[2] The commemoration in 1966, for instance, has been cited as a contributory factor to the outbreak of the Troubles (Higgins 2012) and, as evident in memorial plaques and murals, republican deaths during the conflict are frequently presented as a continuation of the 1916 sacrifices. A century later, with the 'decade of centenaries' upon us, and influenced by transition in a post-conflict Northern Ireland, we can look again at the purpose and nature of commemoration in the region.

This chapter is a consideration of the inclusion of artefacts and histories associated with the Rising in local and national museums in Northern Ireland. What is revealed is a story of absence, of the neglect of an event critical to the history of the island that, for much of the period since, was barely told in the local museums and scantly represented in the collections. That gap is now being slowly filled. There is evidence of a move towards the inclusion of the Rising in the region's museums, amongst the collections, within displays and as the basis of programming.

---

1 Despite presenting this dichotomy, I am aware that there is a multitude of attitudes to the Rising amongst both established and new communities in Northern Ireland.
2 See the CAIN (Conflict Archive on the Internet) website for a chronology of the conflict. http://cain.ulst.ac.uk/othelem/chron.htm. Accessed 7 February 2014.

Museums and the national narrative

The exhibition mounted by the National Museum of Ireland (Joye and Malone, Chapter 16; Cooke, Chapter 18) in 1966 to mark the fiftieth anniversary of the Rising had no equivalent north of the border – the Ulster Museum did not mount a special exhibition and the few other museums that existed were concerned with developing their archaeological and folk life collections. At the time, the Ulster Museum was a relatively new museum – it was established by the Museum Act 1961 (Northern Ireland), which transferred responsibility for the Belfast Museum and Art Gallery from Belfast Corporation to the Government of Northern Ireland.

A national museum has a particular purpose: it is a place of nation-building and an opportunity to establish a preferred historical master narrative. In 1966, the artefacts displayed in the National Museum of Ireland to evoke 1916 were those created to mark the event, such as memorials and new paintings, and authentic material of the period, for example relics and memorabilia. Monuments, commissioned in the early 1920s, were finally completed in time for the 1966 celebrations, and plaques were mounted at significant locations. In addition, Irish artists were encouraged to produce pieces in response to the Rising, later displayed in the Hugh Lane Municipal Gallery in Dublin (Bhreathnach-Lynch 1997; McCarthy 2012), and artworks in the National Gallery were interpreted to match the national sentiment (Higgins 2012, 171–2).

Carew (2013) provides a tantalising glimpse of the 'mock relics' that formed part of the historical collection in the National Museum. Included amongst them were a fan carried by Constance Markievicz, an 'unsightly umbrella' once owned by Patrick Pearse and baby shoes made by the widow of Thomas Clarke. By their association with the Rising, these artefacts would have a 'world of meaning' (Rochberg-Halton 1984, 346) in a newly formed state. Within the museums, in our homes, the objects we surround ourselves with are part of our life experience; they are 'inseparable from who we are' (Csikszentmihalyi and Rochberg-Halton 1981, 16). The life stories embedded in an umbrella, fan and shoes could be used to begin an understanding of the story of the rebirth of the Irish nation. As part of 'who we are' they became 'records of sacrifice, struggle and suffering in the cause of the Republic' (Carew 2013, 11).

By contrast, such exhibitions, art initiatives and collections had no place in the early decades of Northern Ireland; rather, museum plans, collections development and new exhibitions marked a distinct separation from the Irish Free State (and from 1949 the Republic of Ireland). The 'Farm and Factory' exhibition hosted outside Belfast as part of the Festival of Britain in 1951 presented the region as a willing participant in this British nation-building exercise (McBrinn n.d.; McIntosh 1999). A decade later, the Belfast Museum was finally recognised as the national museum and renamed the Ulster Museum – affirmation of the status of the region made more definite (Crooke 2000). Four years later, the Ulster Museum did not contribute to the 1966 commemorations of the Rising, which were taking place in the city and across Northern Ireland (O'Donnell 2006). The Rising was a history the Belfast museum did not comment on. It certainly would not have reflected the identity of the institution, which was firmly associated with a Unionist tradition – as observed by John Hewitt in his time working there up to the late 1950s (Ferguson and White 2013). While the museum was settling into its new status as a national institution, political tension was growing in the region. On the streets of Belfast the Campaign for Social Justice in Northern Ireland (begun in 1964) was bringing discrimination against Catholics to wider attention. Adding to the friction, the Ulster Volunteer Force was re-established in 1966 – apparently in anticipation of the fiftieth anniversary (Higgins 2012, 87). When the time came, the Northern Ireland Government tolerated the republican celebrations of the fiftieth anniversary. Counter-demonstrations were led by Ian Paisley (founder of the Democratic Unionist Party in 1971) in Belfast, including a 'thanksgiving service' to the defeat of the 1916 rebels, held in the Ulster Hall on 16 April 1966 (O'Callaghan and O'Donnell 2006, 206).

All the while, the Ulster Museum kept its distance from the story of 1916. A suggestion of change within the Ulster Museum, and the inclusion of a Rising-related artefact, came about in the mid-1980s with the purchase, from Sotheby's, of a Military Medal awarded to Miss Louisa Nolan at Buckingham Palace in 1917 for her part in helping British soldiers during the battle for Mount Street Bridge in 1916 (Fig. 17.1).[3] According to a curator who worked in the museum at the time, the Ulster Museum was the only institution in Ireland interested in bidding for it.[4] Nolan has no connections with Northern Ireland so what could her medal, and the story behind it, mean for Northern Ireland? If 1916 is to be represented in the Ulster Museum, what better story than that of a heroine who chanced gunfire to drag wounded (British) soldiers to safety? Nolan is described as passing 'calmly through a hail of bullets' to comfort soldiers (National Museums Northern Ireland, 2014). We can only speculate about her motive – possibly in empathy with the British soldiers, as only eight months earlier her brother had been killed on the Western Front (National Museums Northern Ireland, 2014). In Northern Ireland in the

---

3 A brief account can be found online, which is the extent of the museum's current knowledge of the medal. www.nmni.com/um/Collections/History/Militaria/Miss-Louisa-Nolan-s-Military-Medal. Accessed 4 February 2014.
4 R. Heslip (personal communication, April 2013).

17.1   Military medal awarded to Miss
Louisa Nolan for the part she played as a
civilian in helping British soldiers involved
in the Easter Rising, 1917.
Courtesy of National Museums Northern
Ireland

mid-1980s, with the Troubles at its height, the medal becomes a reminder of an earlier conflict. It can be interpreted as a celebration of the bravery of woman-folk, telling a story of someone willing to chance enemy fire. The medal can also be associated with the sacrifice of British soldiers, when their territory is under threat. Each of these aspects can be read as significant lessons suited to Northern Ireland in the 1980s. But, when displayed in the permanent modern history galleries *Plantation to power-sharing* (2009–14) at the Ulster Museum, no such links were made; instead, a label briefly documented the provenance of the medal and, in a gallery crowded with objects and text, it was passed with barely a glance by most visitors.

Across the rest of Northern Ireland, the majority of museums come under the remit of local government, such as Fermanagh County Museum, Down County Museum and Mid-Antrim Museums Service. These museums have barely anything in their collections to tell the story of the Rising; it could be said that the material culture is conspicious in its absence. The paucity of artefacts of the Easter Rising in museums of Northern Ireland can be explained by the factors mentioned so far. A crucial issue to understanding the current museum holdings is the fact that collections development in the region is relatively young. Armagh County Museum and Fermanagh County Museum were both founded in 1976, Down County Museum in 1981 and the Tower Museum in Derry in 1992. Only in the late 1990s did we see the formation of Causeway Museums Service and Mid-Antrim Museums Service. When these first museums were founded, archaeology and folk life material tended to be the chief focus. As the years went on, the contested histories of the early decades of the twentieth century were absent in the displays and object collections (Crooke 2001). In addition, links to significant political personalities were rarely made within the collections. In more recent years, although there is a trend for museums or heritage organisations to mark notable individuals, however tenuous the association, there is little in Antrim to mark the life of Roger Casement, the executed revolutionary, who was brought up by Protestant relatives in Galgorm Castle, County Antrim, and educated at Ballymena Academy – hardly befitting a person who was knighted for his work exposing human rights abuses in the Congo and Peru (Daly 2005) but no doubt a reflection of a man whose history was thought of as 'officially embarrassing and publicly discomforting' (Mitchell 2009, 253), as both a traitor to unionism and an uneasy fit in the canon of Irish nationalism.

Recovering the hidden histories

It was awareness of the lack of collections relating to the social and political context of the early twentieth century that prompted *Connection and division*, undertaken as a collaborative initiative between Fermanagh County Museum, Derry Museum Service and the Inniskillings Museum (a regimental museum) from 2009 to 2012.[5] The project's objective was to 'challenge preconceptions and highlight hidden histories' of the period. Focusing on Home Rule, the First World War, the Easter Rising, the War of Independence, Partition and the Irish Civil War the museums wanted to bring together collections that would fill gaps in provision and provide new perspectives.

One such artefact, bought by Fermanagh County Museum, was an early twentieth-century Christmas card that had been made and sold to raise funds for Sinn Féin (Figures 17.2a and 17.2b). The designer was George Irvine (1877–1954), a Protestant from Fermanagh who later became a prominent republican. Irvine was a member of the Irish Republican Brotherhood, and was sentenced to death for his role in the Easter Rising (later commuted). He is an example of the many 'Protestant rebels', who, according to historian Martin Maguire, regarded themselves as 'neither traitor, not fools, nor mad

---

5   The project was funded by the Heritage Lottery Fund *Collecting Cultures* initiative
    with the purpose to expand museum collecting.

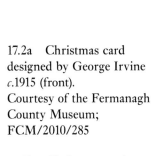

17.2a   Christmas card designed by George Irvine *c.*1915 (front).
Courtesy of the Fermanagh County Museum; FCM/2010/285

17.2b   Christmas card designed by George Irvine *c.*1915 (back).
Courtesy of the Fermanagh County Museum; FCM/2010/285

They rose to guard their fatherland—
In stern resolve they rose,
In bearing firm, in purpose grand,
They met their country's foes.

Ꙅꙅ

Ꙅo ꝺꞇuꞡꙇꝺ Ꝺꙇꙁ
ꞑoꝺꙇꙁꙅ ꞅꙇꙇꞇ Ꝺuꞇ.

(May God give you a Happy Christmas.)

POST CARD.

THIS SPACE MAY BE USED FOR PRINTED OR WRITTEN MATTER.

THE ADDRESS ONLY TO BE WRITTEN HERE.

POWELL PRESS, DUBLIN.

"Let Erin remember" series, designed and published by G. Irvine.

but as politically active citizens' (Maguire 2008–9, 164). Along with his brother William, George was educated in Portora Royal School, Enniskillen, and Trinity College Dublin. George Irvine joined the Gaelic League in 1905 and later formed the Church of Ireland Gaelic Society. He joined the IRB in 1907 and was known to go to church wearing his Irish Volunteer uniform (Brand 2009). Fermanagh-based historian Gordon Brand describes Irvine's involvement in the Rising to be 'a baptism of fire, but short lived' (Brand 2009, 20). Involved in a gun attack at Rialto Gate, when overwhelmed by British fire Irvine called out 'Don't shoot! Don't shoot! We surrender' (Brand 2009, 22).

While George Irvine was active in republican politics in Dublin, his brother William was serving in the Great War with the Royal Inniskillings Fusiliers and Dublin Fusiliers. This difference in familial allegiances did not pass by William Copeland Trimble, editor of a Fermanagh newspaper, who was scathing of George Irvine's politics. Writing in the *Impartial Reporter* in 1917, Trimble described William Irvine as 'loyally serving his country' and George Irvine as 'one of those traitors who tried to stab our army in the back while fighting in France'. Trimble went on to tell his readers 'O for a battalion or two of the 16th Irish Division to deal with these traitors in Ireland, for the Irish soldiers make no secret of what they would do to those who not only deserted them but assisted the enemy' (Fermanagh County Museum 2012). Trimble's opinion, written in the local newspaper, was included in a short article that described a Gaelic Feis and Sinn Féin demonstration that had recently taken place in Enniskillen, at which George Irvine spoke. A well-known Unionist, Trimble was critical of those in Dublin who took the opportunity to rebel at the time of the war in Europe – possibly made all the more bitter because he had lost his son in the Battle of the Somme.

Similar condemnation of the Irish rebels was expressed elsewhere. Stephen Gwynn, a Nationalist MP who served in the war with the Connaught Rangers, wrote that fellow men felt they had been 'stabbed in the back' by those who had taken part in the Rising (Jeffery 2000, 54). The opinion voiced by Trimble, and the story of George and William Irvine, go some way to demonstrating the challenges at the root of the commemoration of the Rising in Northern Ireland. Falling during the same period, the events have long been seen as 'belonging' to different political traditions, and one contrary to the other. Graff-McRae refers to the Somme and the Rising as 'irreconcilable myths' (2010, 85): for Protestants the Somme is a reminder of the 'bravery and loyalty' of Ulstermen and for nationalists the Rising is a story of 'martyrdom, sacrifice and redemption' (2010, 85–6). Faced with these two critical events in British and Irish history, contemporary commemoration becomes a complex marking of religious, political and national difference and 'an explicit barrier, used to divide and exclude' (Jarman 1999, 180).

The introduction of the Sinn Féin postcard into the Fermanagh County

Museum collection may seem minor, but it signified the changing ambitions of the local museum services in the region. The *Connection and division* project, which funded the purchase of the card, and many other items reflecting the period's 'hidden histories', marked willingness amongst the three museums involved in this project to engage with non-traditional stories to challenge perceptions of the period. During the *Connection and division* exhibition (30 March–30 June 2012), which was spread between the neighbouring Fermanagh County Museum and Inniskillings Museum (and also displayed at the Tower Museum Derry), the contrary histories of the regiments and the Rising became more apparent with new stories emerging. For the first time, the Inniskillings museum volunteers became aware that members of the regiment took part in the Ulster Composite Battalion during the Rising.[6] Since the exhibition, both the Sinn Féin postcard and the extract from the *Impartial Reporter* were used in a learning pack produced as a legacy of the project. Working through the packs, young adults in local schools were encouraged to reflect on 'political views [that] appear unexpected given their political background' (Fermanagh County Museum 2012). *Connection and division* demonstrated the willingness of those working in museums to engage with artefacts that reveal the complexity of Northern Ireland's political history and challenged the 'two-traditions' model that is such a common interpretation. Simply by purchasing new items for their collections the museums could add 'critical mass' to their existing holdings. With a greater number of items from this period, an opportunity was provided to explore new stories. The agency and impact of individual items, now in a larger collection, were enhanced.

Conclusion: shared histories

The Rising and the Great War are crucial events marked by the 'decade of centenaries' (2012–22). In Northern Ireland, the official narrative of the commemorations is underpinned with the notions of 'reflection, inclusivity, tolerance, respect, responsibility and interdependence' (Northern Ireland Executive 2012a). In the context of the continuing peace negotiations in Northern Ireland, the commemorations are a means for politicians and agencies across the region to reinstate their commitment to the various 'good relations' or 'shared futures' strategies of recent years. Coverage of Junior Minister Jennifer McCann speaking at the launch of *Shared histories*, an exhibition marking the decade of centenaries at Belfast City Hall in August

---

6 I am indebted to Mark Scott for this detail (email correspondence, 26 April 2013). A brief outline of the exhibition is available. www.inniskillingsmuseum.com/connection-and-division-exhibition. Accessed 4 February 2014.

2012, emphasised this very aspect. She described this commemorative period as 'an historic opportunity to revisit the past, to understand where we have come from, and to come to a shared understanding about where we wish to go to in the future' (Northern Ireland Executive 2012b). Such objectives were also embedded in projects emerging from the museum sector. This was demonstrated by projects marking the period within Northern Ireland museums, such as *On the brink: the politics of conflict 1914–1916* at Mid-Antrim Museums Service and, in Down County Museum, *Transformations: politics and protest in County Down 1900–1920*. Both of these community projects were made possible by external funding, and in their rationales were closely tied to the good relations agenda.[7]

Although the period is underrepresented in Northern Ireland's museum collections, changing museum practice, focused upon a more inventive story-based approach, encourages curators to build upon community knowledge to tell a local story. The sanctified position of the object within a museum collection is under debate (Alberti 2005; Conn 2009); while this is ongoing, it is certain that the role of material culture within museums has evolved. Museums are now concerned with life stories, which can be told with or without the artefact. This approach builds upon the community-based museum practice that works in partnership with the wealth of knowledge and skills outside the museum (Crooke 2007). More often the method is now one of co-production and co-curation, when community groups have an active and engaged role in producing programmes and exhibitions. In such cases the museum (and the initiatives it enables) becomes an opportunity and a venue for that collaborative process. This shift is fundamental to our understanding of the current role of material culture of the Rising in Northern Ireland's museums – the existence of collections, and the importance of individual items, is not the key rationale for new initiatives. Instead, the driving force is a purposeful remembering undertaken with communities. In Northern Ireland, with contemporary concerns in mind, the potential of remembering 1916 lies in the re-imagining of objects and past events, reinterpreted for a 'shared future'.

Acknowledgment

I am indebted to those working in Northern Ireland's museums for their generosity in sharing information about their projects.

---

7 *On the brink* is funded by the Heritage Lottery and *Transformations* through funding from the European Union's PEACE III Programme. J. Clarke (personal communication, 2014); L. McKenna (personal communication, 2014).

18

History, materiality and the myth of 1916

Pat Cooke

The period lying between the outbreak of the Northern 'Troubles' in 1969 and the Good Friday Agreement of 1998 can be summarised as one of intense ideological 'Revisionism', revolving around interpretations of modern Irish republicanism and nationalism and the events that comprised it. As part of that debate, historians engaged in sometimes fierce polemics about the meaning of the 1916 Rising. But while the controversy surrounding the Rising's interpretation had made it probably the most 'revised' subject in modern Irish history, it remained one of the most under-researched in terms of actual scholarship.

However, more recently there has been a transformation in the approach to the subject. In the more temperate intellectual climate that set in following the 1998 Agreement, not only has significant original research emerged, but the growth of interdisciplinary and material culture studies as legitimate fields of academic enquiry has added an unprecedented depth and richness to our understanding of the event. This shift was presaged by a wider intellectual challenge to the text-based complacency of liberal historiography. Most notably, Raphael Samuel questioned the supercilious attitude of academic historians to the growing heritage phenomenon, accusing them of suspecting the visual while indulging in 'fetishisation of archives' (Samuel 1994, 268). There is reason to hope, therefore, that the scholarly contribution to the centenary commemoration will offer in place of revision*ism* a revised understanding of the event, deriving primarily from interdisciplinary syntheses of literary-historical and material culture perspectives.

Yet, the authentically literary nature of the event poses significant challenges for those wishing to revise how it is understood in the light of material evidence. No fewer than four of the 1916 Proclamation's seven signatories were writers, so it was perhaps inevitable that their prose, poetry

18.1a   Commemorative
match-box holder
with a photograph
in elliptical frame on
either side, this side
Thomas MacDonagh.
Courtesy of the
National Museum of
Ireland; NMI/EW/5616

and dramatic writings would transform the Rising by what Declan Kiberd calls 'remorseless textualisation' into an 'instantaneous martyr to literature' (Kiberd 1995, 213). A recent study observes that the Rising's literary imprint led to it being persistently analysed 'as if it were a text to be read rather than a failed insurrection during which over four hundred people died' (Higgins 2012, 5). While this acknowledges the mythologising process as an essentially textual matter, it suggests that delving into the stubborn material reality of what happened can reveal the disenchanted, counter-textual actuality of what occurred. However, the discussion following will suggest that the relation between the textual and the material traces of the Rising are interwoven in ways that are not so simply unravelled, and that curating nationalist history, of which the Rising is but one facet, raises many formidable questions, particularly in relation to the role of aesthetics in historical interpretation.

The first layer of complexity arises from the ways in which word, image and object can be inscribed within a single semiological process. In what was already the age of mechanical reproduction, the words and last words of the patriot dead were combined with their reproducible images to convey the meaning of the event. In the immediate wake of the Rising, the monthly *Catholic Bulletin* provided some of the first emotionally charged biographies of the Rising's leading protagonists. The December issue devoted a full page to a montage of portraits of the wives and loved-ones of the leaders (see Fitzpatrick, Chapter 7). This was only nineteen years after the mass-printing

18.1b Commemorative match-box holder with a photograph in elliptical frame on either side, this side Joseph Mary Plunkett. Courtesy of the National Museum of Ireland; NMI/EW/5616

of photographs had become possible.[1] Print technology allowed memorial cards of the leaders to be circulated as intimate mementoes that could be secreted in wallet or handbag. Their photographic likenesses were even reproduced on badges and other bijouterie. A fine example is the matchbox holder featuring the images of MacDonagh and Plunkett on opposite sides (Figs. 18.1a and 18.1b). It was now possible to broadcast the images of heroes through the everyday and the disposable without, apparently, trivialising their mythic import.

That word and image could work so powerfully together to shape the image of 1916 as a mass-mediated event testifies to the modernity of the moment. But the historical significance of a hat, a shoe, a discarded gaol biscuit, even a flag, uniform or rifle, could not be made to serve the process of communal myth-making quite so immediately. The transformation into public icons of a whole miscellany of totemic, quirky, idiosyncratic things claiming an authentic link to the people and events of the Easter Rising would take more time. The institutionalisation of such objects in museum collections did not begin to happen until twenty years after the event itself.

There are two main reasons why the process of creating public memory from the relics of Easter Week took more time. First, because the Rising was a revolt against the prevailing government, keeping or collecting objects

---

1 It was only possible to reproduce photographs on printing presses running at full speed from 1897.

18.2   Toffee axe from Sackville Street sweet shop, reputedly thrown by a looter during the 1916 Rising.
Courtesy of the National Museum of Ireland; NMI/EW/5699

associated with it belonged (initially and in some cases illicitly) to the personal and private domain. Most of the 1916 objects now in public collections started out as items of personal and familial memory. They were preserved from loss and destruction by being hoarded as keepsakes and souvenirs. As Susan Pearce so eloquently writes of souvenirs, 'they make public events private, and move history into the personal sphere, giving each person a purchase on what would otherwise be impersonal and bewildering experiences' (Pearce 1994, 196). 'Bewildering' is an important word that reflects the vertiginous flow of events leading to the 1916 Rising and culminating in sixteen executions. One of the most moving things about the last letters of some of those executed is their painfully bewildered sense of having to say goodbye to wives and families in the face of events that had unravelled so rapidly. With only hours left before being shot, most of these men had to reconcile themselves to the personal implications of their public sacrifice. As they wrote their last letters, some of them added poignant keepsakes for loved-ones along with them. James Connolly enclosed a lock of hair, Michael O'Hanrahan a button from his Volunteer uniform.

But things were also grabbed, picked up and pocketed by history's lesser players, who may not at the time have attributed much importance to them. Take, for example, the axe used for breaking toffee in a Sackville Street sweet shop (Fig. 18.2). It was reputedly thrown by a looter at a Mr Daly, whose son donated it to the museum in 1980. This one object might serve as a perfect prop for O'Casey's *The Plough and the Stars*, a metonym for all the things looted by the poor of Dublin when the fighting broke out on Easter Monday, things guiltily secreted at the time, only for the pilferer, or a relative, to realise their true significance later. This is not the kind of thing that immediately springs to mind as fitting into the more conventional narrative of the Rising. The objects that end up privately representing historical events are the products of innumerable individual acts of hoarding and meaning-making. Their sheer promiscuity and variety make them resistant to being woven too readily into history's grand narrative. Another quirky example is the cricket bat that stood in the window of Elvery's sport shop on Sackville Street. It was presented to the National Museum in 1981 by a member of the Elvery family, with a rifle bullet fired during Easter Week still lodged in it. It is notable that both these objects took almost the same time (sixty odd years) to find a place in to the national collection of 1916 material.

The second reason it took time for such material to emerge in public collections was that the museum had to become the kind of place that both sanctioned their collection and inspired a patriotic spirit of donation. The Dublin Museum of Science and Art, Ireland's nascent National Museum, was not in 1916, or for many years after, that kind of place for Irish nationalists. Since its opening in 1890, the museum had to all intents been a unionist and imperial institution. Nevertheless, when the moderate Home Rule nationalist George Noble Count Plunkett became director in 1907, it seemed to signal a tilt in the direction of moderate nationalism. In that year's annual report, Plunkett referred to the museum as the 'National Museum of Science and Art'. But if his main goal was to make the Dublin museum the 'Museum of Ireland', he was still, as late as 1914, following sound Home Rule logic by seeking to enhance it 'as much as possible from the resources of the empire'. To this end, he had set up a system of exchange with colonial museums.[2] Sadly, the involvement and subsequent execution of his son Joseph in the Rising cost Plunkett his job. It is hard not to wonder how different might the fate of the National Museum have been had the father of one of the 1916 leaders been allowed to keep his post during the following tumultuous years. As it transpired, the museum remained without a full-time director until Adolf Mahr was appointed in 1934.

An effort to transform the National Museum into a place that might better conform to the self-image of an independent nation began in 1927 when a special committee was appointed by the Minister for Education, Professor J.M. O'Sullivan. Among the committee's recommendations was a proposal to set up one – and only one – new collection category: a division

2 *Irish Times*, 11 April 1914.

dedicated to Irish folklife. Remarkably, the committee had nothing at all to say about a role for the National Museum in building a collection dealing with the struggle for national independence. When the museum finally began to collect such material in earnest it was parked, somewhat anomalously, in the Art and Industry Division.

This was perhaps a missed opportunity. Nationalists continued to view the National Museum and indeed all of the national institutions with suspicion. Writing in 1936, *Ireland Today's* art critic, John Dowling, thought all of the national institutions tainted, describing them as 'potential enemies … as alien now as the day we inherited them' (Dowling 1936, 64).

But change was afoot. 'What a change has been brought about in the National Museum since the last of the State Carriages was trundled out of the hall to its deserved obscurity in a Dublin Castle lumber room' the *Irish Press* reported with approval in 1937, 'and since imperial war medals and uniforms disappeared from the Central Court'.[3] In tandem with this clear-out, the museum staged a temporary exhibition on the period of the War of Independence in 1935 and embarked on a campaign to build a permanent collection of such material (for details of an earlier exhibition in 1932, see Joye and Malone, Chapter 16). A notice in the *Irish Independent* in 1935 stated that the museum was putting together 'a collection of relics dealing with the struggle for National Independence during 1915–22' and would be glad to hear from anybody willing to lend or donate items for that purpose.[4] The initiative was probably motivated by a looming sense of the twenty-fifth anniversary of the Rising in 1941. Éamon de Valera, leader of the government since 1932 and the only surviving leader of a 1916 garrison, played a discreet and influential part in the project. An examination of the initial items donated to the collection reveals that he not only presented material of his own but used his personal influence to encourage others to do likewise. When the exhibition was formally opened on Easter Saturday 1941, Keeper Liam Gogan acknowledged de Valera's generosity in donating some important items to it.[5]

A military historian of distinction, Dr Gerard Hayes-McCoy, curated the 1941 exhibition, ensuring that it would be framed largely as a military narrative. From the outset, the presence of guns, ordnance, uniforms, bullet- and shell-damaged objects became central to the material representation of the Easter Rising. However, this first effort to orchestrate these objects into an exhibition revealed a deeper dependence upon the prevailing textual understanding of the event.

---

3   'Our Irish folklore', *Irish Press*, 27 May 1937.
4   'Relics of national struggle', *Irish Independent*, 9 January 1935.
5   'Taoiseach's souvenirs of 1916', *Irish Press*, 15 April 1941.

The extent to which the Rising's meaning came to be centred upon Patrick Pearse's writings, and visually crystallised in his photographic profile, cannot be overstated. His image was given a pivotal role in the *mise-en-scène* of the 1941 exhibition. An *Irish Independent* report melodramatically recounted how at the heart of the museum's central court 'on a towering vast base, a triumphant catafalque in white surrounded by a mass of palms and green at its base, stands Oliver Sheppard's noble bust of Patrick Pearse'.[6] An account of the exhibition by David Hogan in the *Irish Press* concluded pharaonically, 'and over it all looking to the East is the bust of Pearse'.[7] The pre-established orchestration of the Easter Rising around Pearse's writings provided a cue for how a heterogeneous range of objects associated with the event could visually be organised, with centripetal force, around his image.

Less obviously and more subliminally, the 1916 exhibition added a wholly new dimension to the museum's language of display. The demotic everydayness of much of the contents found an echo in the contemporary lives of its audience, powerfully reinforcing a sense of identification with the lost leaders of 1916. Connolly's fedora hat, for example, would still have been a fashionable item in the early 1940s, an era when no adult male went abroad without a cap or a hat on his head. Despite being constrained by the textualised narrative that informed their arrangement, much of the exhibition's contents could act as cues for personal responses, and appeal directly to the living memory of anybody over thirty years of age, prompting that more intimate question that momentous historic events give rise to: 'where was I on Easter Monday 1916?'

The 1941 exhibition represented the museum's first effort to embrace a popular culture of nationalist sentiment. Moreover, given that the Easter Rising was overwhelmingly a Dublin event, and that the War of Independence was fought substantially in urban contexts, the exhibition was also subliminally about the Irish experience of modernity. It contained fully functional arms still in contemporary use, photographs of people caught in the informal and casual poses enabled by the mass availability of the box-brownie camera, hats and flat caps, cheques drawn on the Munster and Leinster Bank, Christmas cards and postcards, pocket and wrist watches, wire-rimmed spectacles, a typewriter. For almost all of the twentieth century, the nationalist collection in the National Museum was perhaps the only place where everyday objects reflecting modern Irish social experience could find a home, however inadvertently. The museum instantly realised it had a popular hit on its hands. An unprecedented 9,000 visitors saw the

6 'National memorial', *Irish Independent*, 12 April 1941.
7 'Hall of friendly ghosts', *Irish Press*, 14 May 1941.

exhibition on Easter Monday 1941 – the biggest number for a single day in its history.[8]

Yet this development sat uncomfortably within the museum's institutional history. The very populism of the exhibition was not entirely to the taste of those who remained devoted to the museum's founding values as a Victorian institution dedicated to the improvement of public taste. These values were fundamentally aesthetic and scientific and underpinned the museum's divisional structures of Archaeology, Art and Industry and Natural History. The most prominent critic of the departure represented by the new exhibition was Thomas Bodkin, who had been a member of the 1927 committee that reviewed the museum, and director of the National Gallery from 1927 to 1935. In his *Report on the arts in Ireland*, Bodkin vented his distaste for the 1916 room in the National Museum. He described it as 'a tendentious collection', filled largely with objects that were 'trivial or ridiculous and owe their inclusion to misconceived sentimentality'. Such a display should not, he thought, be allowed to 'distort our historical perspective', and needed badly to be 'weeded' (Bodkin 1949, 12).

Bodkin's aesthetic predilections remained consistent with the collecting logic of the Art and Industry Division: he asserted that exhibitions of the modern period should consist of things chosen for their artistic or craft value. His mindset, however, was fairly typical of museum curators of his day, one that betrayed a reflexive distaste for the promiscuous display of relics and souvenirs whose primary value lay in their emotive appeal.

Efforts to construct a version of 1916 from its material remains worked both to reinforce and to subvert the dominant literary narrative. At the macro level, the centring of the exhibition (in the central hall) upon Pearse's iconic image signalled the didactic curatorial intent. But the capacity of individual objects to command the gaze of the visitor, to act as 'triggers of chains of ideas and images' (Jordanova 1989, 23), to set off a miscellany of personal memories and associations, worked against this schematic purpose. Contemporary museum educationists recognise the ways in which personal interests underpin and determine the particular set of memories that each individual takes away from the museum experience (Falk and Dierking 2013, 206–7). These interests are existential. Huyssen in *Twilight memories* insists that 'the temporal status of any act of memory is always the present' and not as some 'naïve epistemology' would have it, the past (Huyssen 1995, 2). It is 'the live gaze that endows the object with its aura' (Huyssen 1995, 31). Try as Hayes-McCoy and others might to determine curatorially the didactic terms on which the exhibition narrative might be publicly or

---

8 'Thousands see 1916 exhibition', *Irish Independent*, 19 April 1941; '1916 Exhibition draws record attendance', *Irish Press*, 19 April 1941.

communally assimilated, the ideological purport of exhibitions is at least in part susceptible to subversion by the power of its individual components to command a personal response in the viewer.

Yet, in a broader temporal context, exhibitions can take on a monumental quality through the inertia of 'permanence', as the subsequent fate of the 1941 exhibition shows. Soon after the initial excitement subsided, the exhibition was moved from the central court to a room on the east side of the building, where it was to remain for over 50 years. The 1966 exhibition (fiftieth anniversary) had substantially the same content as the 1941 exhibition, expanded to include some new acquisitions. The 1991 display (seventy-fifth anniversary) showed little change from the one that had stood there since 1966.[9] While a wave of revisionism engulfed Irish historical debate in the 1990s, the National Museum's exhibition languished unaltered in a room that had come to be commonly referred to, with memorial fixity, as 'the 1916 room' (see also Joye and Malone, Chapter 16).

Material absences

So far, the discussion has revolved around what was collected, chosen and exhibited in the National Museum's construction of a narrative of 1916 through material culture. But, in the material constitution of historical narrative, absences, gaps in collections and the ways in which the spatial deployment of selected objects and images in public display can ignore or elide potentially dissonant readings of the same phenomena require a more conscious effort of retrieval. In this section, the implications of such absences for the narrative of Irish nationalism will be examined in the context of Kilmainham Gaol, a site that not only carried its own direct associations to key events in the history of Irish nationalism and republicanism, but also housed a museum collection on that theme that rivalled the National Museum's in scope and content.

The original visitor's booklet to the gaol produced in the early 1960s stated that 'the fabric itself is a museum piece, a document in stone illustrating the social conscience of the eighteenth and nineteenth centuries' (Kilmainham Gaol Restoration Society 1961). This suggested that the gaol was an object that would receive special attention in the interpretation of the

---

9 A state-of-the-art video wall, telling the story of the 1916 Rising, which the author had produced for an exhibition arranged around the Cuchulainn statue in the General Post Office for the seventy-fifth anniversary of the Rising in 1991, was later relocated to become part of the 1916 exhibition in the National Museum, where it remained for a number of years.

site to the public. But this is not what happened. When the gaol opened as a shrine to Irish nationalism in 1960, its interpretation was organised around those heroic personalities associated with the struggle for Irish political freedom that spanned the 125 years between the gaol's opening in 1796 and the ending of the War of Independence in 1921. As they were led around the building, visitors had pointed out to them the places associated with the leading patriotic figures imprisoned in Kilmainham: Robert Emmet's cell, Anne Devlin's 'dungeon' cell, the yard where five of the Invincibles were hanged, the cells where the 1916 leaders were held. The tour culminated, as it does today, in the execution yard, where fourteen men were shot in the early days of May 1916. The exhibition that opened at Easter 1966 in the gaol's east wing mirrored and corroborated this narrative. Together, the guided tour and exhibition dovetailed into a single, cohesive narrative, describing an ultimately triumphant struggle for national independence.

And yet, despite the unquestionable authenticity of the museum's contents and the historical accuracy of the associations between people and locations on the course of the tour, they amounted to a story of Kilmainham Gaol that was selective and prescriptive. When I became director of the gaol in 1986, it was clear that there was a gaping lacuna in the story then being told: there was hardly a single reference to the place's long history as the County of Dublin Gaol, a place in which thousands of men, women and children were imprisoned for over a century from the time it opened in 1796.

How to explain this? In Richard Slotkin's interpretation of the myth of the American West, the idea of it as a 'fatal environment' (the phrase comes from a poem of Walt Whitman's to describe the circumstances of Custer's 'last stand') is central to all mythologising processes:

> An environment, a landscape, a historical sequence is infused with meaning in the form of a story, which converts landscape to symbol and temporal sequence into 'doom' – a fable of necessary and fated actions. (Slotkin 1998, 11)

Kilmainham's architecture provided a sublime backdrop, an analogously 'fateful environment' for a patriotic story of bondage and sacrifice, culminating in national liberation. The extent to which a poeticised image of the fettered patriot had become a trope of the nationalist imagination (a central image, for example, in the song that became all but a national anthem, 'A nation once again') was crystallised in President de Valera's speech at the opening of the 1966 exhibition. He referred to 'this old dungeon fortress' in which there had been 'so much suffering and courage so that Ireland should be a nation not only free but worthy of its great

18.3   East wing of
Kilmainham Gaol.
Courtesy of the Office
of Public Works

past'.[10] Yet, the east wing of the gaol in which he delivered these words represented an especially fine example of Victorian prison architecture (Fig. 18.3). Completed in 1866, it was thirteen years younger than the city's main and still active prison, Mountjoy Jail. But the teleology of heroic patriotism demanded an image of incarceration purified of any association with common criminality. And so the trope of 'this old dungeon fortress' worked to elide the potential dissonance between nationalist narrative and architectural history.

In *The construction of heritage* (Brett 1991), the first major critical study of the contemporary heritage phenomenon in Ireland, David Brett alerted us to the way a building moulds our response to the heritage experience it contains. 'Our encounter with objects from the past is mediated by the

10   *Irish Press*, 11 April 1966.

circumstances in which we meet them,' he wrote. His term to describe this process is 'narrative topology', which he defines as 'the arrangement of spaces and the connections between them such that they set up, suggest or assert relationships between whatever is displayed in those spaces' (1991, 91). The problem he identified with heritage was a tendency to achieve its effects through the spatial aestheticisation of history. He thought the only effective antidote was by 'the exercise of critical method', as 'only scholarly narrative admits of this level of self-conscious fashioning, it is there that historical narrative achieves its maximum coherence and integration, or "truth"' (Brett 1991, 6).

But it is doubtful whether historical scholarship has the power so effectively to disenchant when dealing with the material and spatial dimensions of historic experience. As visual modes of communication, exhibitions can never fully escape the spatial, optical and inherently theatrical qualities of the *mise-en-scène*. And, as already suggested, museum objects are not entirely amenable to critical rationality. Samuel makes the superb point that we do not have a way of putting quotation marks (metaphorically speaking) around old photographs. They retain a power to seduce and charm us into reverie, so that we are constantly at the mercy of what he calls the 'optical unconscious' (Samuel 1994, 339–40). James Clifford has written about the fetishistic power of objects to 'fixate rather than simply … to edify or inform' (Clifford 1994, 266), and Jim McGuigan has criticised overly rational notions of the public sphere predicated on 'an excessively cognitive and rationalistic conception of the citizen', a disposition that leads to the denigration of affect and emotionality as inherent qualities of the cultural experience (McGuigan 2010, 25). Anthropologist Daniel Miller insists on a poetics of material culture. In *The comfort of things* he writes that 'objects store and possess, take in and breathe out the emotions with which they have been associated' (Miller 2008, 38).

In Kilmainham Gaol, evolving curatorial practice suggested that confronting the material contexts and contents of myth required more, not less, aesthetics, given the experiential essence of the material cultural experience. As Edward Casey, summarising Merleu-Ponty, writes, 'the world of places is densely sedimented in its familiarity and historicity and its very materiality, while, at the same time, it is animated and reanimated by the presence of the lived body in its midst' (Casey 1998, 241). Throughout the 1990s, the involvement of artists and arts practice in visual, operatic and theatrical forms became the major modes by which Kilmainham's difficult history was opened up to interrogation and exploration. Among the highpoints were a staging of Beckett's play 'Catastrophe' in 1999, dedicated in 1968 to Vaclav Havel when he was a prisoner of conscience, a performance of 'The Emperor of Atlantis' in 2002, an opera written by two Jewish inmates of Teresienstadt concentration camp, and a major art exhibition 'In a state' in 2001, in which twenty-one leading Irish visual artists, from North and South and from Catholic and Protestant backgrounds, were invited to make work evoked by the history and symbolism of Kilmainham Gaol (Cooke 2013).

The presence and performance of artworks became a prime means of exploring contested meanings, of introducing dissonance and ambivalence into the interrogation of settled narrative structures, of disrupting the elision of space, objects and experience in the over-determined and ultimately reductive trope of the 'dungeon fortress'. James Joyce declaimed in *A portrait of the artist as a young man*: 'When the soul of a man is born in this country there are nets flung at it to hold it back from flight. You talk to me of nationality, language, religion. I shall try to fly by those nets' (Joyce 1960, 203). The image is one of flight and escape from an imprisoning nationality, and the means of Stephen's escape is an artistic disposition that embraces nuance, ambivalence, irony – all tactics that were to become central features of arts practice in the modern period, and even more so in the period of postmodernity.

But this was not to abandon the role of critical historical method in favour of an entirely aesthetic approach. New research into the prison records and registers in the National Archives revealed an epic story of the common life of Dublin's poor in the nineteenth century. Kilmainham, it transpired, was the main transportation depot for convicts along the length of the east of Ireland, bound for Australia. Over 7,000 of them passed through the gaol before transportation ceased in the 1850s. More poignantly still, the number of men, women and children incarcerated in the gaol in the late 1840s shot up from an average of some 600 a year to over 9,000. Desperately hungry, they sought arrest and imprisonment for the life-saving fare it offered at the height of the Great Famine. Meanwhile, Sinéad McCoole worked to recuperate an all but invisible dimension of the nationalist narrative itself – the role of women in the struggle for independence, culminating in an exhibition and book, both entitled *Guns and chiffon* (McCoole 1997). In the new exhibition of the gaol's history that opened in a dedicated building in 1996, the ground floor was dedicated to the common prisoners' history, contextualised as a story of penal punishment and reform and prison architecture. The more orthodox nationalist tale on the floor above was revised to include the story of women patriots, which had hitherto been largely invisible.

Conclusion

This brief survey has used the 1916 Rising as a case study to explore the complex relation between traditional historical method and material cultural practices in an effort to open up the settled narrative and mythical tropes of nationalism to fresh interpretation and revision. From a curatorial perspective, these goals cannot be adequately served by subordinating objects in space to the putatively transcendent process of critical historical analysis. Curatorial practice must also acknowledge the experiential and epistemological validity of the visual, aesthetic and affective qualities of historic artefacts as encountered by those moving through – and moved by – the topology of place and space.

19

Place versus memory:
forgetting Ireland's sites of independence?

Damian Shiels

Introduction

The history of the revolutionary era is understandably afforded primacy in Irish memory. No other period enjoys the same levels of public interest and no other period is so contested politically. The coming of the 'decade of centenaries' has led to a further intensification of historical study and a new wave of memorialisation to mark these seminal events. For the first time we are also beginning to look at the revolutionary era from an archaeological perspective. Traditionally, the twentieth century has not drawn much notice from Irish archaeologists, with the discipline largely focused on the study of prehistoric and medieval Ireland. However, there is increasing attention being paid to the archaeologies of more recent times, particularly by those interested in the study of conflict (Shiels 2006; 2007). As archaeology relies primarily on the analysis of physical remains to elucidate our understanding of the past, it has the potential to bring fresh perspectives to how we view the period between 1916 and 1923.

Archaeologists view sites of conflicts such as the 1916 Rising in Dublin as battlefield landscapes. Using a multidisciplinary approach, they seek to analyse the environmental setting of the action and to understand how the opposing forces interacted with it. One of the key components of such a study is the identification of what elements of the contemporary revolutionary landscape survive. Given the importance to Irish society of the revolutionary era, it might be expected that many of the key elements of its conflict landscape would remain virtually intact. Analysis is now suggesting that this is not always the case. Indeed, there has been a surprising level of partial or complete destruction and this has often occurred without creating major distress to the very society which cherishes the memory of this period so highly. In order to assess how this has come to pass, it becomes necessary to examine not only the original conflict events but also their subsequent use-history as sites of memory.

The loss of place

On 20 January 1956, Justice Molony of the Dublin District Court issued an order that Liberty Hall should either be taken down, repaired or secured. His instruction came as a result of the poor state of the structure, which at the time was in a dangerous condition and posed a serious health and safety risk. In giving the order, Molony expressed regret that it might result in the destruction of one of the nation's most precious monuments. He added: 'I have no right to say this ... but may I nevertheless say that perhaps in the reconstruction some monument will be set up so that Liberty Hall will not have disappeared'.[1] Liberty Hall was ultimately demolished in 1958. Even during the course of its destruction, the building's links with 1916 were apparent, with the discovery of dummy bullets and other paraphernalia connected with the Irish Citizen Army.[2]

Liberty Hall was one of the key components of the battlefield landscape of the 1916 Rising. It was the site where the Proclamation was printed and where the Irish Citizen Army were headquartered prior to Easter Week. Its ties with early twentieth-century Irish history extend well beyond its association with the Rising, with the building playing a key role in other important events such as the 1913 Lockout. Nonetheless, its destruction in the 1950s did not meet with significant resistance. Newspapers such as the *Irish Times,* while referring to the building's historic past, covered the facts behind the demolition without offering an opinion one way or the other as to its propriety.

Liberty Hall is the most iconic building associated with the 1916 Rising to have been subsequently demolished, but it is not the only one. Sites of garrisons such as the Jacobs Factory and South Dublin Union have also been redeveloped and many others significantly altered. This is perhaps to be expected in a conflict landscape that is centred on the urban heart of a capital city, where necessity demands constant change. However, there is evidence that similar destruction is taking place at rural sites of revolutionary conflict, suggesting there is more at play than simply the relentless march of 'progress'.

On 20 February 1921, members of the 4th Battalion, Cork No. 1 Brigade of the IRA, were surrounded by Crown forces in a farmhouse outside the

---

1 'Liberty Hall said to be "jerry-built"', *Irish Times,* 21 January 1956.
2 'Liberty Hall demolished', *Irish Times,* 1 July 1958.

19.1   Memorial on the site of farmhouse, Clonmult, County Cork.

village of Clonmult in County Cork. In the ensuing firefight, a number of
the IRA volunteers were killed before the building was set on fire, forcing
those still inside to surrender (Ó Conchubhair 2009, 236–40). Although both
sides offer differing accounts of what happened next, the balance of evidence
suggests that some of the men were summarily executed. Patrick Higgins,
an IRA survivor, recalled in his witness statement to the Bureau of Military
History that he and others 'were lined up alongside an outhouse with our
hands up. The Tans came along and shot every man, with the exception of
three'.[3] Clonmult represented the worst loss of life in a single incident that
the IRA experienced during the War of Independence. A total of twelve
volunteers were killed at the farmhouse, with a further two subsequently
tried and executed.

The building in which the IRA sheltered at Clonmult was destroyed
by the 1921 fire and never rebuilt. Today its foundations are situated under
a flowerbed in the yard of what remains a working farm. In the centre of
the flowerbed is a memorial to the ambush and the men who lost their
lives (Fig. 19.1). It remains an important site of memory in the locality and
is regularly visited by both members of the public and political groups.
Clonmult is one of the best-remembered events of the revolutionary period in

3   Irish Military Archives (MA), MA/BMH/WS/1467, 6. Witness: Patrick J. Higgins,
   Captain IRA, Cork, 1921.

east Cork, mainly due to the summary executions which reportedly occurred following the surrender. In 2008, the author conducted a preliminary visit to the site with a view to determining the potential for archaeological analysis of the conflict landscape. Given the destruction of the original farmhouse in 1921, it seemed probable that the most significant survival relating to the action would be the outhouse wall, against which those who had surrendered were shot. While in conversation with the current landowner, it was revealed that this outhouse had in fact been demolished some years previously in order to make way for a more modern shed. Where one might expect that a wall such as this would represent 'hallowed ground' to the local community, it appears that its removal passed largely unnoticed.

Given the importance of the Irish revolutionary period in Irish memory, it seems somewhat incongruous that direct physical links to these iconic events such as Liberty Hall and the Clonmult outhouse could be lost with relatively little fanfare. Potential answers as to how this came to be the case lie in assessing how society interacts with these conflict sites and how we have chosen to remember and memorialise them.

The triumph of memory over place

When examining landscapes of conflict from the revolutionary period, there is one type of feature that stands supreme – the memorial. They are a ubiquitous feature of the Irish town and countryside with hundreds scattered up and down the Republic. These memorials are rich with meaning, with many communicating a very specific and targeted narrative. The motivations behind their erection often went beyond simple commemoration and were intended to serve a dual function by underlining the history of the state while also reflecting party political positions (Higgins 2012, 138). This political meaning is something memorials remain imbued with to this day; addresses by politicians at monuments such as that at Béal na mBláth remain a staple of Irish life.

It is apparent that the memorial landscape constructed after the revolutionary period has played a major role in how subsequent generations have remembered and commemorated the conflict. Another factor to consider is what might be regarded as the 'cult of the individual' which has developed around many of those who participated in the 1916 Rising and War of Independence. This can be seen in those memorials which physically represent those who fought, who are often portrayed in heroic postures (Turpin 2007, 109; Winter 2013, 139–40) and through the favoured preservation of specific sites related to key individuals from the period, such as the childhood homes of Michael Collins in County Cork and Éamon de Valera in Bruree, County Limerick. However, the cult of the individual is most apparent at what are the pre-eminent sites of memory relating to revolutionary Ireland – the graveside of the martyr. There are few sites that are treated more reverentially than these burial places and they continue to serve as major foci of public and political attention. These sites include Glasnevin Cemetery and the graves of the executed 1916 leaders at Arbour Hill – the latter offers an annual opportunity for politicians to associate themselves with the founders of the Republic (see Godson, Chapter 22).

Both culturally and politically, memorials and gravesides have become the two major site types associated with the physical memory of the revolutionary period. They have usurped the surviving elements of the conflict landscape as the people's primary mode of connection to past events. One noteworthy exception to this is the General Post Office, headquarters of the rebels in Dublin during 1916. Reconstructed in 1924, today it is a building in which the rebels are 'amply commemorated' (Jeffery 2006, 13). The General Post Office has successfully combined the roles of both 'place' and 'memorial' (perhaps to the detriment of other 1916 sites) and remains a cornerstone of how the Rising is remembered. However, outside of the General Post Office, the dominance of the memorial and graveside has led to a larger forgetting of place and landscape.

In her analysis of the fiftieth anniversary of the 1916 Rising, historian Roisín Higgins, when speaking of the desire of then Taoiseach Seán Lemass to restore the relics of the national past, posited that Lemass was 'in some sense delegating to the monuments the responsibility for remembering' (2012, 156). This is also a truism in terms of the wider revolutionary landscape, as memorials have today become the main interface between the population and their experience of sites relating to the period. The dominance of the memorial in remembrance has meant that it is war memory rather than the physical remains of the war that drives our direct engagement with the past. For many, the 'memorial' has become the 'place'.

The memorial as place

There are numerous examples of memorials replacing interaction with the physical landscape of the revolution. To return to Clonmult, it is apparent that the memorial has become the embodiment of place at the ambush site, rather than any of the physical elements of the landscape that bore witness to the events. This focus on the memorial as the key place of remembrance meant that the degradation of the site's physical links with the 1921 ambush could occur virtually unnoticed, as the memorial has become the place. A variation of this can be seen in the nearby town of Midleton, County Cork.

19.2   Buildings occupied by the IRA during the Crossbarry ambush on 19 March 1921, part of the surviving battlefield landscape.

Here the Main Street is dominated by a large memorial to the IRA, while those men who lost their lives at Clonmult occupy one of the most prominent positions in the town graveyard. These memorials have come to represent the conflict in the locality. Although Midleton Main Street was itself the scene of a dramatic ambush on 29 December 1920, there is little local awareness of this event, despite the fact that much of the physical landscape of this encounter survives.

One of the strongest examples of a memorial as place is the site of the Crossbarry ambush in County Cork. The engagement at Crossbarry took place on 19 March 1921, when over 100 IRA volunteers under the leadership of Tom Barry engaged multiple columns of Crown troops. After an initial ambush and protracted firefight, the IRA were ultimately successful in inflicting significant losses on the enemy before retiring to safety. Crossbarry is regarded as one of the most significant actions of the War of Independence and was certainly one of the largest. Detailed descriptions of the fighting survive, as does a map of the action prepared by Tom Barry (Barry 1989, 122–31). These sources allow for a detailed analysis of the battlefield landscape, which survives largely intact. The site is spread over a large area and consists of buildings which were occupied

19.3   The Crossbarry memorial in context, Crossbarry, County Cork.

by the IRA during the battle, field boundaries that were used as defensive positions and routeways that were employed for both attack and defence by the opposing sides (Fig. 19.2). None of these contemporary features is readily accessible to the public. What is accessible is the large memorial, situated at the extreme eastern edge of the battlefield landscape (Fig. 19.3). Removed from the core area of the fighting, the isolation of the memorial has been further accentuated by recent road-straightening works, which have led to the monument now forming part of a cul-de-sac. There is no information to inform visitors as to the course the fighting took or to alert them to the fact that a large part of the battlefield landscape survives. For all intents and purposes, the memorial is presented as the Crossbarry ambush site, and for the vast majority of visitors this is how it is viewed – a visit to the memorial is a visit to Crossbarry, just as visits to the memorials at Béal na mBláth or Kilmichael have come to represent the experience of these important revolutionary era sites.

Controversy over the planned construction of a new memorial on the site of the Kilmichael ambush in County Cork serves to illustrate the dominance of the memorial as the primary form of memory at such locations. Plans by the Kilmichael Historical Society and Kilmichael and Crossbarry

Commemoration Committee to refurbish the existing memorial sparked heated debate across the country, as it was proposed that a representation of a Crossley Tender might be included to mark the presence of Crown forces in the action.[4] A further suggestion that the Crown dead might be named at the site was met with outrage. The Commemoration Committee moved quickly to stress that these elements were not being included in the proposed works.[5] The entire debate and associated controversy surrounding the refurbishment centred on who was being remembered and why, but never on the implications the development had for the site itself. Planning permission was granted for 'preserving and enhancing the area around Kilmichael ambush site to include alterations to the existing monument, provision of walkways, information signs, amenity areas and provision of a lay-by for parking, upgrading of existing access track and associated landscape works'.[6] The impact this development will have on the battlefield landscape of Kilmichael is unknown, as the extent and nature of that landscape have never been established. It is notable that the debate surrounding the redevelopment was entirely focused on memory and memorialisation, with place and landscape afforded only secondary consideration.

Conclusion

The long neglect of the physical remains of our revolutionary sites is something that needs to be addressed. The prospect of their survival is little better now than when Liberty Hall was demolished in 1958. It required the imminent proposed demolition of Nos. 14–17 Moore Street, the last headquarters of the provisional government during Easter Week 1916, to mobilise groups to lobby for the appropriate preservation of that historic location. Now declared a National Monument, it is one of only a tiny number of sites from this period that enjoys legislative protection. The lack of any form of protection for the overwhelming majority of 1916 and War of Independence landscapes means that their preservation is not taken into consideration as part of the planning process. Ireland now finds itself in a position where its prehistoric and medieval heritage enjoys significantly superior protection than those locations connected with the independence of the state; indeed the age-bias in protecting monuments means that many of

---

4 'Call for more public debate on Kilmichael ambush interpretation', *Southern Star*, 7 August 2013; 'Kilmichael monument debate', *Irish Examiner*, 26 August 2013.
5 'British forces will not be commemorated at Kilmichael ambush site', *Irish Examiner*, 15 August 2013.
6 'Call for more public debate on Kilmichael ambush interpretation', *Southern Star*, 7 August 2013.

these ancient sites are now significantly more numerous than those relating to the island's twentieth-century history.

The focus of memory on memorials and at gravesides has had a detrimental impact on the physical remains of our revolutionary landscapes. By failing to study and define these landscapes, they have been exposed to inadvertent destruction and are also largely unavailable as tools for interacting with the history of this period. The continued focus on memory at the expense of place and landscape will inevitably lead to the further erosion of our direct physical links to the 1916–23 period. This is a model that seems set to continue during the decade of commemorations, although the increasing focus may also present opportunities for the reintroduction of place into our memory of the Irish revolution.

20

'Of all the trials not to paint ...': Sir John Lavery's painting *High Treason, Court of Criminal Appeal: the Trial of Roger Casement 1916*

Catherine Marshall

There was considerable opposition in critical and social circles in 1916 to John Lavery's decision to paint the appeal trial of Roger Casement against his conviction for treason and sentence of death in July of that year.[1] Yet Lavery went doggedly ahead with it, enduring hostility in newspapers that were widely read by the class to which he owed his most significant patronage. To get a sense of the influences governing the production and subsequent fate of this painting we need to look at the political and social as well as the artistic and personal contexts out of which the painting emerged.

John Lavery (1856–1941) was well known for paintings of high society in the United Kingdom and wherever British aristocrats socialised abroad, in France, Italy, Germany and North Africa, where, like his clients, he owned a substantial villa and shared the same social rituals. He had risen to fame, at the age of 25, with his painting of Queen Victoria's visit to the Scottish Royal Academy in 1881, and cemented this with such paintings as the *Tennis match*, purchased by the Government of Bavaria in 1901, which became one of the most highly regarded and expensive paintings of the decade. His fame was rewarded and his career further enhanced when he married Hazel Trudeau, née Martyn – herself a painter as well as a well-known socialite and beauty – in 1910. Lavery's rising star was firmly endorsed when he was invited to paint King George V and Queen Mary, who posed for him in Buckingham Palace and who gave over the palace's

---

1 Roger Casement (1864–1916) was knighted for his work as a British consul in Africa and South America where he was outspoken in his condemnation of colonial abuses of human rights. Opposed to imperialism, he supported the Irish rebellion and was arrested and tried as a traitor, following a mission to Germany in search of support for the Easter Rising. The selective leaking of the Black Diaries by the British Government during his imprisonment did much to discredit him as a homosexual. He was hanged as a traitor at Pentonville Prison in August 1916.

20.1a   John Lavery, *High Treason, Court of Criminal Appeal: the Trial of Roger Casement 1916*, 1916–*c*.1930, oil on canvas, 2,140 mm × 322 mm.
Government Art Collection, London, on loan to the Honourable Society of King's Inns, Dublin

White Drawing Room as a studio for the duration of the work. It is said that the two men bonded to such a degree that Lavery gave the king a brush to paint the Garter Ribbon himself. The cordiality did not end there. The Laverys were further honoured by a royal visit to their studio in South Kensington in April 1913. The artist's biography lists the rich and famous sitters who posed for his brush, among them prime ministers and their families, opera singers, prima ballerinas and later Hollywood film stars (Lavery 1940). It is not remarkable then that when the word got out that he was bent on painting the Casement appeal trial (Fig. 20.1a) the press showed surprise, one commentator exclaiming:

> Girls in white, girls on the sands in full sun, or girls on horseback – such used to be Lavery's themes. But the penalty of fame has brought him other subjects including a Coronation and a trial. Of all the trials not to paint, the Casement trial I should have thought would have had first place. But Lavery has gone right through with the painful task. ('Another trial': unidentified press-cutting, Lavery scrapbook, private collection, cited in McCoole 2010, 66)

Another commentator went further, saying:

> Much astonishment has been caused in artistic circles by the statement,
> so far uncontradicted, that Mr John Lavery is engaged in painting the
> final scene in the Casement trial ... Mr Lavery ought not to paint his
> picture without knowing the contents of the two diaries ... from all of
> which it follows that the forthcoming picture is sure to attract immense
> attention but scarcely the kind of notice that so popular an artist is
> seeking. (*Weekly Dispatch*, 22 October 1916, cited in McCoole 2010, 66)

What led Lavery to take on this project? An orphan from Belfast, who had
worked in a Glasgow pawnshop as a child, John Lavery wanted recognition.
History painting was the genre which above all others was considered,
in the European academic canon, to be the mark of the truly great artist.
Kenneth McConkey quotes the artist as saying that he did not care much for
history but that he wanted to paint a 'great picture of Mary, Queen of Scots'
(McConkey 1984–5, 19). Sadly the picture he was referring to, *Dawn after the
Battle of Langside* (1887), falls well short of the artist's ambition for it. When
the First World War broke out, Lavery, like his younger Irish contemporary,
William Orpen, became a war artist. Sadly for him, he was quickly forced
to recognise that his attempts at painting such events as the *Surrender of the
fleet* were, as he admitted, merely 'charming colour versions, as if painting a
bank holiday on Hampstead Heath' (Lavery 1940, 149). He admitted that all
he was able to feel in the face of dramatic action was excitement about colour.

In his biography, Lavery says that he was asked by Lord Justice Darling,
the presiding judge, whom he had painted previously, to paint the Casement
trial. It is possible that he saw this as a means to combine that earlier
ambition with his proven ability as a portrait painter. He began the picture,
with sketches and notes in the actual courtroom during the trial in July 1916,
but he did not finish it for over a decade. In the meantime, his Irish rival,
Orpen, had painted another historical group portrait, *The signing of the peace
at the Hall of Mirrors, Versailles* (1919, Imperial War Museum), which Lavery
greatly admired, referring to it and a sketch for it as 'the most powerful
historical documents of the war' (Lavery 1940, 138).

Lord Darling may have asked him to paint the trial, and he certainly
helped the artist by arranging access to the court for him and persuading
people to sit for him, but he did not buy the finished painting. When Lavery
was knighted in 1918, Darling wrote to him saying, 'You will, I hope, take it
as an expression of the will of HM's Government that you should complete
your picture of Casement's trial, one of their victories over the benches'
(letter to Lavery, 1 January 1918, cited in Cullen 2004, 208).

The leaders of the 1916 Rising were executed in Dublin but Roger

Casement was taken out of the country to London to stand trial. In Lavery's painting he is isolated again, placed almost in the centre of the canvas, with the opposing legal teams seated at the benches in the foreground, the judges in their red robes on the left and a packed courtroom on the right. Casement is dressed in the sober garb of a convicted felon, stripped of his honours, and flanked, as Lavery himself described it, by 'hard-faced warders' on either side (Lavery 1940, 189–90).

An introduction to some of the participants might throw some light on the reasons for the picture's subsequent history. Casement's legal team was led by George Gavan Duffy, son of the Fenian Charles Gavin Duffy, at that time a partner in a successful London Law firm. He was warned that if he represented Casement he would have to resign his position, but he took the case anyway. Duffy had considerable trouble finding a barrister, as those he approached initially all turned down the brief. Eventually, his brother-in-law, Serjeant Sullivan, reluctantly took the case, following advice from Chief Baron Palles, and in return for an exorbitant fee, which could only be met by donations raised from figures such as Arthur Conan Doyle, Sir Arthur Cadbury and donors in the USA. Mrs Margaret Gavan Duffy sits to the right of her husband at the centre of the counsel bench, and another of the hatted women has been identified as Gertrude Bannister, Casement's cousin, who lost her teaching job directly as a punishment for her 'traitorous actions' in helping her cousin (McGuiggan 1999, 158). A lesson for the artist in all of this is that too close an identification with the prisoner might have negative effects on his future career.

The artist's sympathies, however, seem to have been with the sitter, as the language of the painting subtly suggests. Casement is shown, like Jesus Christ in Renaissance paintings, in the only full frontal pose in the entire painting. His face is picked out fully by a beam of light, reaching downwards from the balcony on the top right. In the painted sketch for the painting this balcony is shown more fully and was filled with Irish sympathisers such as Eva Gore Booth and Ada MacNeill. Just as the perspective lines in Renaissance paintings direct the eye to the hero at the centre, most notably in Leonardo da Vinci's *Last Supper* fresco, here too they seem, at first glance, to lead the eye straight to Casement, quietly elevating him above the gowned lawyers. In fact, Lavery was more subtle than that and an analysis of the perspective reveals that he abandoned the clarity of Renaissance perspective in order to make a definite separation between the judges and the prosecution on the left and the other participants on the right. He achieved this by using not one but two main vanishing points, one of which is consistent for the prosecution group and the space they occupy, while the other defines a space which embraces the viewer, including the artist, the prisoner in the dock and his supporters (Fig. 20.1b).

20.1b   Perspectival analysis of Lavery, *High Treason, Court of Criminal Appeal: the Trial of Roger Casement 1916.*
Courtesy of Nicky Coghlan, 2013

Casement himself, during the two-day appeal hearing, felt that the artist supported him. His cousin Gertrude Bannister wrote to Lavery that Casement saw a woman (Hazel Lavery) with the painter: 'I thought I knew her face. It was very sad,' he said, and he commented also that he felt that Lavery himself 'came dangerously near "aiding and comforting", if not indeed "compassing" from the way he eyed Mr. Justice Darling delivering judgment' (Lavery 1940, 189–90). That compassion that Casement intuited is revealed in the painting, in the understated dignity of the figure in prison attire in the dock surrounded almost suffocatingly by the robes and wigs of officialdom. Much of the artwork's power lies in the artist's ability to present this contrast.

Lavery claimed in his biography that he was only persuaded to paint Irish political subjects because Hazel recommended that he should 'use his art to reconcile both sides in Irish politics' (Lavery 1940, 216). In any case, as early as 1914 he had requested that Edward Carson, leader of the Ulster Unionists, and John Redmond, leader of the Irish Home Rule Party, should sit for him, on the grounds that their portraits would one day hang together. Lavery described these portraits as 'the first attempt to bind up the contending forces in the bond of holy paint' ('Sir John Lavery, his works, a record of modern life', *Sunday Times, c.*1930, cited in McCoole 2010, 63).

Carson believed that the Redmond portrait was better, and said to Lavery (a Belfast Catholic), 'It is easy to know which side you are on' (Lavery 1940, 208). By the time he painted Casement's trial, the executions following the 1916 Rising had already taken place and opinion was becoming radicalised. Lavery's subsequent donation of the Carson and Redmond portraits to a sale in the Mansion House in aid of those who were wounded in 1916 suggests a genuine sympathy for the revolutionaries.

If his natural sympathies led in a particular direction, Lavery's political position suggests a level of naivety. When Hazel said, 'John why don't you do something for your country?', he said that he was not interested in conflict or difference.

> To which Hazel replied 'Just agree with them all, as you do anyway'. So it struck me that I might be some use in making my studio neutral ground where both sides might meet ... My interest in politics is nil, although I did allow myself to express a decided opinion in a letter from Armagh. (Lavery 1940, 216)

The letter referred to here was addressed to Winston Churchill. It is undated but was probably written in 1920 when the Laverys were in Armagh to paint Cardinal Logue, and purports to speak freely as one artist to another. Lavery writes, 'My Dear Minister of War ... I believe that Ireland will never be governed by Westminster, the Vatican, or Ulster, without continuous bloodshed. I also believe that the removal of the "Castle" and all its works, leaving Irishmen to settle their own affairs, is the only solution left' (Lavery 1940, 211–12).

It is Lavery's strongest statement about the Irish political situation, and untypically forthright. His rather optimistic view in 1940, that Lloyd George had 'settled the Irish question (more or less)' in 1921 (Lavery 1940, 183), and his disarming remark about the experience of painting Éamon de Valera in London in the same year ('I was naturally more interested in what he looked like than in what he said' (Lavery 1940, 223)), reveal the superficiality of his political thought and add to the view that it was his wife who was really interested in Irish affairs.

The context for paintings of Irish historical subjects is particularly interesting in this period. For colonial reasons, Irish history had been almost completely ignored for centuries, so much so that James Ward, headmaster of the Metropolitan School of Art, in an effort to promote the genre in Ireland, introduced a prize for the best painting of a 'Figure subject from Irish History, Legend and Romance in the College' in 1912–13 (Metropolitan School of Art, Headmaster's Report, 1912–13). To give his students experience in this field of work, he offered, with their assistance,

20.2   James Ward and others, *Brian Boru addressing his army before the Battle of Clontarf, 1014 AD*, 1914–19, spirit fresco on stone, 124 cm × 248 cm (approx.). Courtesy of City Hall, Dublin

to undertake a series of history paintings to decorate Dublin's City Hall in 1913. The subject matter was suggested by the Sinn Féin Alderman, Thomas Kelly, and depicted scenes from the history of medieval and early modern Dublin. The scheme was uncontroversial because the scenes it depicted were so remote chronologically that they were unlikely to disturb the peace in the present, and work continued, unaffected by the Rising or by the politics of its aftermath. When the pictures were unveiled in 1919, in a city aroused by the events of 1916 and the outbreak of the War of Independence, they generated little interest (Fig. 20.2). The scheme did not make Ward famous and did nothing to spawn a generation of eager history painters.

One of Ward's pupils, did, however, find herself painting a revolutionary subject. By pure coincidence, Kathleen Fox stumbled across the scene of the arrest of Countess Markievicz outside the College of Surgeons in Stephen's Green. Shocked, especially as she had known Markievicz as a regular visitor to the art schools, Fox did sketches on the spot, and later, as she recorded it herself, with her nationalist feelings aroused by the executions of the leaders, she finished the painting. Fearful, however, that it would mark her out as a troublemaker, she had the picture smuggled out of the country, and only brought it back when, under the Free State, she felt it safe to recover it for the Thomas Davis commemorative exhibition in 1946. Fox was not alone. It is widely believed that Estella Solomon destroyed portraits of her friends among the Sinn Féin leaders in the War of Independence, although conclusive research on this is still pending.

But it is the dependence of visual art on the whims of power and patronage that is most disturbing. Jerome Connor's three big Irish commissions for commemorative sculpture, including his 1916 patriot monument, were aborted because, among other reasons advanced, in 1929 and 1930, they were not thought to be sufficiently 'Catholic'. The absence of deserted and crumbling cottages in Paul Henry's west of Ireland paintings show that the Free State regime was more interested in selling an image of primitive cosiness than a country from which people were still emigrating to escape economic privation. Ironically, even Lavery's painting *The tennis match* was a victim of politics. Following Germany's defeat in the First World War, the Bavarian authorities sold it out of their collection. It is now in private ownership.

Where, then, could Lavery's painting of Casement's trial be accommodated? Since Lord Darling, having encouraged the artist to paint it, did not purchase it, Lavery sought other homes for the painting. During the 1930s there were a number of proposals to buy it. Although initially one of those opposed to the painting, Lord Birkenhead (F.E. Smith), an acquaintance of Lavery's who had led the case against Casement, expressed interest in having the painting bought for the Law Courts, this did not happen. John H. Morgan, legal adviser to the court, also considered purchasing it. It was offered in Lavery's will to the National Portrait Gallery in London, with the Royal Courts of Justice as residuary legatees. However, the Trustees of the Portrait Gallery did 'not consider the occasion important enough for representation here' (Cullen 2004, 207).

After the war, it was given to the Royal Courts of Justice and hence to the Government Art Collection in Britain. It was hung, out of public view, in the office of the senior clerk of the Court of Criminal Appeal, for fear, the Lord Chancellor said, that it might provoke 'undesirable demonstrations by people who considered Casement a martyr' (Cullen 2004, 208). In 1950, Serjeant Sullivan, now retired to Ireland, asked if it could be given to the King's Inns Benchers in Dublin. The Lord Chancellor agreed, saying 'We can adopt the suggestion of lending it to the King's Inns on indefinite loan which means that we can forget to ask for its return'. He wrote to Sullivan saying that the loan was repayable on demand but that 'such a demand is unlikely to be hurried' (His Honour Judge Bradbury, Colchester County Court, June 1997, quoted in McGuiggan 1999, 157–9). It was unveiled by President Seán T. O'Kelly in the King's Inns, in Dublin in 1951, where it has remained ever since.

In case anyone should feel complacent about post-Independence Irish openness to similar historic projects, it is important to remember, as

20.3   Oisin Kelly,
Roger Casement,
bronze, 2.2 m,
completed 1971,
erected 1984 at
Ballyheigue, near
Banna Strand,
County Kerry

Fintan Cullen has pointed out (Cullen 2004, 209), that the statue of Roger Casement, commissioned on behalf of the Irish government from Oisin Kelly for Glasnevin cemetery in the 1960s, suffered a similar fate. Because of growing republican activity in Northern Ireland, the statue was not installed there but was placed, instead, far from the public gaze, at Ballyheigue Park, near Banna Strand in Kerry (Fig. 20.3). History painting and sculpture remain vulnerable to the whims of patronage and political expediency.

21

'Dusty fingers of time': photography, materials memory and 1916

Justin Carville

There is an old Russian aphorism which neatly encapsulates the preoccupation of much recent historical inquiry into the Easter Rising and the struggle for control of the representation of 1916 in public and political commemoration (Boyce 1996; Daly and O'Callaghan 2007; Higgins 2012; O'Dwyer 2007). With an appropriately ironic inflection, the saying goes: 'we know the future will always be certain, for us it is the past that is unpredictable'. In a society where the interpretation of historical events continues to be contested in both the academy and in public discourse, the uncertainty of how the past is reconfigured into meaningful representations in the present is a salient feature of Irish public culture. That the historical landscape of Ireland is a minefield littered with potentially volatile interpretations of the past that lie dormant just beneath the surface of historical consciousness is thus a familiar state of affairs. However, the decade of centenaries of 1912–22 has thrown into sharp relief that it is no longer just past historical events that appear on the horizon as unpredictable interruptions to contemporary historical consciousness; rather, it is how that past has been and continues to be commemorated that now results in the formation of new uncertainties surrounding the interpretation of Irish historical events.

As the decade of centenary commemorations progresses, historical analysis has increasingly turned to the cultural practices and spaces across which historical memories are sedimented into the fabric of Irish society. As Ian McBride (2001, 5–6) has observed, 'questions of collective memory and commemoration have assumed a new prominence', not only within Irish history but also across the mass media, international relations and public discourse, and, as Oona Frawley's four-volume series *Memory Ireland* also demonstrates, there is a burgeoning interest in the cultural politics of memory across the humanities more broadly. The commemoration of 1916 and the legacy of its aftermath have sharpened this focus on the politics of memory in ways that illuminate that how Irish society has interpreted the past through practices of commemoration is as contested and unpredictable as the contemporary representation of the historical events themselves. Such is the political and cultural legacy of the semi-centennial commemorations of 1966, for example, that Mary Daly and Margaret O'Callaghan go so far as to claim that the 'struggle for control of the representation of the nature of the 1966 commemoration has accreted to the debate of 1916 itself in a way that has made it constitutive of it' (Daly and O'Callaghan 2007, 2).

In this chapter, I engage with the politics of the commemoration of 1916 through one of the most ubiquitous forms of material visual culture, the photographic image. In identifying this as a feature of the commemoration of the Rising, it is not my intention to claim for photography a distinct exceptionality in the politics of Irish cultural memory. Instead, what I work towards demonstrating is how the photograph as a material image-object has the potential to connect, rupture and intervene into the practices of commemoration of 1916, both in the past and in more recent acts of commemoration. In the discussion that follows, I explore a range of 'photographica' of the Easter Rising, not as historical documents of a fixed and immutable past but for their affective qualities in commemorating the events of 1916 and their aftermath. This chapter then is not concerned with what the photographs mean, that is to say I am not interested in the rhetoric of the image, nor am I interested in measuring the photograph against a perceived historical reality. The aim of this chapter is simply to explore what these photographs potentially *do* in the context of the commemoration of 1916 in popular culture.

Materialising memory

Expressing such a sentiment as the unpredictable past at the beginning of a discussion on photography and a historical event such as the Easter Rising might appear somewhat counterintuitive to our understanding of photography's capital as the 'real' and its capacity to preserve the past. Our commonsense view of photographs is that they in fact fix history. As André Bazin (1960, 8) would have it, photographs rescue time from its 'proper corruption'. In photographs, the past is believed to have become petrified through its exposure to the shadowy silver halides of film and, increasingly, of course, the numerical sequencing of digital code. Photographs, it is commonly believed, reaffirm not only that the past is history by clearly demonstrating that we are separated from it, they also confirm that what is depicted within the geometric frame of the image is indeed history by reflecting back to the viewer their own non-existence in what they see represented on what John Tagg has acerbically described as the 'paltry paper' surface of the photograph (Tagg 1988, 65). Roland Barthes (who capitalised the word 'History' throughout his writing and who wrote on historical discourse and the French historian Michelet) observed this affective quality of the photograph on the viewer's sense of separation with the past (Barthes 1981a; 1981b, 64–5; 1987). Opining that it was the same century that was responsible for the invention of both history and photography (Barthes 1981b, 93), Barthes proclaimed that with the advent of the photograph 'what we see on paper is as certain as what we touch' (Barthes 1981b, 88).

In Irish historical scholarship, this certainty of what is seen within the frame of the photograph is privileged over that of the material connection to the past through the haptic sense of connection to the material object. Pádraig Óg Ó Ruairc's visual survey of the revolutionary decade of 1913–23, for example, reproduces photographs from illustrated commemorative publications of the Easter Rising and weds them to the chronology, person-alities and place of historical events (Ó Ruairc 2011). Any sense of the photographic image as itself being the historic is overshadowed by a burden of authenticity weighed in the openness of the photograph to being mined for historical data. Yet, it is precisely the materiality of the photographic image, its tangible existence as a physical object, that has the potential to connect the viewer in unpredictable ways to the past and with the shifting contours of remembrance.

As the historical, the photographic image's circulation through time and across space subjects it to varying practices of looking and cultural use. Drifting in and out of view, its impact on the historical imagination is impossible to chart accurately. To borrow a phrase from Régis Durand (1995, 146), 'the object itself lacks all "certainty"'. It is precisely the very ambiguity of the materiality of the photographic images of 1916 and their continuous circulation that makes them such unpredictable conduits to the politics of cultural memory. Photographs of the personalities and events of 1916 have appeared in a number of material forms ranging from illustrations in print media such as newspapers and pictorial magazines, to postcards, visual histories, commemorative booklets, lockets, medallions, memorial cards, personal scrapbooks, diaries and documentary films.

While context is not only important but always necessary, the recontex-tualisation of photographs through different material forms is not all that is at issue here. The material form of the same photograph configured as a different type of image-object frequently commands different practices of looking. The organisation of these practices of looking may be designated towards purely technical ocular exercises, others directed at more physical investments in the photograph attached to mnemonic processes and haptic associations with the past. The range of 1916 photographica circulating in popular culture in variegated material form frequently necessitates different types of attention. Often shaped by their historical situated-ness, these various forms of attention are themselves frequently confronted with the uncertainty of the photograph as an image-object.

Photographs, it is important to accede, have multiple social uses that subject the image-object to a range of cultural practices of ocular and haptic dimension. Amongst the numerous collections of photographs of the Easter Rising and its aftermath held in the photographic archives of the National Library of Ireland is an album compiled by the engineer J.W. O'Neill. The album of 29 photographs taken in May of 1916 depicts the damage to the exterior of the General Post Office and the destruction to its internal mechanised infrastructure.[1] An assistant engineer at the General Post Office, O'Neill's photographs are, in the vernacular of the instrumental uses of photography, 'documents'. As Steve Edwards has observed, most people are familiar with the look of the photographic document and have a sense of their function, but, as they tend to be banal and visually dull, pay little if any attention to such photographs (Edwards 2006, 12–39).

Indeed, the historical understanding of the photographic document and its attendant practices of looking has largely been lost within the historiography of the photographic image. In what is perhaps the most sympathetic exploration of the historical significance of the photographic document, Molly Nesbit notes that the document sat comfortably within a culture that lacked an extensive lexicon with which to describe the photographic image. She emphasises that with photographic documents 'a technical look took command', which dissected the photograph 'surgically and brought away what it needed' (Nesbit 1992, 17). This was a practical looking that searched the document for technical signs 'lodged in the very appearance of the picture'. Photographic documents were scrutinised without too much elaboration, being read silently by an observer who knew exactly what sort of information they required from the photograph: 'For a document was actually defined by an exchange, which is to say, by a viewer reading a certain kind of technical information from the picture and by the picture's ability to display just that technical sign' (Nesbit 1992, 17).

O'Neill's photographs, with their utilitarian visual depiction of dry facts, required their corollary in the engineer's eye to put them to work as documents. A specialised, methodical and productive look took command of the document and laboured over its quiet visual depiction of technical information. However, O'Neill's photographs, despite the technical intentions of their taking, are now part of that official repository of cultural memory, the national archive. In cultural practices of commemoration, such clinical

---

1   National Library of Ireland (NLI), NLI/MS/ALB107.

observation of the photograph as required by the document rarely fulfil the work of cultural memory. They require a different type of gaze, an alternative practice of looking. For the most part, photographs are looked at retrospectively if not with a certain degree of hindsight. Looking at the photograph here to the past event then, the gap between is filled with the fantasies, anxieties and expectations of cultural memory. What is collectively known of the events of Easter Week 1916, its sometimes tragic consequences and its periodic emergence into popular consciousness and political discourse, continually permeate the space between the taking of the photograph and our looking at it now.

Photographs are thus not static and predictable in their photo-chemical traces of the past but are continually open to affective responses generated through the performative exchange between viewer and image-object. They are an unpredictable past precisely because the space between our looking from here to then is open to fluctuating and sometimes unstable perceptions and aspirations of cultural memory. This is the paradox of the photograph as a material object, despite its reconfiguration from one physical place (the engineer's office) to another (the archive), from one constituency of social use to an alternate sphere of cultural meaning, the photographs can still carry and return to their original state and historical position within the visual culture of 1916. This migratory pattern of the photograph, sometimes emerging simultaneously in various material forms of image-object or at other times transformed into photographica in different historical contexts, reflects a much more flexible and elastic sense of the photograph's relationship to history and memory.

For the sake of theoretical expediency, I want to refer to this quality of the photographic image as 'materials memory'. The concept is borrowed from Richard Terdiman's theorisation of modernity's destabilisation of recollection through technologies of representation (Terdiman 1993, 31–71), but I want to adapt it here to the uncertainty of the photographic object. Materials memory, or what is more commonly termed 'smart materials', are physical objects that return to their original form after being distorted, compressed, manipulated or crushed. The photographic image contains these properties in so far as despite its serial reproduction, its cropping and assemblage into textual print, its montage into the visual and audio projection of cinema and televisual broadcasting and its migration into the photographica of recollection, it still retains and has the potential to return to its original form. This stretching and migration of the photograph into various forms of image-object is a particularly potent form of memory production, allowing multiple temporal engagements and practices of commemoration to connect and intervene with one another while retaining an attachment to the past event through the materiality of the photograph and its historical affect.

Photography and the mnemonic economy

Most accounts of the 1916 jubilee celebrations of 1966, such as those by Rory O'Dwyer and Roisín Higgins's extensive account of the politics of the commemoration, *Transforming 1916*, concentrate on pageantry, TV, film and art exhibitions at both the National Gallery and the Municipal Art Gallery rather than the paltry paper photograph. Yet in the immediate aftermath of the Rising it was photography that was first mobilised in the processes of commemoration. In the weeks following the Easter Rising at least five commemorative pamphlets illustrated with photographs were commercially published for public sale, in addition to numerous supplements printed by the national and international print media. The most prominent of these include: *The Rebellion in Dublin, April 1916* (Eason's); *The 'Sinn Féin' revolt illustrated* (Healy's); *Dublin and the 'Sinn Féin rising'* (Wilson Hartnell & Co.); and *Dublin after the six days' insurrection* (Mecredy, Percy & Co.). Six years later, several other photographically illustrated pamphlets appeared that incorporated photographs of 1916 with images commemorating the Civil War of 1922. The *Catholic Bulletin* (1916) and the *Irish Times* in their *Sinn Fein Rebellion Handbook* (1917) also included photographs in their special publications on the Rising in addition to the numerous postcard series and photographically illustrated memorial cards of portraits of signatories to the Proclamation and those subsequently executed by the British authorities. Albums of personal photographs were also produced, including one by the celebrated antiquarian Thomas J. Westropp, and numerous commemorative albums and scrapbooks were compiled from newspaper photographs, postcards and memorial cards by the public.

The swift publication of photographs and their circulation as commemorative objects of the Rising and its aftermath was in part due to technological advances in cameras and mechanical reproductive processes such as half-tone printing, which greatly expanded the earlier emergence of photojournalism in the print media. *Survey Graphic*, one of the first publications to utilise half-tone printing for photographs, also published a photo-essay on the Rising and its impact on the residents of Dublin. However, photography was already becoming increasingly incorporated into cultural expressions of memory independent of the increasing industrialisation of photographic processes. Bernd Hüppauf (1995, 100) has noted that the sudden presence of war images during the First World War 'contributed to shaping the collective memory and public discourse of war'. Photography was established as a prominent feature in the commemoration of the First World War, not only through the collection of photographs and postcards of the war-scarred landscapes of Europe, but also as the photographic process itself was used to overcome the palpable sense of loss of loved ones

Irish Rebellion, May, 1916

Holding a Dublin street against the Re

21.1 'Irish Rebellion, May, 1916: Holding a Dublin street against the Rebels'.
Postcard, 1916.
Author's collection

21.2 'Irish Rebellion, May, 1916: Sackville Street in Flames. A photograph taken
by a *Daily Sketch* Photographer under fire'. Postcard, 1916.
Author's collection

Irish Rebellion, May, 1916.

Sackville Street in Flames. A photograph taken by a
"Daily Sketch" Photographer under fire.

21.3   Dust jacket of *Dublin and the 'Sinn Féin rising'*, Wilson & Hartnell, 1916

21.4   'Corner of Sackville St and Eden Quay', from *The rebellion in Dublin*, Eason's, 1916

through spiritualism's exploitation of portraits of the war dead (Dixon 2004; Matheson 2006).

The resonance of the First World War was incorporated into attempts to find a legible lexicon to describe the ruined streetscapes of the city in the aftermath of the Rising, and the language used to describe the war was utilised to animate the affect of photographically illustrated pamphlets commemorating 1916. James Stephens (1992, 73), reflecting on the aftermath of the events on Sackville Street (Fig. 21.2), remarked:

> The Insurrection is over, and it is worth asking what has happened, how it happened, and why it happened? The first part is easily answered. The first part of our city has been blown to smithereens, and burned to ashes. Soldiers amongst us who have served abroad say the ruins are more complete than anything they have seen at Ypres, than anything they have seen in France or Flanders.

The *Freeman's Journal* similarly drew on the visual cartography of the First World War's technological destruction of the cityscape when one journalist exclaimed, 'The greatest thoroughfare in Europe has been reduced to a smoking reproduction of the ruin wrought at Ypres by the mercilessness of the Hun'.[2] The resonance of the First World War also found its way into the discourse of photographic commemoration. The commemorative album *Dublin and the 'Sinn Féin rising'* captioned a vignette photograph on the cover of an elevated view of the ruins beneath the statue to Daniel O'Connell 'Ypres on the Liffey' (Fig. 21.3). The same photograph was also reproduced in sepia form inside the covers of Eason's *The rebellion in Dublin* with a caption in the pictorial space of the image inscribed 'Corner of Sackville St. & Eden Quay' (Fig. 21.4). This simultaneous publication of the same photograph in various mediated forms of popular memory, and their attachments to two different spaces and historical events, is an example of both the uncertainty of the material form of the image–object and the affective resonances of the photograph to topographies of memory and historical events. This malleability of the photograph as a mnemonic register is particularly efficacious in its material connection to the past in practices of commemoration.

The urban ruin, the demolished buildings and detritus of technological warfare are a prominent feature of postcards and photographs reproduced in commemorative pamphlets of the Rising. The photographic ruin appeared in these forms as a sort of proto-late photography, a trace of a trace, as it were (Campany 2003). It is important, however, that these urban ruins are

---

2 *Freeman's Journal*, 5 May 1916.

not reduced to the iconography of technological warfare. As several commentators have noted, it is the affective qualities of photographic ruins and their efficacy in dramatising for the viewer their own sense of distance and loss that made photography such a salient feature of collective memory of war. As Julia Hell and Andreas Schönle (2010, 6) have recently observed, 'revolutions unavoidably produce a rhetoric of ruins', the greatest expression of which is to be found in the photographic image.

The cultural significance of the photographic ruin lies not in the aestheticisation or spatialisation of history but in its affect on the temporal and cultural ambivalence of the photograph. It is important to be cognizant that photographs are never memory in and of themselves: rather, they are material objects through which memory is performed, through the sifting through the photographs themselves and/or the oral and multi-sensory experiences of the image-object (Edwards 1999). To borrow a phrase from W.J.T. Mitchell (2005, 257), the photograph is not a sovereign visual experience but rather 'braided' with haptic, aural and oral sensory experiences in the performance of commemoration. It is this perfomative mnemonics through the materiality of the photograph and its cultural affect – the haptic engagement with the photograph as the historic – which has the potential to intervene in the politics of cultural memory. I want to turn briefly to a photograph from the 1916 jubilee year commemorations to think through the performative mnemonics of photography and its implications for the politics of cultural memory in Ireland (Fig. 21.5).

During the extravagant and hugely popular fiftieth anniversary commemorations of the Easter Rising, Joseph Cashman photographed a group of passers-by looking into the window of the Irish Press newspaper offices on Dublin's O'Connell Street. The passers-by are engaged in a collective, and it must be noted, masculine gaze on history. The window they have crowded around has been framed by a large white border as if it has itself been transformed into a picture, and across the top of the window a sign reads 'Historic Photo's' [*sic*].

The window contains a display of photographs taken by Cashman during his career as a photojournalist (Redmond 1992). Working as a photoengraver and photographer for the *Cork Examiner* during the first decade of the twentieth century, Cashman returned to Ireland from Wales to take over the running of the photo-engraving department of the *Freeman's Journal* newspaper in 1911 and established both the photographic and photoengraving departments of the Irish Press in 1929 at the request of Éamon de Valera (O'Brien 2001). In this image, his photographs of political and revolutionary events had been organised into a cohesive display commemorating the fiftieth anniversary of the 1916 Easter Rebellion. That these photographs taken by Cashman had been labelled 'historic' suggests just how quickly

21.5   Joseph Cashman, 'Historic Photo's' [*sic*], 1966
© RTE Still Library

the moment of the camera's snapshot turns memory into history. Writing on modern urbanisation, Walter Benjamin observed that amongst the innovations that share the common practice of 'one abrupt movement of the hand triggering the process of many steps' the 'snapping of the photographer has had the greatest consequences'. With mechanical forms of recording the fleeting and transitory experiences of the city, 'a touch of the finger now sufficed to fix an event for an unlimited period of time. The camera gave the moment a posthumous shock, as it were' (Benjamin 1973, 171). Benjamin recognised that modern photography disrupted the mnemonic process by transforming the consciousness of an event into an object. Photography quickened memory by turning the past event into an individual, historical trace decontextualised from actual experience.

For the men looking into the window display of Cashman's 'Historic Photo's', the Easter Rebellion just about persisted to exist as unmediated, spontaneous memory; for others, recollection of the Rising was generated through what Benjamin described after Marcel Proust as *mémoire volontaire* – 'voluntary memory'. Cashman's display of 'historic photo's', an example of the techniques of the camera to 'extend the range of the *mémoire volontaire*' permanently to record an event in sight and sound (Benjamin 1973, 170–1, 182–4), thus functioned as visual stimuli for the conscious recollection of the Rising. They simultaneously marked a separation with the past event and a connection to it.

In Cashman's photograph, memory would appear to have given way under the weight of history. The window of the Irish Press offices has been transformed into what Pierre Nora has described as a *lieu de mémoire* – a site of memory – an assemblage of historical paper traces, temporarily unified in a commemorative display. The commemorations of 1966 marked a moment of *lieux de mémoire*, occurring, as Nora describes it, 'at the same time that an immense and intimate fund of memory disappears, surviving only as a reconstituted object beneath the gaze of critical history' (Nora 1989, 12). In the years following the jubilee anniversary, commemorations of 1916 became less visible as a public spectacle, and the generation of '66, as the poet Michael O'Loughlin described them, became more cynical of the Irish state, while national history came under sustained attack by a critical, historical revisionism (Tóbín 1993, 5). The historian D. George Boyce has observed that the fiftieth anniversary celebrations of 1916 encouraged closer scrutiny of the Rising by historians, ushering in a 'genuine interest in recovering a past that was not necessarily the past that politicians and public were commemorating' (Boyce 1996, 163, 165). As Nora goes on to state of the moment of *lieux de mémoire*, 'This period sees, on the one hand, the decisive deepening of historical study and, on the other hand, a heritage consolidated' (Nora 1989, 12).

Cashman's photograph of the men looking into the window of the Irish Press offices records a moment when the everyday experiences of involuntary memory began to give way to official, state-sanctioned commemoration of the Rising. When Cashman's display of 'historic photo's' was removed from the office window on O'Connell Street, the photographs found their way into another manifestation of *lieux de mémoire*, that repository of the material remains of memory, the archive of the National Museum. Amongst the photographic imagery taken by Cashman that circulated in popular culture in the years leading up the fiftieth anniversary of the Rising, and which still exists as a photographic souvenir, and indeed in three-dimensional form as a sculpture on O'Connell Street, is a photograph of the labour leader James Larkin with arms outstretched giving a speech to trade unionists on his return from America in 1923. The men looking into the window are looking at a similar photograph, which is just visible above the head of a man standing to the centre right of the window. Separated from these men in time and space, others before and after them joined in their looking at history photographically; they saw, and continued to see, what these viewers in 1966 have seen. Yet their historical position as 'observers' (Crary 1992, 5) amidst the jubilee commemorations suggests that looking at these photographs took on added significance as triggers of the mnemonic process.

What I am suggesting here is that Cashman's photograph of the men gathered around the window of 'Historic photo's' provides a departure for 'a history of looking' at photographs as memory objects, which reveals the complexities of the photographic image as a mnemonic device in commemoration. In their retention of the past moment, photographs appear to conform to those other cultural forms of modernity that convert memory into history. In Cashman's photograph, the men see the same photographed event as those viewers of the photograph before and after them. However, their continued circulation across time suggests that their popular currency in shaping memory in the present is not as fixed or as certain as other forms of spatial memory such as monuments and museums. As material objects that were exchanged, bought and sold as commodities and souvenirs, their value as a register and trigger of memory fluctuated and changed over time. As Barthes (1981b, 88) describes it, 'the past is as certain as the present, what we see on paper is as certain as what we touch'. Thus while bringing the past to the present and preserving it for the future through its fixing of time, the photograph is also open to shifting and competing demands, accruing as well as expending value as memory object (Carville 2009).

Conclusion

As Richard Terdiman points out, memory has a history (Terdiman 1993, 3). He reminds us of this not only to reinforce that the differences between history and memory are important, but that history and memory are constantly in dialectical tension with one another. One continually reconfigures the other, drawing on the energy of each to reinforce their relevance in cultural politics. The history of memory in modernity is its increasing externalisation: the gramophone, diary, typewriter, cinema, photographs and of course now the ubiquitous memory stick. These forms of externalising experience, of memory inscription, as Paul Connerton defines it, should not be regarded as memory, nor as it happens as anti-memory, but rather as salient cultural forms through which commemoration is performed (Connerton 1989). As we move towards another milestone in the commemoration of the Rising, it is worth concluding by reflecting on the continued position of photography within the politics of cultural memory of 1916 and its interpretation of history.

In 1966, the *Capuchin Annual* published an essay by a former volunteer, Éilis Ní Chorra, amongst facsimile reproductions of artefacts, photographs and postcards, which it printed to commemorate the Easter Rising. The essay began by evoking the vagaries of memory through the realm of the pictorial, with the author declaring that 'Memory is like a picture gallery where some colours, untouched by the dusty fingers of time, still glow as brightly as when first painted, while others have faded and blurred and nothing remains but a vague outline of something that once was clearly etched' (Ní Chorra 1966, 292). An evocative expression of how some memories gleam or fade with the passing of time, it nevertheless privileges the ocular in the mnemonic process of remembrance. The brute opticality of the visual is perceived as the illuminating energy of recollection while the grubby residuum of touch threatens to dull the luminosity of fast-fading memories. In a culture that has concentrated memory of 1916 in the external spaces of the archive, the museum and monument, the ocular has indeed been bestowed with a privileged status in the commemoration of the Rising. However, this spatial and visual concentration of memory of 1916 places it out of reach from everyday experience. The localisation of memory objects and choreographed displays of silver jubilee, golden jubilee and centennial commemorations is as much about the orchestration of cultural amnesia as it is about regulating how we remember: out of touch, out of mind.

In 2006, during the nintieth anniversary commemorations of 1916, a series of photographs were fly-posted on a wall just off the main thoroughfare of O'Connell St as the military procession and flag-lowering ceremonies took place at the General Post Office. Reproductions of memorial cards to the executed signatories to the 1916 Proclamation, the photographs were accompanied with the caption 'Executed by British Imperialists, 1916'. What is at stake here is not that photography provides a radical rupture to the culture of memory and the state-sanctioned practices of commemoration, but rather that the photograph's material elasticity facilitates alternative mnemonic performances and connections to history. These fading portraits, re-mediated and fly-posted onto the very fabric of the city, may not have seared the memory of 1916 with their vivid colour, but their affective evocation of history are a reminder that the externalisation of memory can be redeemed through our ability to touch the material memories of the past.

22

Ritual, religion and the performance of memory in the Irish Free State

Lisa Godson

In *How societies remember*, Paul Connerton discusses how social memory has been promoted by elites through 'rituals that claim continuity with an appropriate historic past, organising ceremonies/parades and mass gatherings, and constructing new ritual spaces' (Connerton 1989, 51). This short chapter addresses the material aspects of the commemoration of the Rising at one particular ritual space, from 1923 to 1933.

During the War of Independence, Joseph Lawless was detained for a number of months in Arbour Hill.[1] He later recounted how the detention barracks became so overcrowded that there was little room for exercise 'in the immediately adjoining' yard. Instead, prisoners were allowed access to one further away. In that outer yard, 'probably through a whisper from one of the British N.C.O.s', they learned the 'precise spot' in the north-east corner where fourteen of the 1916 leaders had been buried in a trench almost five years previously, although the ground showed 'no sign whatever that any grave existed'.[2] The bodies had been buried in Arbour Hill after the executions in Kilmainham Gaol through the orders of the military governor General Maxwell. He refused the release of the remains to the bereaved families, and reasoned to the Prime Minister that otherwise 'Irish sentimentality' would

---

1 Lawless was detained at Arbour Hill from December 1920 to March 1921 and then Rath Internment Camp at the Curragh until his escape in October 1921. He had participated in the Rising in Ashbourne, supplied cars and ran a munitions factory in Parnell Street, Dublin, and joined the National Army for a short time in February 1922, rejoining on the outbreak of the Civil War in June 1922. See Irish Military Archives military service pensions files MA/24/SP/2912 as well as his witness statement to the Bureau of Military History (entitled 'Recollections of the Anglo-Irish War 1916–1921'), MA/BMH/WS 1043. Witness: Joseph V. Lawless, Member IV, Fingal, 1916; Officer IRA, Dublin, 1921.
2 MA/BMH/WS 1043.

turn the graves into 'martyrs' shrines' and annual processions would be made to them 'which will cause constant irritation in this country' (Townshend 2005, 301).[3] As such, by denying a tangible materiality to the leaders' graves, Maxwell tried to ensure they could not be sacralised.

However, within a day or two of discovering its location, prisoners started gathering at the burial site of the dead leaders 'to recite the rosary each day for the repose of their souls and for the triumph of the cause for which they had died'.[4] Through the daily prayers, the invisible grave was activated from the unvariegated surface and achieved a presence, called into being through religious gesture, rite and utterance, typical 'acts of separation' to mark the different spheres of the sacred and profane (Agamben 2007). The praying at the grave by Lawless and his colleagues was looked upon by the prison authorities as 'a political demonstration' and after a few days the prisoners were debarred from that outer yard.

Within a couple of years, the grave at Arbour Hill was more fully materialised as a ritual site. Historians have written that 1924 was the first year an official state ceremony was held at Arbour Hill to commemorate the 1916 Rising (Fitzpatrick 2001, 196; Ferriter 2007, 200; Wills 2010, 136).[5] However, in the dying days of the Civil War one year earlier, the National Army held a ceremony that fixed the official commemorative format for decades to come. The event's precedence was noted in the *Freeman's Journal*: 'it is probable that yesterday's ceremony will be an annual one'.[6]

This was on 3 May 1923, the anniversary of the execution of Patrick Pearse, Thomas Clarke and Thomas MacDonagh, when rituals commenced 'early in the morning' with a parade of more than 1,000 troops at Collins Barracks. Then 'headed by their brass and reed and fife and drum bands, which rendered the solemn strains of the Dead March,'[7] the soldiers marched the short distance from the barracks to the garrison church at Arbour Hill for Solemn Requiem Mass, where they were joined by the President and members of the government and armed forces.

Afterwards, the soldiers marched to the yard where the bodies had been buried, uncoffined, in a quicklime pit. By now, the site was simply indicated by a 'small, green, moss-covered cross'.[8] The rosary was recited in Irish,

---

3 Townshend quotes from Maxwell to H.H. Asquith, 25 May 1916, Bodleian Library, Oxford, MS Asquith 43.
4 MA/BMH/WS 1043.
5 For arrangements and planning of the official ceremonies, see National Archives of Ireland, Department of the Taoiseach files TSCH/3/S9815 A [Easter Week commemorations 1925–41] and TSCH/3/S9815 B for 1949–54.
6 'A historic event', *Freeman's Journal*, 4 May 1923.
7 'A historic event'.
8 'A historic event'.

three volleys fired over the grave, and the Last Post sounded. Through its timing and form, the ceremony's identity as a commemoration of the event or action of the Rising of 24–29 April was ambiguous. Although characterised as 'the annual observence of the Republic's proclamation on Easter Monday' (Fitzpatrick 2001, 196), in fact it aligned remembrance to the deaths of the martyred leaders and not the dates of the Rising nor the moveable feast of Easter. Its central 'commemorative' ceremony was a requiem anniversary Mass, its format dictated by the rubrics of the Catholic Church and military funerary ceremony.

However formal and fixed the ritual was, in 1923 it was represented in terms that suggested the pro-Treaty side derived their moral and military authority from the martyrs of 1916. Newspapers reported the event in terms of the army paying tribute, mourning and laying claim to *its* dead – the *Freeman's Journal* described Pearse as 'the first Commander-in-Chief of the Irish Army' and suggested that he and his comrades 'may be regarded as the foundation stones of the new Irish state'.[9] The *Irish Independent* described the men in front of the leaders' graves as 'the victorious Army they created', and presented that army as the direct descendants of the 1916 heroes, as 'rigid ranks of soldiers clad in the uniform the men they honoured had sanctified with their blood'.[10] As such, the relationship of 1916 to the army was represented in terms of a 'myth of origin', 'the instrument of a teleology' (Ozouf 1988, 276).

For the next few years, the format for official memorialisation changed little, remaining a quasi-private religious ceremony behind the well-guarded gates of Arbour Hill, and almost always on the anniversary of the deaths of at least some of those buried there,[11] whereas republican parades to Glasnevin cemetery took place around Easter. The sense that the anniversary was a natural demonstration of the army being descended from the dead of 1916 was rarely suggested overtly after 1923.

While the chief mourners at the first of the anniversaries at Arbour Hill were the army, in subsequent years the gates creaked open slightly to admit by invitation the relatives of 'those who fell in action' in 1916. Many stayed away, including almost all of those whose family members

---

9 'A historic event'.
10 'The Dead of 1916', *Irish Independent*, 4 May 1923.
11 For example, in 1923 and 1927, the ceremonies were held on 3 May, the anniversary of MacDonagh, Pearse and Clarke; in 1924 and 1925 on 4 May, the anniversary of Joseph Mary Plunkett, Edward Daly, Michael O'Hanrahan and Willie Pearse; in 1926 on 5 May, anniversary of John MacBride; in 1928 on 9 May, anniversary of Thomas Kent, executed and buried in Cork; in 1929 on 8 May, anniversary of Éamonn Ceannt, Conn Colbert, Seán Heuston and Michael Mallin. The specific day of the week the ceremonies were held on varied from year to year.

were buried there.[12] So although Jay Winter, the historian of mourning and memory, writes that 'practices of public commemoration respond directly to individuals' need for consolation' (Winter 1995, 29), in the early years the Arbour Hill ceremonies were an irritant for those who most needed consoling, as were other Free State commemorative events (see Dolan 2003). The Civil War had fractured a unitary 'collective' memory of 1916 and the state's control of the graves of the leaders in effect prohibited mourning at the very place and by the very people that it meant the most to. When the site came under the control of Fianna Fáil following their election in 1932, Kathleen Clarke, whose husband Tom and brother Ned Daly were buried in Arbour Hill, wrote that she had 'never seen those graves' and never intended to visit them 'on a permit from any source',[13] and, in an ironic twist, for that year's ceremonies, Éamonn Ceannt's widow 'who had never seen her husband's grave' could not be present as she was attending the funeral of Michael Mallin's widow, one of the few relatives who had attended the ceremonies since 1923.[14]

From 1925, the general public were allowed to visit the graves following the formal ceremonies.[15] Some flourishes were added, the sight and sound of the event spilling into public space (and probably within earshot of republican prisoners in Arbour Hill prison); by 1925, troops from Portobello and from Phoenix Park marched to Collins' Barracks, 'where they paraded with other units taking part in the display' and as the buglers within the walls of Arbour Hill began to sound the last bar of the Last Post at the graves, 'echo buglers in Collins Barracks and at G.H.Q. Parkgate St started to sound the "Last Post" and a strikingly impressive effort was produced'.[16] A guard of honour of four men was mounted on the grave from the firing party until the gates were closed again at 6 o'clock.[17]

By this stage, the church and the yard had been more permanently marked as a site of remembrance. A tripartite stained glass window by Earley and Company had been inserted in the wall of the chancel in 1925 bearing a dedication to the men who had died for Ireland (the inscription reads 'i ndíl-chuimhne na bhfear a fuair bás ar son na hÉireann, 1916–1924');[18]

---

12 Of the executed men, only Michael Mallin's widow attended in earlier years; by 1928, a couple of the relatives of Eamonn Ceannt and James Connolly were in attendance. See 'The Men of 1916', *Irish Independent*, 10 May 1928.

13 'The graves in Arbour Hill: touching letter from Mrs. Tom Clarke', *Meath Chronicle*, 19 March 1932.

14 'The graves at Arbour Hill', *Irish Press*, 3 May 1932.

15 'Tribute: Arbour Hill display', *Irish Independent*, 5 May 1925.

16 'Tribute: Arbour Hill display'.

17 'Tribute: Arbour Hill display'.

18 'Patriots of 1916: a beautiful memorial', *Irish Independent*, 5 May 1925.

the graves were now 'fenced off by a low white railing' and 'very simply and effectively decorated'.[19] These subtle changes edged the complex of churchyard commemoration closer to becoming a 'ritual-architectural event', a term devised by architectural historian Lindsay Jones to describe sacred architecture in hermeneutic terms (Jones 2000). The lack of individual names on the mass grave suggested that the significance of the place was public ceremony, not private mourning. In recognition of its use as a ceremonial site, what had previously been described as a yard was soon termed a 'parade ground'.[20] But, under Cumann na nGaedheal, there was little innovation in the ceremonial repetoire employed at these events – in action, temporality and spatial practice, they were circumscribed by existing ritual formats that gave a gloss of transcendence to the events rather than representing the historicity of the Rising.

In terms of a 'usable past' (Commager 1967) that could be easily represented as inevitably leading to the present, the Easter Rising was clearly fraught with problems for Cumann na nGaedheal as leaders of the compromised Free State rather than upholders of the Republic declared in 1916. With the legitimacy of the Free State, including Cumann na nGaedheal's 'right' to invoke 1916, coming under severe challenge in the years immediately after the Civil War, the religious nature of the 1916 ceremonies is understandable. In Maurice Bloch's influential analysis of ritual, he asserts that political and religious power is generally asserted through extreme formalisation in ritual, thus diminishing propositional force (Bloch 1989, 33), and the form of a requiem mass with its fixed rites was unassailable. It also spoke to other ways the government mobilised religious ritual to assert its legitimacy.

A fundamental way the Cumann na nGaedheal government addressed uncertainty in its early years was through drawing on the 'superabundant reserves of political legitimacy' held by the Catholic Church (Garvin 1996, 180). While generally represented in legal and individual terms, for example, the new politicians enacting laws 'enforcing public morality' along Catholic lines and politicians 'making their personal piety publicly known' (Garvin 1996, 181), it was also through drawing on what, to the minds of the Catholic population, was actual spiritual power. State rituals of celebration and of commemoration were cast in religious terms. The *Irish Catholic Directory*'s annual record of ecclesiastical events traces the way that, while there was just one desultory (secular) attempt to celebrate the foundation of the Free State (Fitzpatrick 2001, 199), most of its offices, agents and works were publicly blessed and even consecrated, thus emphasising the confessional identity

19 'Tribute: Arbour Hill display'.
20 *Irish Press*, 24 March 1932.

of the nation. For example, the new national police force (the Civic Guard, later to become the Garda Síochána) was solemnly consecrated to the Sacred Heart in a ceremony of 15,000 men in April 1923.[21] The army, so central to the Arbour Hill ceremonies, were consistent, eager and prominent participants in many specifically religious events. This was partly through their role as ceremonial functionaries, for example, by providing a guard of honour to visiting ecclesiastical dignitaries and to the Eucharist at Corpus Christi processions. The armed forces also demonstrated their religious credentials in more self-selected ways: as early as March 1922, Irish troops in Beggars Bush barracks publicly paraded to mass in the Pro-Cathedral,[22] and public parades to mass became a convention, as did participation in pilgrimages.[23]

Whereas Cumann na nGaedheal 'commemorations' had tightly focused on the anniversaries, and on the church, barracks and burial yard, when Fianna Fáil came to power in 1932, they expanded the scope of Arbour Hill better to assert their more fulsome inheritance of 1916. First, they opened access to the burial site on Easter Sunday and Monday, linking it more generally to the Rising.[24] Although initially represented as for the public, Fianna Fáil used this as an opportunity to make political speeches.[25] From 1933, they publicly extended the invitation to the annual anniversary ceremonies to the relatives of the '77' executed during the Civil War alongside those of the 1916 dead, symbolically enlarging the burial site and the concept of anniversary.[26] Another form of 'enlargement' was the initiation of processions through the city to Arbour Hill, soon involving parades by a variety of organisations.[27] The General Post Office became the central focal point for state commemoration of the Rising from 1934, and although anniversary ceremonies continued at the burial site, interest diverted eastwards to O'Connell Street.

21 *Irish Catholic Directory* (henceforth *ICD*), 1924, 566.
22 *ICD* 1923, 569.
23 For a sense of the persistence of this role for the army, see 'Adjournment matters – army presence at religious ceremonies', 3 June 1992, *Seanad Éireann Debates*, 132(17), 9.
24 'Arbour Hill graves open to public at Easter', *Irish Press*, 24 March 1932.
25 A 1916 memorial event with political speeches is still held by Fianna Fáil every Easter at Arbour Hill – for example, on 27 April 2014, publicised as 'Annual Fianna Fáil Easter Rising 1916 Commemoration'. www.fiannafail.ie/content/pages/9707. Accessed 10 March 2014.
26 'Arbour Hill ceremony', *Irish Press*, 3 May 1933.
27 See, for example, 'Arbour Hill: where leaders lie', *Irish Independent*, 17 April 1933.

Afterword
Lost city of the archipelago:
Dublin at the end of empire

Nicholas Allen

In 1916, the citizens of Dublin, rebels and soldiers inhabited a moment of profound change in Ireland and the wider world. The nineteenth-century expansion of European imperial power had given shape to Irish politics, even as the desolation of the Famine preceded a convergence of late nineteenth-century Atlantic economies. In Dublin, the reality of dreadful poverty was obscured by the growing consumption of imported goods as the British Empire rose to the zenith of its trading power and as increasing wages made the objects of trade accessible to a wider population (O'Rourke and Williamson 1999, 147–8). This phase of imperial globalisation began its end in 1914 with the advent of war. The siren of this change in Ireland was the Easter Rising, a rebellion led by a cohort of militants and idealists, a significant number of whom were radicalised by their own complicated experiences of migration. I argue here that the intensity of Irish separatism can be understood better in relation to its imperial counterparts of exchange and capital flows. John Darwin (2011, 7) notes that in 'national' histories links forged by the circulation of goods and ideas retreat to the margins, or form the static backdrop to a national 'project'. The lens of late imperialism captures the global complexity and hybrid experience of Ireland in the period in question. The rebellion crossed two worlds. It was a product of the old order and a prototype for the new, an early sign of the other revolutions still to come in other empires: as Doherty and Keogh (2007, 23) argue,

> the events of 1916 can best be understood, neither as a starting point (though it clearly gave the republican cause a momentum that it had previously lacked) nor as a terminus (crucial though it undoubtedly was, for example in the subsequent collapse of the Irish Party), but rather as a decisive turning point in the history of Ireland over the *longue durée.*

This afterword considers elements of Dublin's cultural, material and architectural renderings in relation to the expanding British world system of the late nineteenth and early twentieth centuries, as befits the study of a radical generation born largely in the 1870s and 1880s (McMahon 1999, 138). This requires us to search to find new terms and revised forms, such as archipelago and empire, to map the world moment onto 1916 (e.g., Pocock 2005; Kerrigan 2008; Darwin 2011). Empire had militarised Irish culture in the decades previous to the war, and Ireland's experience of militarisation must be situated within a pan-European if not a global context (Bartlett and Jeffery 1997; Horne 2008). It had also exposed the island to an expanding global economy while providing increased access to education and trade. One result of this was a transformation in the nature of goods available. In general, the

> consequence for consumers in Britain of the shifts of entrepreneurs, administrators, and workers out to and around the Empire was tea from Ceylon, cocoa from the Gold Coast, sugar from Mauritius, bananas from Jamaica, sago from Malaya, wheat from Canada, and New Zealand lamb for dinner. Industry absorbed palm-oil from Nigeria, wool from Australia, cotton from the Sudan, and metal ores from Northern Rhodesia. (Constantine 1999, 164)

These material developments underpinned the cultural and political movements that fed the rebellion.

After 1918, the emergence of new nations (and the restitution of old ones) obscured the imperial cultures of their seceding populations. The archives are a last repository of the traces that indicate the existence of these old alignments (and one of the ironies of the commemoration planning of the rebellion's centenary is the degree to which the now public documents, like the witness statements and pension records, tell us at least as much about the material history of Ireland's imperial culture as they do about the political ideology of separatism). The fabric of this late imperial society in Ireland was rich and torn, and its many threads were unpicked as material to dress the national tapestry after independence. The rags of this past are bound to a material history that has survived hidden in plain sight for a century – a material history stored and exhibited in state collections according to the demands of the evolving national narrative, while at the same time facilitating private remembrance through the personal collections of individual citizens.

The British Empire spanned the world's oceans, its territories joined by a network of coastal stations that linked the most remote landing to the wharves of London. Its myriad trades extended beyond its formal boundaries as other empires overlapped its sea routes and pathways. The potential for conflict was constant, even as this British world was at its zenith: as David Cannadine (2001, 71) writes,

> On the eve of the First World War, and notwithstanding the participation of France, Germany and Belgium in the 'Scramble for Africa', the British Empire was still very much the greatest and the grandest in the world. Taken together, the dominions of settlement, the Indian Empire and the tropical colonies comprised an imperium that was without rival in terms of its territorial extent, its mixture of variety and coherence, and its unifying characterisitcs of hierarchy and tradition.

All of Ireland's major cities were ports, as were many of its important secondary towns. Dublin retained its architectural advantage in the eighteenth century layout of its centre. It was further networked into the island as a whole though the system of docks and canals that brought its imports to the inland heart of the country, a distribution inhibited by the lack of a closely sited railway station. Mary Daly observes that despite major investment in the North Wall and Alexandria Basin, 'Dublin singularly failed to develop a significant deep-sea trade and the return on capital invested in berths and quay space for overseas shipping was low' (Daly 1995, 7); so every orange in the west of Ireland came there through Liverpool.

Cork had a centuries-old history as a centre of provisions for the Americas. After 1914, it was guardian to the Atlantic approaches and a major sea port in the defence of Britain (Nolan and Nolan 2009). Belfast was brash and less planned because its nineteenth-century growth was rapid and industrial. The city was built on stilts as it crept into the sea and these uncertain, alluvial foundations have given the poets a metaphor for Belfast's instability. Louis MacNeice's 'Valediction' (2002, 52) describes a city 'devout and profane and hard / Built on reclaimed mud, hammers playing in the shipyard'. Galway, Limerick and Derry were barrack towns that supplied steady streams of migrant workers into the northern archipelago of the British coast. Each of these places, and others, like Waterford in the south, had their individual histories of imperial contact and culture. In addition, a significant but variable volume of people moved through the Irish ports to seasonal work on the other island. The *Irish Times* reported in the early summer of 1916 that after the rebellion the

> military authorities in Ireland have now advised that the port of Londonderry will be open from to-day for the departure of migrating labourers to Scotland. In normal times the number of such migrants through this port at the harvest (hay and corn) season is about two

thousand, but it is not expected that the number will be nearly so large this year.[1]

In 1916, Dublin, like Belfast and Cork, was a hub of global exchange. The impact, depth and texture of its cultural, historical and political place within the world system of overlapping empires underpins the work of its great laureate, James Joyce, and his magical sensibility of objects, a sensibility that has historical form. From the early days of the Atlantic trade, the populations of Britan and Ireland thought of the colonies as the commodities they produced (Chaplin 2011, 229; Davis and Huttenback 1986). Joyce's realism is less a picture of the world as it was than a rendering of the empire as it was experienced through the senses. Again, this has colonial provenance. The discovery of the Americas brought vanilla, tobacco and scent to Europe. James Joyce's *A portrait of the artist as a young man* was first published in New York in December 1916. It begins with a passage that brings the senses and the sea together:

> He was baby tuckoo. The moocow came down the road where Betty Byrne lived: she sold lemon platt.
> *O, the wild rose blossoms*
> *On the little green place.*
> He sang that song. That was his *song*.
> O, the green wothe botheth ...
> His mother had a nicer smell than his father. She played on the piano the sailor's hornpipe for him to dance. He danced
> *Tralala lala,*
> *Tralala tralaladdy,*
> *Tralala lala,*
> *Tralala lala.*
>
> (Joyce 2007, 5)

As the colours of the imperial world fade like so many old uniforms hung in back corners of a falling house, so has that imperial world's effect on the senses diminished. Considering 1916 offers a glimpse into Ireland's part in a world system that was under stress and soon to crack. If the future was still obscure after the Easter Rising, the present was crowded still with refugees from before the war, art and objects the late emissaries of a culture that led to the war, but was not of it. Touch, sight, smell and hearing are fundamental registers of historical context in James Joyce's work. This is true from *Dubliners* to *Finnegans wake*. Up to *A portrait* these

---

1 *Irish Times*, 2 June 1916, 4.

sensations are bound in perceivable ways to the productive life of objects. Ivory, coins, sugar and tea impel their consumers to hold a picture of the world in their mind. That world was bound by the brutal execution of a global trade secured in part by military force and cultural colonialism. This was as obvious in Ireland as it was in the further colonies: Liam de Paor (1997, 81), for example, makes a point of remembering that many of the Chinese objects that came to Britain at the beginning of the twentieth century were possessions won from the defeat of the Boxer Rebellion in 1900. The sensual presence of this imperial world is legible in the interior life of the objects that populated Ireland's kitchens, libraries and drawing rooms. By thinking about things, as Stephen reflects in *A portrait*, you can understand them (Joyce 2007, 37).

The interpenetration of the material world with the historical and the political has made it difficult to unpack the idea of empire. Further, the attempt to consider any aspect of Irish culture as imperial can provoke the reaction that this is but another attempt to legitimise a British presence in Ireland. There is merit in this argument, if only because the new British studies that precipitated the general debate about island histories coincided with a wider conversation about devolution within what remained of the Union. Again, this is fraught in the context of Ireland, in part because of the situation in the north.

The British Empire was a dynamic and sometimes chaotic mechanism by which the interests of a vast swath of territories and people was governed (or at best managed). Ireland had a complex and multifocal relationship with Britain, as did India, Canada and Australia. What was good at one point in time was not at another, as the war proved. Men died for an idea of Britain that they would have died to defeat at another time. Many of the Volunteers were trained by soldiers from the British Army and many members of the Irish Republican Army fought first in the Great War. Like their counterparts in continental Europe, they found demobilisation a possible step towards separatist politics. There remains much work to be done in the systematic and analytical recovery of the relationship between members of the British Army, the Irish Volunteers, and later that between soldiers who survived the war and the republican movement. This question might extend into the formation of the Free State and its various forces. Emblematic figures like Tom Barry are well known; the intricacies of family, community and political ties are less familiar and may do more to inform us of the long bridging moment between empire and independence. The effect on public life of these individuals was often in gross disproportion to their actual number.

Empire faltered as a system of governance and possession after 1914. Hovering in the visible future were new political systems, which in Ireland included Home Rule, liberal democracy, constitutional monarchy, republicanism and mutual aid. Perched on the edge of the Atlantic, Ireland was a transit hub for emerging ideas of global significance. If the actual scale of Ireland's participation, or not, in world wars and treaties was insignificant in terms of its resident population, its laboratory status made Ireland almost uniquely problematic. Ireland was half in and half out of the dominant world arrangement. Its population was subject further to long-term dispersal to America and the British colonies. Owing to circumstance and history, nineteenth- and then twentieth-century Ireland operated in a world exchange whose fulcrum was about to break. Caught nearest the churning cogs, and in no small part responsible for their malfunction, Ireland was remade rapidly and radically. As empires threatened to collapse inwards, Ireland was the last of the old nations and the first of the new. As Darwin (2009, 7) suggests, "'British connections" were dynamic not static. Their strength and solidity at any particular time were powerfully (perhaps decisively) shaped by the play of economic and geopolitical forces at the global not just imperial level'. Belfast, Dublin and Cork were imperial cities in their administration, architecture and, to contested degrees, their public culture (see, e.g., Dickson 2005; Kilfeather 2005; Connolly 2013). All were connected to a network of other cities and empires, each of which was its own patchwork of local history and transnational association. Their imperial ties were not restricted to the British. They were also French, Austro-Hungarian and German (and, with some licence, American).

If empire was a construct combined of goods and force then an individual's sense of objects and authority reflects an imperial culture that was weakened by the war and destroyed by rebellion. The witness statements that were stored in the Bureau of Military History are now open to full public access. Historians have made much of their significance to the political genesis of separatist violence in Ireland. But the witness statements are at least as important as a cultural resource. In explaining the social context for volunteer activity, they illustrate the intimate textures of late imperial life in Ireland. The great sense of confusion that attended the rebellion as it unfolded suggests the degree to which a national separation was inconceivable to a population the fabric of whose daily life was generated by imperial trade.

Stock reports show how profit was chased around the world. Bonds were dealt with Brazil, Peru and China, shares traded in railways that ran through Africa and interest taken in ships that steamed to Port Said; a single page of the *Irish Independent* listed dividends from South African Mines, Mexican Eagle Oil and British American Tobacco, among many others.[2] Ireland's claim to a share in this speculation was formed in part from its contribution to the construction of this system in the first place, and part

2   *Irish Independent*, 22 December 1916, 5.

from the threat it posed to the whole if it broke off. The actual consequences of secession were unknown. Britain's global network was represented as a force of civilisation, imagined to exist as organic and progressive. In reality it was haphazard and provisional, formed of local arrangements and chance opportunities: Hyam (2010, 1, 21) proposes the idea of 'informal empire', 'a loose aggregation of diffuse elements, often uncertain, inherently complex, endlessly uneven in its impact' (see also Darwin 2009, xi). Imperial authority was elastic and, as the rebellion showed, unpredictable in its application. There was no simple relation between centre and periphery. Dublin and London were open, imperial cities. Although different in history, culture and contemporary wealth, Daly (1985, 4) has observed of Dublin that 'A comparison of the city's spread of occupations, derived from the population censuses reveals a city much closer to London in the variety of its activities than to any English or Irish provincial city' and, furthermore, that '23% of migrants, mostly in the elite public service and business positions, were born outside Ireland, indicating Dublin's position as a colonial city where many of the most privileged occupations were filled by outsiders' (Daly 1985, 16). Dublin, London and many other cities besides were ports in the archipelago of empire. They were transit hubs for objects and ideas, crossing points for populations that could live their lives in the empire without ever attending to its core metropolis. If the story of Ireland in 1916 is profligate and uncertain, its many forms still have something to tell us of this cultural moment that, if not unique, underlies much of the national architecture today.

For the privileged, empire was a sensorium of objects arranged in the domestic space of the home. For the less well off, its projected image was inscribed in the public spaces of the museums and libraries. Its emblems were carved into the statuary and buildings of its cities. It permeated popular culture because it attached itself to every aspect of the traded commodity, which by the turn of the twentieth century was one of the bedrocks of the Irish economy. A large part of the population experienced the imperial presence as symbolic and material, not political. The urban population of Dublin knew Britain through their home city's architecture: the population living in Irish towns and cities rose dramatically between the Famine and the First World War, so that more people than ever before had access to Dublin as an imperial city (O'Rourke and Williamson 1999, 150). Dublin Castle, the gaols and the barracks were the bones of the imperial skeleton. Trinity College faced Grattan's parliament, which had been sold to the Bank of Ireland in 1803. This transaction heralded the coming of the nineteenth-century empire. Education and trade were twin pillars of a global economy that promised unprecedented access to unclaimed wealth. There were equivalents in Belfast and Cork with their new universities and strong merchant princes, and all of them depended on the sea as a conduit for global trade. Cork had been involved in a transatlantic business since at least the settling of the Caribbean colonies, which the province of Munster did so much to provision (Rogers 2007). Belfast took the opportunity one stage further and began to build the ships that sailed the seas. Edward Harland and Gustav Wolff transformed the industrial capacity of the northern city. The profits of that period are visible still in the baroque grotesquerie of the City Hall. By 1916, Ireland was a major exporter of food to the other British isles. In 1913, it had sold 33 million tonnes of provisions there, equal to volumes from the USA. Two out of every five cattle fattened in Britain were imported from Ireland.[3] So prolific was the supply of aeroplane canvas that Lord French said the 'war in the air was won on Belfast wings' (Moore 1922, 162).

British power was veiled in the senses. Empire was tasted, smelled and seen. Walter Benjamin wrote in the *Arcades project* that 'To write history means giving dates their physiognomy' (cited in Olsen 2010, 107). If the archive represents a material repository of historical experience, then the history of lost or destroyed objects, as may be recovered only in memory or in fragments, is imaginable in a language of sensation. Empire offered pleasure before persecution, so long as there was happy access to the table. Its pathways were open to the experience of cultures beyond its borders. The Mediterranean and the Americas were the preserve of many powers. Participation in the British Empire gave access to a multiple world of experience that exceeded the drab conditions of life in the provinces (which was part of the allure of military service). Joyce registered these perceptions in *Dubliners*. The final story of that collection is 'The Dead', which is celebrated as a forensic examination of the cultural aftermath of the famine. In it Gabriel Conroy finds that his wife Gretta has harboured a love for a dead boy in the west of Ireland. Michael Furey died of consumption, a pun worthy of the connection between capital and infection. The setting for this miniature tragedy is Gabriel's aunts' house on Usher's Island on the south side of the Dublin quays. The splendour of the Christmas dinner is a ploy to provoke the imagination to picture the abomination of famine to follow. But it is also a map of the world that took shape in Dublin through the experience of objects. As Gabriel worries over his speech the narrator takes the reader on a tour of imperial imports. The table is book-ended with a goose and a side of beef, with a plump ham in between:

Between these rival ends ran parallel lines of side-dishes: two little

---

3   National Library of Ireland (NLI), NLI/MS/15262/3, John Redmond papers, figures from briefing notes for the Department of Agriculture attached to a letter from T.P. Gill to John Redmond, 18 March 1916.

minsters of jelly, red and yellow; a shallow dish full of blocks of blancmange and red jam, a large green leaf-shaped dish with a stalk-shaped handle, on which lay bunches of purple raisins and peeled almonds, a companion dish on which lay a solid rectangle of Smyrna figs, a dish of custard topped with grated nutmeg, a small bowl full of chocolates and sweets wrapped in gold and silver papers and a glass vase in which stood some tall celery stalks. In the centre of the table there stood, as sentries to a fruit-stand which upheld a pyramid of oranges and American apples, two squat old-fashioned decanters of cut glass, one containing port and the other dark sherry. (Joyce 1996, 196)

Dinner is a map of the world organised on imperial principles. Goods are arranged on military lines, in squads and sashes suitable to their value. The almonds, figs and nutmeg signal Dublin's connection to an exchange of the senses. Irish nationalists created their own propaganda in response to this trade expansionism. They promoted a culture of national purity that was aggressively critical of the jobbery they associated with constitu-tional nationalists in the Irish Parliamentary Party. In their formation, an independent Ireland would return to its pre-invasion condition of utopic self-sufficiency. Whatever the reality of such a proposition, the ideal had immense imaginative appeal since it proceeded from the domestic familiarity through which Irish people had integrated into imperial culture. The fabric of daily life in Dublin, Cork and Belfast was interwoven with things from elsewhere. They could be food, or its wrappings, furniture, decoration or the paper on which the minority wrote. The poor who could not afford these things saw advertisements plastered on walls or goods in shop windows. The war turned this domestic world inside out. The regular notice of dead men in the trenches was followed by advertisement of their goods by auction in the newspapers of record. Mahogany tables and walnut sideboards had empanelled the interior of the Irish upper middle-classes with the scented texture of the Far East; ivory piano keys and ornaments brought Africa to the drawing rooms.

The decades following the First World War secured the idea of grand armies caught in stalemate, with the occasional flare up in peripheral theatres. The public understanding of the war was more sophisticated than this at the time, not least because so many relatives were caught up in its campaigns. Beginning in no man's land and stretching to the prisoner of war camps, the barracks and the refugee centres, Europe, and at its extremity, Ireland, churned with the movement of people. The ideas, books and belongings these people carried changed the environments they encountered by contacts that took force as much from their frequency as from their substance. This exchange was part of Ireland's history. Emigration, forced or otherwise, was one established route into the wider world. Trade, education and imperial service had offered other entries into global communication. This process was well-established in the nineteenth century. The advertisements for Dublin's auction houses map a previous generation's practices of acquisition: mahogany panels and ivory-keyed pianos suggest that Africa, India and the Americas had their place in the city's suburbs. These collections extended into the provinces. The estate of a Mr Tuite was advertsised for sale in two auctions in Dublin and Mullingar. It included:

> his collection of coins, medals, antiques, Irish Antiquarian articles … objects of eastern furniture and other such items, pictures and … books, many of which are of local and antiquarian interest, including 'Lyons' Grand Juries of Westmeath', with supplement written up to the year 1909; musical instruments, Italian Statuary, Cameras with special lenses, photographic apparatuses, book cases, many objects of Eastern and other furniture and art, etc., etc.[4]

The war changed the conditions of these transactions. As the imperial economy turned to military production, the trade in surplus goods thinned out. The bureaucracy that served this global exchange was drained quickly by the war. Increasingly, the demand for soldiers from the home countries was difficult to meet. For the Irish abroad, patriotism chimed with a call home. Dublin became a new global capital whose currency was the letters of the dead and wounded. Working in a Dublin asylum, Thomas King Moylan noticed a package addressed to one of the residents. Mother to a soldier killed in Gallipoli, she received a package of effects, which included a card to a Warwickshire girl. It read:

> On active service. Please post this to the following … 'Dear Norah – if I am Killed in action someone may be kind enough to post this to you. Good By for ever. E. Byrne.'[5]

The material history of the Easter Rising draws us inevitably into the tangled complex of late empire. This world, in which ideas of Ireland, Turkey and England overlap in a battle between the British, Ottoman and other empires, is anomalous with regard to the national narratives that overtook imperial hegemony at the war's ending. The material and symbolic power of these dead global arrangements attach still to the objects that once underpinned these empires built on trade. Material culture is in itself a rich

4 *Westmeath Examiner*, 23 December 1916, 4.
5 NLI/MS/9620, Thomas King Moylan diary, 8 February 1916.

resource for new thinking about the past. It is, however, in Ireland's case more than this again. Object history is the orchestration of global questions in concert with a sequence of material contexts. It is the prompt to think of the insular history of nations in comparative context even as the situation of these objects in their cultural moment compels us to reconfigure the place in which we have put them. In the last century, that place was more frequently the storage room and the library archive. The commemoration of the rebellion and of the war, and the work of generations of scholars, has opened a door into these dusty spaces. The challenge that remains is to keep the objects uncovered in public view if only because sight of them reminds us all how contemporary the global past can be.

References

Adams, M. 1990. *Great adventure: male desire and the coming of World War I.* Indianapolis, IN: Indiana University Press.

Agamben, G. 2007. *Profanations* (trans. J. Fort). New York, NY: Zone Books.

Ahern, B. 2009. *The autobiography.* London: Hutchinson.

Albert (Fr.) OFM Cap. 1935. How Seán Heuston died. *Capuchin Annual*, 161–4.

— 1942. How Seán Heuston died. *Capuchin Annual*, 343–4.

Alberti, S. 2005. Objects and the museum. *Isis* 96, 559–71.

Allen, N. and Brown, T. 2011. Publishing after partition, 1922–1932. In Hutton, C. and Walsh, P. (eds) *The Oxford history of the Irish book*, vol. 5, *The Irish book in English, 1891–2000*, 702. Oxford: Oxford University Press.

Aloysius (Fr.) OFM Cap. 1942. Easter Week 1916: personal recollections. *Capuchin Annual*, 211–20.

Alter, P. 1987. Symbols of Irish nationalism. In O'Day, A. (ed.) *Reactions to Irish nationalism, 1865–1914*, 1–21. London: Hambledon.

*An bhratach náisiúnta/*The national flag. 1953. Dublin: Stationery Office.

Appadurai, A. (ed.) 1998. *The social life of things: commodities in cultural perspective.* Cambridge: Cambridge University Press.

Arnold, B. 1998. *Jack Yeats.* New Haven, CT/London: Yale University Press.

Ash, J. 2010. *Dress behind bars. Prison clothing as criminality.* London: I.B. Taurus.

Attfield, J. 2000. *Wild things: the material culture of everyday life.* Oxford: Berg.

Barnard, T. 2005. *A guide to sources for the history of material culture in Ireland, 1500–2000.* Dublin: Four Courts Press.

Barnes, J. 2012. *Through the window: seventeen essays (and one short story).* London: Vintage Books.

Barrett, R. 2010. *Twice condemned: Irish views of the Dreyfus affair.* Dublin: Original Writing.

Barry, T. 1989. *Guerilla days in Ireland.* Dublin: Anvil Books.

Barth, F. 1969. *Ethnic groups and boundaries*. Boston, MA: Little, Brown and Co.

Barthes, R. 1981a. The discourse of history (trans. S. Bann). In Shaffer, E.S. (ed.) *Comparative criticism: a yearbook*, vol. 3, 7–20. Cambridge: Cambridge University Press.

— 1981b. *Camera lucida: reflections on photography* (trans. R. Howard). London: Flamingo.

— 1987. *Michelet* (trans. R. Howard). London: Hill & Wang.

— 1993 [1957]. *Mythologies* (trans. A. Lavers). London: Random House.

Bartlett, T. and Jeffery, K. (eds) 1997. *A military history of Ireland*. Cambridge: Cambridge University Press.

Barton, B. 2002. *From behind a closed door: secret court martial records of the 1916 Easter Rising*. Belfast: Blackstaff Press.

Batchen, G. 2004. *Forget me not: photography and remembrance*. New York, NY: Princeton Architectural Press.

Battaglia, D. 1990. *On the bones of the serpent: person, memory and mortality in Sabarl island society*. Chicago, IL: University of Chicago Press.

Bazin, A. 1960. The ontology of the photographic image. *Film Quarterly* 13(4), 4–9.

Beegan, G. 2008. *The mass image: a social history of photomechanical reproduction in Victorian London*. Basingstoke: Palgrave Macmillan.

Benjamin, W. 1968. Theses on the philosophy of history. In Benjamin, W. *Illuminations* (trans. H. Zohn), 253–64. New York, NY: Harcourt Brace Jovanovich.

— 1973. On some motifs in Baudelaire. In Benjamin, W. *Illuminations* (trans. H. Zohn), 152–90. London: Fontana.

Bennett, A. 2004. *The history boys*. London: Faber and Faber.

Bhabha, H.K. 1994. *The location of culture*. London and New York, NY: Routledge.

Bhreathnach-Lynch, S. 1997. The Easter Rising 1916. Constructing a canon in art and artefacts. *History Ireland* (spring), 37–42.

— 2007. *Ireland's art/Ireland's history: representing Ireland, 1845 to the present*. Omaha, NE: Creighton University Press.

Blackstone, W. 1837. *The commentaries on the laws of England in four books* (3rd edn). London: John Murray.

Bloch, M. 1989. *History, ritual and power: selected papers in anthropology*. London: Athlone Press.

Bodeman, M.Y. 2002. *In den Wogen der Erinnerung*. Munich: dtv.

Bodkin, T. 1949. *Report on the arts in Ireland*. Dublin: Stationery Office.

Bouch, J.J. 1936. *The republican Proclamation of Easter Monday 1916: a paper read before the Bibliographical Society of Ireland*. Dublin: At the Sign of the Three Candles.

Bourdieu, P. 1977. *Outline of a theory of practice*. Cambridge: Cambridge University Press.

Boyce, D. 1996. 1916, interpreting the Rising. In Boyce, D. and O'Day, A. (eds) *The making of modern Irish history: Revisionism and the Revisionist controversy*, 163–87. London: Routledge.

Braidotti, R. 2013. *The posthuman*. Cambridge: Polity.

Brand, G. 2009. George Irvine from Enniskillen and the 1916 Dublin Rising. *Spark* 22, 19–22.

Braudy, L. 1999. Acting: stage vs screen. In Braudy, L. and Cohen, M. (eds) *Film theory and criticism*, 419–25. Oxford: Oxford University Press.

Breen, D. 1981. *My fight for Irish freedom*. Dublin: Anvil Books.

Brett, D. 1996. *The construction of heritage*. Cork: Cork University Press.

Brown, B. 2001. Thing theory. *Critical Inquiry* 28(1), 1–22.

Brown, K. 2013. Thomas MacGreevy and Jack B. Yeats. In Schreibman, S. (ed.) *The life and work of Thomas MacGreevy: a critical reappraisal*, 203–16. London: Bloomsbury.

Buchli, V. 2010. Presencing the immaterial. In Bille, M., Hastrup, F. and Sørensen, T. (eds) *An anthropology of absence: materializations of transcendence and loss*, 185–206. Berlin: Springer.

Buchli, V. and Lucas, G. (eds) 2001. *Archaeologies of the contemporary past*. London/New York, NY: Routledge.

Bull, G. (ed.) 1987. *Michelangelo: life, letters, and poetry*. Oxford: Oxford University Press.

Bunreacht na hÉireann/Constitution of Ireland. 1937. Dublin: Stationery Office.

Bunreacht na hÉireann/Constitution of Ireland. 2012. Dublin: Stationery Office.

Caden, S. 2007. *The alderman: alderman Tom Kelly (1868–1942) and Dublin Corporation*. Dublin: Dublin City Council.

Campany, D. 2003. Safety in numbness: some remarks on problems of late photography. In Green, D. (ed.) *Where is the photograph?*, 123–32. Brighton/Maidstone: Photoworks/Photoforum.

Campbell, L. 1946. A contemporary Irish master. Laurence Campbell RHA at work on his statue of Seán Heuston. *Capuchin Annual*, 336–52.

Candlin, F. and Guins, R. (eds) 2009. *The object reader*. Oxford: Routledge.

Candon, A. 2012. What place for contemporary collecting at the National Museum of Ireland? In Barresti, J. (ed.) *Que reste-t-il du présent? Collecter le contemporain dans les musées de société*, 176–8. Bayonne: Festin.

Cannadine, D. 2001. *Ornamentalism: how the British saw their empire*. Oxford: Oxford University Press.

Capuchin Annual. 1945. The Association of Patrons of the *Capuchin Annual*. *Capuchin Annual*, 382–3.

Carew, M. 2013. Patrick Pearse's 'unsightly umbrella'. *Archaeology Ireland* (summer), 10–11.

Carr, G. 2011. Engraving and embroidering emotions upon the material culture of internment. In Myers, A. and Goshenska, G. (eds) *Archaeologies of interment*, 129–45. New York, NY: Springer.

— 2012. 'God save the King!' Creative modes of protest, defiance and identity in Channel Islander internment camps in Germany, 1942–1945. In Carr, G. and Mytum, H. (eds) *Cultural heritage and prisoners of war: creativity behind barbed wire*, 168–85. London: Routledge.

Carty, X. 1978. *In bloody protest: the tragedy of Patrick Pearse*. Dublin: Able Press.

Carville, J. 2009. Visualizing the Rising: photography, memory and the visual economy of the 1916 Easter Rising. In Kadar, M., Perreault, J. and Warley, L. (eds) *Photographs, histories and meanings*, 91–109. New York, NY: Palgrave Macmillan.

Casey, C. 2005. *The buildings of Ireland: Dublin. The city within the grand and royal canals and the circular road*. New Haven, CT: Yale University Press.

Casey, E.S. 1998. *The fate of place: a philosophical history*. Berkeley, CA: University of California Press.

Cashman, R. 2008. Visions of Irish nationalism. *Journal of Folklore Research* 45(3), 361–81.

Chambers, C. 2012. *Ireland in the newsreels*. Dublin: Irish Academic Press.

Chaplin, J. 2011. The British Atlantic. In Canny, N. and Morgan, P. (eds) *The Oxford handbook of the Atantic World c.1450–c.1850*, 219–34. Oxford: Oxford University Press.

Clare, A. 2011. *Unlikely rebels: the Gifford Girls and the fight for Irish freedom*. Dublin: Mercier Press.

Clark, K. 1942. Jack Yeats. *Horizon* 5(25), 40–1.

Clifford. J. 1994. Collecting ourselves. In Pearse, S.M. (ed.) *Interpreting objects and collections*, 258–68. London: Routledge.

Cohn, N. 2005. *Warrant for genocide: the myth of the Jewish world conspiracy and the protocols of the Elders of Zion*. London: Serif.

Colum, M. 1947. *Life and the dream*. New York, NY: Doubleday.

Commager, H. 1967. *The search for a usable past, and other essays in historiography*. New York, NY: Alfred A. Knopf.

Conn, S. 2009. *Do museums still need objects?* Philadelphia, PA: University of Pennsylvania Press.

Connerton, P. 1989. *How societies remember*. Cambridge: Cambridge University Press.

Connolly O'Brien, N. 1980. James Connolly. In MacEoin, U. (ed.) *Survivors: the story of Ireland's struggle as told through some of her outstanding living people recalling events from the days of Davitt, through James Connolly, Brugha, Collins, Liam Mellows, and Rory O'Connor, to the present time*, 183–215. Dublin: Argenta Publications.

Connolly, J. 1914. The ballot or the barricades. *Irish Worker*, 24 October.

— 1915. Street fighting – summary. *Workers' Republic*, 24 July.

— 1949a. *Labour in Ireland*. Dublin: At the Sign of the Three Candles Press.

— 1949b. *Labour and Easter Week*. Dublin: At the Sign of the Three Candles Press.

— 1991. Socialism and revolutionary traditions (1900). In Deane, S. (ed.) *The Field Day anthology of Irish writing*, 988–9. Derry: Field Day Publications.

Connolly, S.J. (ed.) 2013. *Belfast 400: people, place and history*. Oxford: Oxford University Press.

Constantine, S. 1999. Migrants and settlers. In Brown, J. and Louis, W.R. (eds) *The Oxford history of the British empire*, vol. 4, *The twentieth century*, 163–87. Oxford: Oxford University Press.

Coogan, T.P. 2003. *Ireland in the twentieth century*. London: Hutchinson.

Cooke, P. 1986. *Scéal Scoil Éanna. The story of an educational adventure*. Dublin: Office of Public Works.

— 2009. Patrick Pearse: the Victorian Gael. In Higgins, R. and Ní Chólltáin, R. (eds) *The life and after-life of P.H. Pearse*, 45–62. Dublin: Irish Academic Press.

— 2013. Art and Kilmainham Gaol: negotiating art's critical intervention in the heritage site. In Russell, I.A. and Cochrane, A. (eds) *Art and archaeology: collaborations, conversations, criticisms*, 83–98. New York, NY: Springer.

— n.d. Kilmainham Gaol: interpreting Irish nationalism and republicanism. *Open Museum Journal* 2, 1–11.

Cosgrove, D. 1984. *Social formation and symbolic landscape*. London: Croom Helm.

Coulter, R. and Kennedy, R. 2013. It is only by learning to fully understand the past that we can most easily come to realise the significance of the present: Thomas MacGreevy, art critic and art historian. In Schreibman, S. (ed.) *The life and work of Thomas MacGreevy: a critical reappraisal*, 51–64. London: Bloomsbury.

Crary, J. 1992. *Techniques of the observer: on vision and modernity in the nineteenth century*. Massachusetts, MA: MIT Press.

Crooke, E. 2000. *Politics, archaeology and the creation of a National Museum of Ireland – expressions of national life*. Dublin: Irish Academic Press.

— 2001. Confronting a troubled history: which past in Northern Ireland's museums? *International Journal of Heritage Studies* 7(2), 119–36.

— 2007. *Museums and community*. London: Routledge.

— 2014. The active museum: how concern with community transformed the museum. In McCarthy, C. (ed.) *Museum practice: critical debates in the contemporary museum*. Oxford/Malden, MA: Wiley-Blackwell.

Crowley, B. 2009. 'I am the son of a good father': James and Patrick Pearse. In Higgins, R. and Ní Chólltáin, R. (eds) *The life and after-life of P.H. Pearse*, 19–32. Dublin: Irish Academic Press.

— 2013. *Patrick Pearse: a life in pictures*. Dublin: Mercier Press.

Csikszentmihalyi M. and Rochberg-Halton, E. 1981. *The meaning of things: domestic symbols and the self*. Cambridge: Cambridge University Press.

Cullen, F. 2004. *The Irish face: redefining the Irish portrait*. London: National Portrait Gallery.

Curran, C.P. 1966. Griffith, Mac Neill and Pearse. *Studies: an Irish quarterly review* 55(217), 21–8.

Daly, M. 1985. *Dublin: the deposed capital: a social and economic history 1860–1914*. Cork: Cork University Press.

— (ed.) 2005. *Roger Casement in Irish and World History*. Dublin: Royal Irish Academy.

Daly, M. and O'Callaghan, M. (eds) 2007. *1916 in 1966: commemorating the Easter Rising*. Dublin: Royal Irish Academy.

D'Arcy, M. and Arden, J. 1986. *The non-stop Connolly show*. London: Pluto Press.

Darwin, J. 2011. *The empire project: the rise and fall of the British world system, 1830–1970* (revised edition). Cambridge: Cambridge University Press.

Davis, F. 1992. *Fashion, culture, and identity*. Chicago, IL: University of Chicago Press.

Davis, L. and Huttenback, R. 1986. *Mammon and the pursuit of empire: the political economy of British imperialism, 1860–1912*. Cambridge: Cambridge University Press.

de Paor, L. 1997. *On the Easter Proclamation and other declarations*. Dublin: Four Courts Press.

Desai, R. and Eckstein, H. 1990. Insurgency: the transformation of peasant rebellion. *World Politics* 42(4), 441–65.

Dickson, D. 2005. *Old world colony: Cork and South Munster, 1630–1830*. Cork: Cork University Press.

Dixon, R. 2004. 'Where are the dead?' Spiritualism, photography and the Great War (Frank Hurley). *History of Photography* 28(2), 247–60.

Doherty, G. and Keogh, D. 2007. Introduction. In Doherty, G. and Keogh, D. (eds) *1916: The long revolution*, 21–3. Cork: Mercier Press.

Dolan, A. 2003. *Commemorating the Irish Civil War: history and memory, 1923–2000*. Cambridge: Cambridge University Press.

Dolmen Press, 1960. *The Easter Proclamation of the Irish Republic, 1916*. Dublin: Dolmen Press.

— 1975. *The Easter Proclamation of the Irish Republic, 1916*. Dublin: Dolmen Press.

Dowling, J. 1936. Art: the National Gallery. *Ireland Today* 1(6), 64–5.

Doyle, R. 1999. *A star called Henry*. London: Jonathan Cape.

Dudley Edwards, R. 1977. *Patrick Pearse and the triumph of failure*. London: Victor Gollancz.

Duffy, C., Sigerson, G. and Hyde, D. 1973. *The revival of Irish literature*. New York, NY: Lemma.

Dunlevy, M. 1989. *Dress in Ireland*. London: Batsford.

Durand, R. 1995. How to see (photographically). In Petro, P. (ed.) *Fugitive images: from photography to video*, 141–51. Bloomington, IN: Indiana University Press.

Durney, J. 2004. *The Volunteer: uniforms, weapons and history of the Irish Republican Army 1913–1997*. Naas: Gaul House.

Dusselier, J. 2012. The arts of survival: remaking the inside spaces of Japanese–American concentration camps. In Carr, G. and Mytum, H. (eds) *Cultural heritage and prisoners of war: creativity behind barbed wire*, 81–97. London: Routledge.

Edwards, E. 1999. Photographs as objects of memory. In Kwint, M., Breward, C. and Aynsley, J. (eds) *Material memories: design and evocation*, 221–36. Oxford: Berg.

Edwards, H. 1929. The historical pageant. In Stephens, E.M. (ed.) *Dublin Civic Week official handbook*, unpaginated. Dublin: Civic Week Council.

Edwards, S. 2006. *Photography: a very short introduction*. Oxford: Oxford University Press.

Elliott, J. 2012. Communicating advanced nationalist identity in Dublin, 1890–1917. PhD thesis (unpublished), University of Warwick.

Evans, S. 2007. *Mothers of heroes, mothers of martyrs: World War I and the politics of grief*. Montreal: McGill-Queen's University Press.

Falk, J.H. and Dierking, L.D. 2013. *Museum experience revisited*. Walnut Creek, CA: Left Coast Press.

Fentress, J. and Wickham, C. 1992. *Social memory: new perspectives on the past*. London: Wiley-Blackwell.

Ferguson, F. and White, K. (eds) 2013. *John Hewitt. A north light. Twenty-five years in a municipal art gallery*. Dublin: Four Courts Press.

Fermanagh County Museum. 2012. 'Connection and Division'. Education pack. Enniskillen: Fermanagh County Museum.

Ferriter, D. 2004. *The transformation of Ireland, 1900–2000*. London: Profile Books.

— 2007. Commemorating the Rising, 1922–65: 'a figurative scramble for the bones of the patriot dead'? In Daly, M. and O'Callaghan, M. (eds) *1916 in 1966: commemorating the Easter Rising*, 198–218. Dublin: Royal Irish Academy.

FitzGerald, D. 1968. *Memoirs of Desmond FitzGerland, 1913–1916*. London: Routledge & Kegan Paul.

Fitzpatrick, D. 2001. Commemoration in the Irish Free State: a chronicle of embarrassment. In McBride, I. (ed.) *History and memory in modern Ireland*, 184–203. Cambridge: Cambridge University Press.

Fitzpatrick, J.D. 2009. Rewriting the past: historical pageantry in the Dublin Civic Weeks of 1927 and 1929. *New Hibernia Review* 12(1), 20–41.

Foucault, M. 1979. *Discipline and punish: the birth of the prison* (trans. A. Sheridan). New York, NY: Vintage Books.

Fox, R.M. 1935. *Rebel Irishwomen*. Dublin: Talbot Press.

— 1943. *History of the Irish Citizen Army*. Dublin: James Duffy.

Foy, M. and Barton, B. 2011. *The Easter Rising*. Stroud: History Press.

Fraser, N. 2007. Transnationalizing the public sphere: on the legitimacy and efficacy of public opinion in a post-Westphalian world. *Theory, Culture and Society* 24(4), 7–30.

Frawley, O. 2010. *Memory Ireland*, vol. 1, *history and modernity*. Syracuse, NY: Syracuse University Press.

— 2012. *Memory Ireland*, vol. 2, *diaspora and memory practices*. Syracuse, NY: Syracuse University Press.

—— 2014. *Memory Ireland*, vol. 3, *the Famine and the Troubles*. Syracuse, NY: Syracuse University Press.

Frawley, O. and O'Callaghan, K. 2014. *Memory Ireland*, vol. 4, *James Joyce and cultural memory*. Syracuse, NY: Syracuse University Press.

Garvin, T. 1996. *1922: the birth of Irish democracy*. New York, NY: St Martin's Press.

Gayle Backus, M. 2008. 'More useful washed and dead': James Connolly, W.B. Yeats, and the sexual politics of 'Easter 1916'. *Interventions: International Journal of Postcolonial Studies* 10(1), 67–85.

Gell, A. 1998. *Art and agency: an anthropological theory*. Oxford: Oxford University Press.

Gifford, S. 1974. *The years flew by: the recollections of Madam Sydney Gifford Czira*. Dublin: Gifford and Craven.

Gilligan, S. 1993. Image of a patriot: the popular and scholarly portrayal of Patrick Pearse 1916–1991. MA thesis (unpublished), National University of Ireland, Dublin.

Githens-Mazer, J. 2006. *Myths and memories of the Easter Rising: cultural and political nationalism in Ireland*. Dublin: Irish Academic Press.

Glenavey, B. 1964. *Today we will only gossip*. London: Constable.

González Corona, G. 2009. The Catholic Church in the Irish Civil War. Madrid: Cultiva Comunicación.

Government of Ireland. 1965. *Athbheochan na Gaeilge. The restoration of the Irish language*. Dublin: Government Publications.

Graff-McRae, R. 2010. *Remembering and forgetting 1916: commemoration and conflict in post-peace process Ireland*. Dublin: Irish Academic Press.

Halbwachs, M. 1992 [1951]. *On collective memory*. Chicago, IL: University of Chicago Press.

Hall, M. 2000. *Archaeology and the modern world: colonial transcripts in South Africa and the Chesapeake*. London: Routledge.

Hammer, V. 1987 [1943]. *Manifesto: type design in relation to language and to the art of the punch cutter*. Maple Shade, NJ: Pickering Press.

Haskell, F. 1993. *History and its images: art and the interpretation of the past*. New Haven, CT: Yale University Press.

Hayes-McCoy, G.A. 1970. Museums and our national heritage. *Capuchin Annual*, 128–35.

Hayward, M. 2009. *Rich apparel: clothing and the law in Henry VIII's England*. Farnham: Ashgate.

Heidegger, M. 1962 [1927]. *Being and time* (trans. J. Macquarrie and E. Robinson). Oxford: Blackwell.

Hell, J. and Schönle, A. 2010. Introduction. In Hell, J. and Schönle, A. (eds) *Ruins of modernity*, 1–14. Durham, NC/London: Duke University Press.

Herzog, H. and Shapiro, R. 1986. Will you sign my autograph book? Using autograph books for a sociohistorical study of youth and social frameworks. *Qualitative Sociology* 9(2), 109–25.

Hicks, D. and Beaudry, M. (eds) 2010. *The Oxford handbook of material culture studies.* Oxford: Oxford University Press.

Higgins, R. 2009. Remembering and forgetting P.H. Pearse. In Higgins, R. and Ní Cholltáin, R. (eds) *The life and after-life of P.H. Pearse*, 123–48. Dublin: Irish Academic Press.

— 2012. *Transforming 1916: meaning, memory and the fiftieth anniversary of the Easter Rising.* Cork: Cork University Press.

Hirsch, J. 1981. *Family photographs: content, meaning, and effect.* Oxford: Oxford University Press.

Hirsch, M. (ed.) 1999. *The familial gaze.* Hanover, NH: University Press of New England.

Hobsbawn, E. and Ranger, T. 1983. *The invention of tradition.* Cambridge: Cambridge University Press.

Horne, J. (ed.) 2008. *Our war: Ireland and the Great War.* Dublin: Royal Irish Academy.

Hoskins, J. 1998. *Biographical objects: how things tell the stories of people's lives.* London: Routledge.

Hume, I.N. 1964. Handmaiden to history. *North Carolina Historical Review* 41(2), 215–25.

Hüppauf, B. 1995. Modernism and the photographic representation of war and destruction. In Devereaux, L. and Hillman, R. (eds) *Fields of vision: essays in film studies, visual anthropology and photography*, 94–124. Berkeley, CA: University of California Press.

Huyssen, A. 1995. *Twilight memories: marking time in a culture of amnesia.* London: Routledge.

Hyam, R. 2010. *Understanding the British empire.* Cambridge: Cambridge University Press.

Ingold, T. 2000. *The perception of the environment: essays on livelihood, dwelling and skill.* London: Routledge.

— 2007. Materials against materiality. *Archaeological Dialogues* 14(1), 1–16.

Irish Art Handbook. 1943. Dublin: Cahill and Co.

Jarman, N. 1997. *Material cultures: parades and visual display in Northern Ireland.* Oxford: Berg.

Jeffery, K. 2000. *Ireland and the Great War.* Cambridge: Cambridge University Press.

— 2006. *The GPO and the Easter Rising.* Dublin: Irish Academic Press.

Jennett, S. 1958. Clónna Gaelac(h)a. Irish types: 1571–1958. *British Printer* (February).

Jones, L. 2000. *The hermeneutics of sacred architecture: experience, interpretation, comparison*, vol. 1, *Monumental occasions: reflections on the eventfulness of religious architecture.* Cambridge, MA: Harvard University Press.

Jordanova, L. 1989. Objects of knowledge: a historical perspective on museums. In Vergo, P. (ed.) *The new museology*, 22–40. London: Reaktion Books.

Joyce, J. 1960. *Portrait of the artist as a young man*. Harmondsworth: Penguin.

— 1996. *Dubliners*. Harmondsworth: Penguin.

— 2007. *A portrait of the artist as a young man* (ed. J.P. Riquelme). New York, NY: Norton.

Joyce, P.W. 1906. *A smaller history of ancient Ireland, treating of the government, military system, and law; religion, learning and art; trades, industries and commerce; manners, customs and domestic life, of the ancient Irish people.* London/Dublin: Longmans, Green & Co. and M.H. Gill & Sons.

Joye, L. 2013. The Irish Volunteer uniform. *History Ireland* 21(6). www.history-ireland.com/volume-21/irish-volunteer-uniform/. Accessed 5 February 2014.

Joye, L. and Malone, B. 2006. The Roll of Honour of 1916. *History Ireland* 14(2), 10–11.

Kennedy, C.M. 2010. *Genesis of the Rising, 1912–1916: a transformation of nationalist opinion*. New York, NY: Peter Lang.

Kennedy, R. 2008. Divorcing Jack … from Irish politics. In Scott, Y. (ed.) *Jack B. Yeats. Old and new departures*, 33–46. Dublin: Four Courts Press.

Kennedy, S. 2013. Too absolute and Ireland haunted: MacGreevy, Beckett and the Catholic Irish nation. In Schreibman, S. (ed.) *The life and work of Thomas MacGreevy: a critical reappraisal*, 189–202. London: Bloomsbury.

Kermode, F. (ed.) 1975. *Selected prose of T.S. Eliot*. London: Faber.

Kerrigan, J. 2008. *Archipelagic English: literature, history, and politics, 1603–1707*. Oxford: Oxford University Press.

Kiberd, D. 1995. *Inventing Ireland*. London: Jonathan Cape.

Kiely, B. 1991. Father Senan OFM Cap.: the corpulent Capuchin of Capel Street. In Kennedy, B.P. (ed.) *Art is my life: a tribute to James White*, 121–6. Dublin: National Gallery of Ireland.

Kilfeather, S. 2005. *Dublin: a cultural history*. Oxford: Oxford University Press.

Kilmainham Gaol Restoration Society. 1961. *Kilmainham: the Bastille of Ireland*. Dublin: Kilmainham Gaol Restoration Society.

King, L. 2001. Text as image: the Proclamation of the Irish Republic. In Sisson, E. (ed.) *History, technology, criticism: a collection of essays*, 4–7. Dublin: IADT.

Kopytoff, I. 1986. The cultural biography of things: commoditization as cultural process. In Appadurai, A. (ed.) *The social life of things*, 64–91. Cambridge: Cambridge University Press.

Kwint, M. 1999. Introduction: the physical past. In Kwint, M., Breward C. and Aynsley J. (eds) *Material memories: design and evocation*, 1-16. Oxford: Berg.

Kwint, M., Breward C. and Aynsley J. (eds) 1999. *Material memories: design and evocation*. Oxford: Berg.

Laffan, M. 1999. *The resurrection of Ireland: the Sinn Féin Party, 1916–1923*. Cambridge: Cambridge University Press.

Landsberg, A. 2004. *Prosthetic memory: the transformation of American remembrance in the age of mass media*. New York, NY: Columbia University Press.

Latour, B. 1992. Where are the missing masses? The sociology of a few mundane artefacts. In Bijker, W. and Law, J. (eds) *Shaping technology/building society: studies in sociotechnical change*, 225–58. Cambridge, MA: MIT Press.

— 1999. *Pandora's hope: an essay on the reality of science studies*. Cambridge, MA: Harvard University Press.

— 2005. From *realpolitik* to *dingpolitik* or how to make things public. In Latour, B. and Weibel, P. (eds) *Making things public: atmospheres of democracy*, 14–41. Cambridge, MA: MIT Press.

Lavery, J. 1940. *The life of a painter*. London: Little, Brown & Co.

Le Roux, L. 1932. *Life of P.H. Pearse*. Dublin: Talbot Press.

Leach, D. 2008. Bezen Perrot: The Breton nationalist unit of the SS, 1943–5. *e-Keltoi: Journal of Interdisciplinary Celtic Studies* 4, 1–38.

Lehmann, U. 2000. *Tigersprung: fashion in modernity*. Cambridge, MA: MIT Press.

Levenson, S. 1973. *James Connolly: a biography*. London: Martin Brian & O'Keeffe.

Lewis, J. 1970. *Anatomy of printing: the influences of art and history on its design*. London: Faber.

Lloyd, D. 2007. The political economy of the potato. *Nineteenth-century contexts: an interdisciplinary journal* 29(2–3), 311–35.

— 2008. *Irish times: temporalities of modernity*. Dublin: Field Day.

Lomas, D. 2012. *Mons 1914: the BEF's tactical triumph*. Oxford: Osprey.

Lütticken, S. 2004. Planet of the remakes. *New Left Review* 25 (January/February), 103–19.

Lynam, E.W. 1969 [1924]. *The Irish character in print, 1571–1923*. Shannon: Irish University Press.

MacLiammóir, M. 1961 [1946]. *All for Hecuba: an Irish theatrical autobiography*. Dublin: Progress House.

McBride, I. 2001. Memory and national identity in modern Ireland. In McBride, I. (ed.) *History and memory in modern Ireland*, 1–42. Cambridge: Cambridge University Press.

McBrinn, J. n.d. *Festival of Britain in Northern Ireland*. Belfast: Craft Northern Ireland. http://craftni.org/images/uploads/Festival_of_Britain_Feature.pdf. Accessed 23 March 2015.

McCarthy, M. 2012. *Ireland's 1916 Rising: explorations of history-making, commemoration and heritage in modern times*. Aldershot: Ashgate.

McCay, H. 1966. *Padraic Pearse: a new biography*. Cork: Mercier Press.

McConkey, K. 1984–5. *Sir John Lavery RA, 1856–1941*. Catalogue for exhibition held at Fine Art Society, Edinburgh; Fine Art Society, London; Ulster Museum, Belfast; and National Gallery, Dublin.

McCoole, S. 1997. *Guns and chiffon: women revolutionaries and Kilmainham Gaol, 1916–1923*. Dublin: Stationery Office.

— 2003. *No ordinary women: Irish female activists in the revolutionary years, 1900–1923*. Dublin: O'Brien Press.

— 2010. *Passion and politics. Sir John Lavery: the salon revisited*. Dublin: Hugh Lane Gallery.

McCormack, W.J. 2002. *Roger Casement in death, or haunting the Free State*. Dublin: University College Dublin Press.

— 2012. *Dublin 1916: the French connection*. Dublin: Gill & Macmillan.

McEvansoneya, P. 1999. History, politics and decorative painting: James Ward's murals in Dublin City Hall. *Irish Arts Review* 15, 142–7.

McGarry, F. 2010. *The Rising. Ireland: Easter 1916*. Oxford: Oxford University Press.

— 2011. *Rebels: voices from the Easter Rising*. Dublin: Penguin Ireland.

McGrath, S. forthcoming. 'The darkest hour is before the dawn': the story of Arthur 'Neal' Wicks (1893–1916), English socialist, hotel-waiter and Easter Rising rebel. *Saothar*.

MacGreevy, T. 1942. Three historical paintings by Jack B. Yeats. *Capuchin Annual*, 238–51. Thomas MacGreevy Archive. www.macgreevy.org/index.jsp. Accessed 30 January 2014.

— 1945a. Michelangelo. *Father Matthew Record* (April), 3–4. Thomas MacGreevy Archive. www.macgreevy.org/index.jsp. Accessed 30 January 2014.

— 1945b. Jack B. Yeats: an appreciation and an interpretation. Dublin: Victor Waddington.

McGuigan, J. 2010. *Cultural analysis*. London: Sage Publications.

McGuiggan, J. 1999. A rare document of Irish history: 'High treason' by Sir John Lavery. *Irish Arts Review* 15, 157–9.

McGuinne, D. 1992. *Irish type design*. Dublin: Irish Academic Press.

McIntosh, G. 1999. *The force of culture. Unionist identities in twentieth-century Ireland*. Cork: Cork University Press.

Mack, A. 1975. Why big nations lose small wars: the politics of asymmetric conflict. *World Politics* 27, 175–200.

McKernan, L. 1992. *Topical Budget: the great British news film*. London: British Film Institute.

McLaughlin, J.G. 2002. *Irish Chicago*. Boston, MA: Arcadia.

McMahon, D. 1999. Ireland and the Empire-Commonwealth, 1900–1948. In Brown, J. and Louis, W.R. (eds) *The Oxford history of the British empire*, vol. 4, *the twentieth century*, 138–62. Oxford: Oxford University Press.

McMaster, A. 1953. *Presentation for an Bord Fáilte of the Pageant of St Patrick*. Dublin: Bord Fáilte.

MacNeice, L. 2002. *Collected poems*. London: Faber.

Maguire, M. 2008–9. Harry Nichols and Kathleen Emerson: Protestant rebels. *Studia Hibernica* 35, 147–65.

Marx, K. 1852. *The 18th brumaire of Louis Bonaparte*. www.marxists.org/archive/marx/works/1852/18th-brumaire/ch01.htm. Accessed 23 March 2015.

Matheson, N. 2006. The ghost stamp, the detective and the hospital for boots: light and the post-war battle over spirit photography. *Early Popular Visual Culture* 4(1), 35–51.

Matthews, A. 2010a. *Renegades: Irish republican women, 1900–1922*. Cork: Mercier Press.

— 2010b. *The Kimmage garrison, 1916. Making billy-can bombs at Larkfield*. Maynooth: Maynooth Studies in Local History.

Mauss, M. 1990 [1924]. *The gift: the form and reason for exchange in archaic societies* (trans. W. Halls). London: Routledge.

Metscher, P. 2008. James Connolly, the Easter Rising and the First World War: a contextual study. In O'Donnell, R. (ed.) *The impact of the 1916 Rising among the nations*, 141–60. Dublin: Irish Academic Press.

Miller, D. 1987. *Materiality and mass consumption*. Oxford: Blackwell.

— (ed.) 1998. *Material cultures: why some things matter*. Chicago, IL: University of Chicago Press.

— 2005. Materiality: an introduction. In Miller, D. (ed.) *Materiality*, 1–50. Durham, NC/London: Duke University Press.

— 2008. *The comfort of things*. London: Polity.

Miller, D., Rowlands, M. and Tilley, C. (eds) 1995. *Domination and resistance*. London: Unwin Hyman.

Miller, L. 1960. *A Gaelic alphabet, designed & cut by Michael Biggs; with a note on Irish lettering by Liam Miller*. Dublin: Dolmen Press.

— 1976. *Dolmen XXV*. Dublin: Dolmen Press.

Mitchel Henry, R. 1920. *The evolution of Sinn Féin*. Dublin: Talbot Press.

Mitchell, A. 2009. Beneath the hieroglyph: recontextualising the Black Diaries of Roger Casement. *Irish Migration Studies in Latin America* 7(2), 253–65.

Mitchell, W.J.T. 2005. There are no visual media. *Journal of Visual Culture* 4(2), 257–66.

Monaghan, N.T. 2000. The National Museum of Ireland. In Buttimer, N., Rynne, C. and Guerin, H. (eds.) *The heritage of Ireland*, 404–12. Cork: Collins Press.

Moore, A.S. 1922. *Linen*. New York, NY: Macmillan.

Moran, A. and O'Brien, S. (eds) 2014. *Love objects: emotion, design and material culture*. London: Bloomsbury.

Moran, J. 2005. *Staging the Easter Rising: 1916 as theatre*. Cork: Cork University Press.

Morris, E. 2005. *Our own devices: national symbols and political conflict in twentieth-century Ireland*. Dublin: Irish Academic Press.

Moshenska, G. 2008. A hard rain. Children's shrapnel collections in the Second World War. *Journal of Material Culture* 13(1), 107–25.

Mosley, J. 2010a. The image of the Proclamation of the Irish Republic 1916. *Typefoundry* (6 January). http://typefoundry.blogspot.ie/2010/01/image-of-proclamation-of-irish-republic.html. Accessed 18 March 2014.

— 2010b. The Proclamation of the Irish Republic: notes from Dublin. *Typefoundry* (17 September). http://typefoundry.blogspot.co.uk/2010/09/the-proclamation-of-irish-republic.html. Accessed 20 September 2014.

Mullins, G. 2007. *Dublin Nazi No. 1 – the life of Adolf Mahr.* Dublin: Liberties Press.

Murphy, B. 1989. J.J. O'Kelly, the Catholic Bulletin and contemporary Irish cultural historians. *Archivium Hibernicum* 44, 71–88.

— 2005. *The Catholic Bulletin and Republican Ireland with special reference to J.J. O'Kelly ('Scelig').* Belfast: Athol Books.

Murray, P. and Hennessey, C. (eds) 2007. *Séamus Murphy (1907–1975): sculptor.* Kinsale: Gandon Editions.

Myles, F. 2012. Archaeological assessment. Moore Street and environs, Dublin 1. Unpublished report submitted to the National Museum of Ireland and the National Monuments Service of the Department of Arts, Heritage and the Gaeltacht.

Naji, M. and Douny, L. 2009. Editorial in special issue, 'Making' and 'doing' the material world: anthropology of techniques revisited. *Journal of Material Culture* 14(4), 411–32.

Nally, D. 2011. *Human encumbrances: political violence and the great Irish famine.* Notre Dame, IN: University of Notre Dame Press.

National Museums Northern Ireland. 2014. *Miss Louisa Nolan's Military Medal.* www.nmni.com/um/Collections/History/Militaria/Miss-Louisa-Nolan-s-Military-Medal. Accessed 26 February 2014.

Nesbit, M. 1992. *Atget's seven albums.* New Haven, CT/London: Yale University Press.

Ní Chorra, E. 1966. A rebel remembers. *Capuchin Annual,* 292–300.

Ní Ghairbhí, R. and McNulty, E. (eds) 2013. *Patrick Pearse: collected plays.* Dublin: Irish Academic Press.

Nic Dháibhéid, C. 2012. The Irish National Aid Association and the radicalization of public opinion in Ireland, 1916–1918. *Historical Journal* 55(3), 705–29.

Nolan, L. and Nolan, J.E. 2009. *Secret victory: Ireland and the war at sea, 1914–1918.* Cork: Mercier Press.

Nora, P. 1989. Between memory and history: les lieux de mémoire. *Representations* 26, 7–25.

Northern Ireland Executive. 2012a. Executive statement on decade of centenaries. 15 March. www.northernireland.gov.uk/index/media-centre/executive-statements/executive-statement-on-decade-of-centenaries.htm. Accessed 26 February 2014.

— 2012b. News release. Junior Minister McCann launches 'decade of centenaries' exhibition in Belfast City Hall. 6 August. www.northernireland.gov.uk/news-ofmdfm-060812-junior-minister-mccann. Accessed 26 February 2014.

Ó Broin, L. 1976. *Revolutionary underground: the story of the Irish Republican Brotherhood.* Dublin: Gill and Macmillan.

O Brolchain, H. 2012. *16 lives: Joseph Plunkett.* Dublin: O'Brien Press.

Ó Buachalla, S. (ed.) 1980a. *The letters of P.H. Pearse.* Garrard's Cross: Colin Smyth.

— (ed.). 1980b. *A significant Irish educationalist: the educational writings of P.H. Pearse*. Cork/Dublin: Mercier Press.

Ó Cathasaigh, P. 1919. *The story of the Irish Citizen Army*. London: Maunsel.

Ó Ceallaigh Ritschel, N. 1998 James Connolly's *Under Which Flag*, 1916. *New Hibernia Review/Iris Éireannach Nua* 2(4), 54–68.

Ó Conchubhair, B. (ed,) 2009. *Rebel Cork's fighting story, 1916–21*. Dublin: Mericer Press.

Ó Cuív, B. (ed.) 1969. *A view of the Irish language*. Dublin: Stationery Office.

Ó Duibhir, L. 2013. *Prisoners of war: Ballykinlar internment camp, 1920–1921*. Cork: Mercier Press.

Ó Faoláin, S. 1934. *Constance Markievicz: or, the average revolutionary. A biography*. London: Jonathan Cape.

— 1965. *Vive moi! An autobiography*. London: R. Hart-Davis.

Ó hAodha, M. 1990. *The importance of being Micheál: a portrait of Mac Liammóir*. Dingle: Brandon/Mount Eagle Publications.

Ó Lochlainn, C. 1954. Joseph Mary Plunkett, printer. *Irish Book Lover* 32(5), 57–9.

Ó Ruairc, P. 2011. *Revolution: a photographic history of revolutionary Ireland, 1913–23*. Cork: Mercier Press.

O'Brien, M. 2001. *De Valera, Fianna Fail and the Irish Press: the truth in the news*. Dublin: Irish Academic Press.

O'Callaghan, M. 1984. Nationality and cultural identity in the Irish Free State, 1922–7: the 'Irish Statesman' and the 'Catholic Bulletin' reappraised. *Irish Historical Studies* 24(94), 226–45.

O'Callaghan, M. and O'Donnell, C. 2006. The Northern Ireland government, the 'Paisleyite movement' and Ulster unionism in 1966. *Irish Political Studies* 21(2), 203–22.

O'Casey, S. 1945. *Drums under the windows*. London: Macmillan.

O'Connor Lysaght, D.R. 2009. Count George Noble Plunkett. In McGuire, J. and Quinn, J. (eds) *Dictionary of Irish biography*, vol. 8, 178–9. Cambridge: Cambridge University Press.

O'Connor, J. 1999. *The story of the 1916 Proclamation*. Dublin: Anvil Press.

O'Curry, E. 1873. *Manners and customs of the Ancient Irish*. London/Dublin/New York, NY: Williams & Norgate, Kelly, and Scribner, Welford & Co.

O'Donnell, C. 2006. 1966 and all that: the 50th anniversary commemorations. *History Ireland* 14(2), 31–6.

O'Dwyer, R. 2007. The golden jubilee of the 1916 Easter Rising. In Doherty, G. and Keogh, D. (eds) *1916: the long revolution*, 352–75. Douglas: Mercier Press.

O'Farrell, E. 1917. Miss O'Farrell's story of the surrender. *The Catholic Bulletin* 7(4), 266–70; 7(5), 329–34.

O'Kelly, H. 1986. The rise in national consciousness in Ireland during the Celtic Revival, *c*.1880–1920, and its expression in dress. MA thesis (unpublished), Courtauld Institute, University of London.

— 1992. Reconstructing Irishness: dress in the Celtic Revival, 1880–1920. In Ash, J. and Wilson, E. (eds) *Chic thrills: a fashion reader*, 75–83. London: Pandora.

O'Kelly, J.J. 1916. Events of Easter Week. *Catholic Bulletin and Book Review* 6(12) (December), 697–711.

O'Mahony, S. 1987. *Frongoch: university of revolution*. Killiney: FDR Teoranta.

O'Neill, E. 1935. Patrick Pearse: some other memories. *Capuchin Annual*, 217–22.

O'Neill, M. 2000. *Grace Gifford Plunkett and Irish freedom: tragic bride of 1916*. Dublin: Irish Academic Press.

O'Rourke, K. and Williamson, J. 1999. *Globalization and history: the evolution of a nineteenth-century Atlantic economy*. Cambridge, MA: MIT Press.

Olsen, B. 2010. *In defense of things: archaeology and the ontology of objects*. Plymouth, MA: AltaMira Press.

Ozouf, M. 1988. *Festivals and the French Revolution*. Cambridge, MA: Harvard University Press.

Parrott, F. 2005. 'It's not forever'. The material culture of hope. *Journal of Material Culture* 10(3), 245–62.

Pearce, S.M. 1994. Collecting reconsidered. In Pearse, S.M. (ed.) *Interpreting objects and collections*, 193–204. London: Routledge.

Pearse, M.B. (ed.) 1934. *The home-life of P.H. Pearse, as told by himself, his family and friends*. Dublin: Browne and Nolan.

Pearse, P.H. 1952. *Political writing and speeches*. Dublin: Talbot Press.

— n.d. *Autobiography* (unpublished). Pearse Museum archive, PMSTE.2004.0946.

Perkins, S. 2013. Senan Moynihan. *Dictionary of Irish biography*. Cambridge/ Dublin: Cambridge University Press online and Royal Irish Academy. http://dib.cambridge.org. Accessed 23 March 2015.

Pinney, C. 2005. Things happen: or, from which moment does that object come? In Miller, D. (eds) *Materiality*, 256–72. Durham, NC/London: Duke University Press.

Pocock, J.G.A. 2005. *The discovery of islands: essays in British history*. Cambridge: Cambridge University Press.

Pyle, H. 2005. *Cesca's diary, 1913–916: where art and nationalism meet*. Dublin: Woodfield Press.

Rachamimov, I. 2012. Camp domesticity: shifting gender boundaries in World War 1 internment camps. In Carr, G. and Mytum, H. (eds) *Cultural heritage and prisoners of war: creativity behind barbed wire*, 291–305. London: Routledge.

Reddin, K. 1945. A man called Pearse. *Studies: An Irish Quarterly Review* 34(134), 241–51.

Redmond, L. 1992. *Ireland – the revolutionary years: photographs from the Cashman Collection, Ireland 1910–1930*. Dublin: Gill and Macmillan & RTÉ.

Reeves, N. 2004. *The power of film propaganda: myth or reality?* London: Continuum.

Rochberg-Halton, E. 1984. Object relations, role models, and the cultivation of the self. *Environment and Behaviour* 16(3), 335–68.

Rogers, N. 2007. *Ireland, slavery and anti-slavery*. London: Palgrave.

Rokem, F. 2002. *Performing history: theatrical representations of the past in contemporary theatre*. Iowa City, IA: University of Iowa Press.

Rolston, B. 2010a. 'Trying to reach the future through the past': murals and memory in Northern Ireland. *Crime, Media, Culture* 6(3), 285–307.

— 2010b. *Drawing support: murals in the North of Ireland*. Belfast: Beyond the Pale.

Rose, G. 2010. *Doing family photography: the domestic, the public and the politics of sentiment*. Farnham: Ashgate.

— 2012. *Visual methodologies: an introduction to researching with visual materials* (3rd edn). London: Sage Publications.

Rose, G. and Tolia-Kelly, D. (eds) 2012. *Visuality/materiality: images, objects and practices*. London: Ashgate.

Ryan, D. 1919. *The man called Pearse*. Dublin: Maunsel and Co.

— 1924. *James Connolly*. Dublin: Talbot Press.

— 1949. *The Rising, the complete story of Easter Week*. Dublin: Golden Eagle Books.

Samuel, R. 1994. *Theatres of memory: past and present in contemporary culture*. London: Verso.

Saunders, N. 2003. *Trench art: materialities and memories of war*. Oxford: Berg.

Scully, S. 1986. Moore Street – 1916. *Dublin Historical Record* 39(2), 53–63.

Shapiro, R. and Herzog, H. 1986. Understanding youth culture through autograph books: the Israeli case. *Journal of American Folklore* 97(386), 442–60.

Shaw, G.B. 1962. *The matter with Ireland* (eds D. Greene and D. Lawrence). London: Rupert Hart-Davis.

— 1985. *Collected letters, 1911–1925* (ed. D. Lawrence). London: Max Reinhardt.

Sheehy, J. 1980. *The rediscovery of Ireland's past: the Celtic revival, 1830–1930*. London: Thames & Hudson.

Shiels, D. 2006. The archaeology of insurrection: St Stephen's Green 1916. *Archaeology Ireland* 20(1), 8–11.

— 2007. The potential for conflict archaeology in the Republic of Ireland. *Journal of Conflict Archaeology* 2, 169–87.

Silvestri, M. 2009. The bomb, bhadralok, Bhagavad Gita, and Dan Breen: terrorism in Bengal and its relation to the European experience. *Terrorism and Political Violence* 21(1), 1–27

Sisson, E. 2004. *Pearse's patriots: St Enda's and the cult of boyhood*. Cork: Cork University Press.

Slotkin, R. 1998. *The fatal environment: the myth of the frontier in the Age of Industrialization, 1800–1890*. Oklahoma, OK: University of Oklahoma Press.

Stephens, J. 1992 [1916]. *The insurrection in Dublin*. Gerrards Cross: Colin Smythe.

Stewert, S. 1993. *On longing: narratives of the miniature, the gigantic, the souvenir, the collection*. Durham, NC/London: Duke University Press.

Strachan, J. and Nally, C. 2012. *Advertising, literature and print culture in Ireland, 1891–1922*. Basingstoke: Palgrave Macmillan.

Strathern, M. 1988. *The gender of the gift*. Berkeley, CA: University of California Press.

Tagg, J. 1998. *The burden of representation: essays on photographies and histories*. London: Macmillan.

Tallion, R. 1996. *When history was made: the women of 1916*. Dublin: Beyond the Pale Publications.

Taylor, L. 2002. *The study of dress history*. Manchester: Manchester University Press.

Terdiman, R. 1993. *Present past: modernity and the memory crisis*. Ithaca, NY: Cornell University Press.

Tickner, L. 1988. *The spectacle of women: imagery of the sufferage campaign, 1907–14*. Chicago, IL: University of Chicago Press.

Tilley, C. 1999. *Metaphor and material culture*. Oxford: Wiley Blackwell.

Tobin, M. 1964. Enniscorthy and the national flag. *The Past: The Organ of the Uí Cinsealaigh Historical Society* 7, 141–8.

Tóibín, C. 1993. New ways of killing your father. *London Review of Books*, 18 November, 5.

Townshend, C. 2005. *Easter 1916: the Irish rebellion*. London: Allan Lane.

— 2006. Moore Street 1916. Unpublished report for Dublin City Council.

— 2013. *The Republic: the fight for Irish independence, 1918–1923*. London: Penguin.

Trentmann, F. 2009. Materiality in the future of history: things, practices, and politics. *Journal of British Studies* 48(2), 283–307.

Turpin, J. 2000. *Oliver Sheppard, 1865–1941: symbolist sculptor of the Irish cultural revival*. Dublin: Four Courts Press.

— 2007. Monumental commemoration of the fallen in Ireland, North and South, 1920–60. *New Hibernia* 11(4), 107–19.

Valente, J. 2011. *The myth of manliness in Irish national culture, 1880–1922*. Champaign, IL: University of Illinois Press.

Wall, M. 1969a. The background to the Rising, from 1914 until the issue of the countermanding order on Easter Saturday 1916. In Nowlan, K.B. (ed.) *The making of 1916: studies in the history of the Rising*, 157–97. Dublin: Stationery Office.

— 1969b. The plans and countermand: the country and Dublin. In Nowlan, K.B. (ed.) *The making of 1916: studies in the history of the Rising*, 201–51. Dublin: Stationery Office.

Ward, M. 1995. *Unmanageable revolutionaries: women and Irish Nationalism*. Dublin: Pluto Press.

Warde, B. 1999 [1932]. The crystal goblet. In Bierut, M., Helfand, J., Heller, S. and Poynor, R. (eds) *Looking closer 3: classic writings on graphic design*, 56–9. New York, NY: Allworth.

Weihman, L. 2004. Doing my bit for Ireland: transgressing gender in the Easter Rising. *Éire-Ireland* 39(3–4), 228–49.

Weiner, A. 1992. *Inalienable possessions: the paradox of keeping-while-giving.* Berkeley, CA: University of California Press.

Weizman, E. 2007. *Hollow land: Israel's architecture of occupation.* London: Verso.

West, S. 1999. Introduction. In Tarlow, S. and West, S. (eds) 1999. *The familiar past? Archaeologies of later historical Britain*, 1–15. London/New York, NY: Routledge.

Whelan, Y. 2003. *Reinventing modern Dublin: streetscape, iconography and the politics of identity.* Dublin: University College Dublin Press.

White G. and O'Shea, B. 2003. *Irish Volunteer Soldier, 1913–23.* Oxford: Osprey.

Wills, C. 2009. *Dublin 1916. The siege of the GPO.* London: Profile.

Wilson, E. 1985. *Adorned in dreams.* London: Virago.

Winter, J. 1995. *Sites of memory, sites of mourning: the Great War in European cultural history.* Cambridge: Cambridge University Press.

— 2013. Beyond glory? Cultural divergences in remembering the Great War in Ireland, Britain and France. In Horne, J. and Madigan, E. (eds) *Towards commemoration: Ireland in war and revolution, 1912–1923*, 134–44. Dublin: Royal Irish Academy.

Witmore, C. 2007. Symmetrical archaeology: excerpts of a manifesto. *World Archaeology* 39(4), 546–62.

Yeats, W.B. 1990. *W.B.: the poems* (ed. D. Albright). London: Everyman's Library.

— 1992. *Collected letters.* Charlottesville, VA: InteLex.

Žižek, S. 2002. *Revolution at the gates: selected writings of Lenin from 1917.* London: Verso.

Index